ISLAMIC RADICALISM AND POLITICAL VIOLENCE

Islamic Radicalism and Political Violence

The Templars of Islam
and Sheikh Ra'id Salah

RAPHAEL ISRAELI
Hebrew University, Jerusalem

VALLENTINE MITCHELL
LONDON • PORTLAND, OR

First published in 2008 by Vallentine Mitchell

Suite 314, Premier House,	920 NE 58th Avenue, Suite 300
112–114 Station Road,	Portland, Oregon,
Edgware, Middlesex HA8 7BJ	97213-3786

www.vmbooks.com

Copyright © Raphael Israeli 2008

British Library Cataloguing in Publication Data

Israeli, Raphael
  Islamic radicalism and political violence : the Templars of Islam and Sheikh Ra'id Salah
  1. Salah, Sheikh Raid – Trials, litigation, etc. 2. Islamic fundamentalism – Israel 3. Terrorism – Religious aspects – Islam 4. Islam and politics – Israel
  I. Title
  320.5'57'092

ISBN 978 0 85303 729 3 (cloth)
ISBN 978 0 85303 730 9 (paper)

Library of Congress Cataloging-in-Publication Data

A catalog record for this book is available
from the Library of Congress

All rights reserved. No part of this publication may be reproduced, stored in or introduced into a retrieval system or transmitted in any form or by any means, electronic, mechanical, photocopying, recording or otherwise, without the prior written permission of the publisher of this book.

Typeset in 11.5 pt on 13.5 pt Dante
by Vitaset, Paddock Wood, Kent
Printed in by Biddles Ltd, King's Lynn, Norfolk

Contents

GLOSSARY	ix
ACKNOWLEDGEMENTS	xiii
Preface: Explaining the Templar Metaphor	xv
Chapter One: Religion and Politics: What are the Stakes?	1
Chapter Two: The Arab Minority in Israel	36
Chapter Three: The Islamic Movement in Israel: Ideology and Organization	47
Chapter Four: Sheikh Ra'id Salah: The Shepherd and his Flock	65
Chapter Five: Indictment and Evidence	84
Chapter Six: The Trial and its Resonance	96
Chapter Seven: The Plea Bargain and its Significance	121
Chapter Eight: Consequences of the Trial	138
BIBLIOGRAPHY	159
ENDNOTES	163
INDEX	169

To the devoted young lawyers
Who laboured relentlessly to build this case
Until the unwarranted plea bargain
Put an end to their endeavour
And obstructed justice

Nehemia and Tirtza Levtzion
The exemplary couple and parents
A model of devoted friendship
And lifelong commitment
In memoriam

Glossary

Allah Akbar (God is the greatest) – war cry of the Muslims
Amir al Mu'minin (Commander of the Faithful) – title of the Muslim Caliph
al-Aqsa Mosque – one of the holy shrines of Islam, lent its name to the Aqsa Foundation, the main channel of Hamas moneys to the Muslim Movement in Israel
al-Ard (the Land) – underground group of Arab citizens of Israel
Ashura – days of remembrance of the suffering of Imam Hussein for the Shi'a
Ayatollah (the sign of God) – title of the top clerics in the Shi'ite hierarchy
Al-Azhar – leading university and religious institution in Sunni Islam, located in Cairo
Balfour Declaration – made by the British in 1917 pledging the establishment of a Jewish National Home in Palestine
bid'a (innovation) – a blasphemy in Islam, since the innovator purports to know better than the prescriptions of the Qur'an or the teachings of the Prophet
Bukhari and Muslim – foremost collectors and editors of the *hadith*
caliph (*khalifa*) – successors of the Prophet Muhammed at the head of the Muslim community
dar al-harb (House of War) – territory not yet dominated by the rule of Islam
dar al-Islam (Abode of Islam) – territory under Islamic rule, regardless of the composition of its population
da'wa (call, mission) – propaganda through which Islam is diffused
dhimmi (protected) – refers to non-Muslims, mainly Christians and Jews under Muslim rule, and is a judicial, political, religious, cultural, social and economic status that defines the underpinnings of 'tolerated' people under Islam
fat'h – conquest of territories in the course of Islamic expansion
fatwa – religious verdict pronounced by a Muslim cleric and binding upon Muslims

fida'iyun (self-sacrificing, for a Muslim cause) – precursor of Islamikaze or 'suicide bombers'

FIS (*Front Islamique du Salut*) – Muslim movement in Algeria which rebelled after it was denied the power that it legally won

gama'at (groups) – extremist and militant Muslims who split from the Muslim Brothers and pursued violent attacks against Egyptian targets

hadith (stories) – about the biography of the Prophet, learned as a model for emulation

hajj – Pilgrimage to Mecca, one of the five Pillars of the Faith; also the title that the pilgrim receives after its completion

Hamas (Islamic Resistance Movement) – religious-militant part of the Palestinian people which has opted for the domination of politics by religion

Hanafi – one of the four schools of law in Sunni Islam, the most open and inclusive

Hanbali – the most radical school of law in the Sunna

Hidden Imam – in the Shi'a designates the twelfth and last imam, who has been in hiding and will return as the Mahdi at the Day of Reckoning

hijra (migration) – commemorates the migration of the Prophet from Mecca to Medina in AD 622; also connotes a spiritual migration

Hizbollah (Party of God) – Islamic-Shi'ite movement in Lebanon which has opted to pursue political and religious goals by violent means

Humanitarian Relief Society (HRS) – Islamic movement in Israel front organization

Humanitarian Salvation Committee (HSC) – Islamic movement front organization

Hudaybiyya – place near Mecca where the Prophet signed a precedent-setting truce (*hudna*) for ten years, which he then broke when convenient to Islam

irhab (terror) – Qur'anic version of terrorism, which lend to it legitimacy and justification

imam – in the Sunna it is the leader of prayer or the officiating cleric in a mosque; in the Shi'a, one of the twelve in the holy apostolic chain

Interpal – Palestinian Relief Organization with links to Hamas

intifada (uprising) – of the Palestinians under Israeli rule in 1987–92, and again in 2000–05 (al-Aqsa)

Islamic Jihad – splinter group from the Muslim movement among the Palestinians, pursues an independent campaign of terror

Islamikaze – a term combining Islam and Kamikaze, coined by this author to designate 'suicide bombers'

isra' and mi'raj – nocturnal journey of the Prophet on his winged horse back

to Jerusalem, and his ascension thence to heaven
jahiliyya (ignorance) – refers to the pre-Islamic period, also used to designate any society that leads an un-Islamic life
jihad (holy war) – refers also to spiritual striving and betterment of the self, but connotes mainly the recourse to violence to propagate Islam; *mujahid* is the jihad fighter
jizya – poll tax paid by the *dhimmi*, in return for his 'tolerated' status
Ka'ba – holy stone in Mecca which has become the object of Muslim worship
kafir (infidel) – refers to non-Muslims in general
Karin A – ship aboard which the PLO attempted to smuggle weapons to Gaza, against its obligations under Oslo; the boat was seized by Israel
Karbalah – town in Iraq where Imam Hussein was buried, his tomb becoming a holy shrine for the Shi'ites
Laskar Jihad – a Muslim terrorist organization based in Indonesia
madrasa – traditional school in the Islamic system which trains Muslim scholars and terrorists
Mahdi (Guided One) – who will come and succour the world: for the Shi'a he is, by definition, the returning Imam; among the Sunna he exists only in popular belief
Marj-al-Zuhur (Valley of Flowers) – valley in Southern Lebanon where Hamas members were exiled by Israel for a year (1992)
Mossad (Institution, in Hebrew) – Israeli equivalent of the CIA
mu'azzin – man who calls the Believers to prayer from the top of the minaret
murabit (Camper) – Muslims who settle and dwell in the farthest reaches of Islamdom to defend its border against infidel marauders
musallah – house of prayer which is not a mosque, but improvised for worship
Muslim Brothers – Islamic organization founded in 1928 in Egypt; many of today's Muslim militant movements regard themselves as its followers
Nakbah (Disaster) – way the Arabs refer to the emergence of Israel as an independent state in 1948
Nahdat al-'Ulama (Revival of the 'Ulama) – largest Muslim party in Indonesia and probably the world
al-Qa'ida (the base) – Islamic terrorist organization founded by Osama Bin Laden, the acknowledged perpetrator of 11 September
Ramadan – month of fasting in the Muslim calendar, daily from sunrise to sunset
rashidun (Righteous ones) – refers to the first four caliphs after the Prophet
shahid (martyr) – refers to anyone who died in battle for the sake of Islam, even if death is self-provoked and not only incidentally incurred

Shari'a Law – Holy Law of Islam based primarily on the Qur'an and the *hadith*

Shi'a (faction) – followers of Ali and the 12 Imams, who await the return of the last one; constitute some 12 per cent of the 1.5 billion Believers

shura (council) – council of elders in traditional society, borrowed to refer to any instrument of rule by consensus

sira (biography) – hagiographic curriculum vitae of Muhammed, designed to idealize and idolize him

Sunna (tradition) – mainstream of Islam, follows the traditions of the Prophet, to distinguish from Shi'a

Takfir wa-Hijra (accusing others of apostasy and turning away from them) – small splinter movement from the Muslim Brothers in Egypt, eliminated by the government

Taliban (students) – movement of Afghani students which took over government in Kabul in 1996, before being removed by coalition forces in 2002

Tanzim (Organization) – group of militants among the Fat'h Movement, dedicated to fighting Israel

Temple Mount – place in Jerusalem where according to Jewish tradition the two Jerusalem Temples (Solomonic and Herodian) had been built and destroyed

'Triangle' – area in Central Israel, just east of Tel Aviv, which comprises several Arab towns and villages delineated roughly by Tul Karem and Qalqiliya in the West Bank

'Ulama (scholars of the Holy Law of Islam) – constitutes the class of intellectuals and also the pool from which functionaries like judges and administrators are drawn

umma (nation) – congregation of all Muslims, somewhat equals the Christian notion of ecclesia

Usrat al-Jihad (the Family of Jihad) – underground terrorist organization of the Muslim movement in Israel, dismantled in 1979

Wahhabi – followers of Abd al-Wahhab, a nineteenth-century Hanbalite who swept the entire Arabian Peninsula into his brand of conservative and puritanical Islam

Wailing Wall – remaining vestige of the ancient temples on Temple Mount, a Jewish place of worship

waqf (Holy Endowment) – assets dedicated by their donors to charity and thereby excluded from the economic and fiscal systems of Muslim countries

zakat – giving of alms, one of the five Pillars of Islam; at first a tax, later becoming voluntary

Acknowledgements

THIS VOLUME IS THE fruit of coincidence much more than the product of deliberate and premeditated academic planning. In some of my previous writings on the Arabs in Israel and the rise of Muslim fundamentalism, my attention was drawn to the role that Sheikh Ra'id Salah of Umm al-Fahm, the foremost Muslim town in Israel, played in his constituency. But I had not thought, at that time, that his growing prominence would warrant a special study on him, as a leader who combines spiritual authority with political appeal, religious concerns with organizational wheeling and dealing, and local popularity with international salience. Two developments during the year of 2004 converged to justify the present study of Ra'id's leadership. The first was the fact that Ra'id was arrested and accused of channelling funds to the Hamas organization which has been outlawed in Israel. The second had to do with the structural change in the Truman Institute for the Advancement of Peace, under whose sponsorship this research has been pursued in the past and currently, which now requires that studies be conducted in groups rather than by individual researchers.

On the first score I became directly involved in the case when I was asked by the Haifa District Attorney, who handled the case with the aid of half a dozen young lawyers, to write an 'expert opinion' on the Islamic movement in Israel headed by the chief defendant in the trial, and to prepare myself for cross-examination by the lawyers of the defendants. My consent to the deal was predicated on my former research on the Islamic movement and its ideological affiliation with Hamas, and it was assumed that I could help the case by showing in court the close relationships that existed between the two movements. I stood at the witness box for three consecutive days and was interrogated in depth by the attorneys for the defence.

On the second score, as soon as the new structural reform was announced at the Truman Institute, lone wolves like myself, who had for decades followed their own path, were now obliged to join research groups. I chose an option tentatively dubbed 'Religious Actors in Politics', framed and developed by a variety of researchers and former diplomats headed by Dr Neville Lamdan, a former Israeli ambassador to the Vatican. This book was thus conceived during the many discussions among the ten members of the group, each of whom brought his or her case-study to bear on our theorizing. For those discussions, which were at times frustrating but always fruitful, I am indebted to the other members of the group: Emanuel Sivan, Glora Eliraz, Eldad Pardo, Yitzhak Reiter, Chen Brami, Neville Lamdan, Daphne Tsimhomi, Shelley Elkayam, Aryeh Oded and Reuven Enoch, and especially to Tal Nitsan who held the group together.

While much of this book will probably appear in the collective work of the group, I thought that my unplanned personal involvement in Ra'id's trial necessitated a more detailed study than the group's common endeavour would manage in a single comparative volume. Hence my decision to step outside the group and present this as an independent work. I alone am responsible for any mistakes in facts or interpretation.

I would like to thank the Truman Institute, its staff and facilities for the unfailing assistance I have received during this research, and the president and staff of the Haifa District Court, as well as the Haifa District Attorney and her assistants for all the help and encouragement they extended to me beyond their call of duty to make possible the collection of documentation and to enable me to bring this book to fruition. However, since my request to both the claimants and the defendants to make available to me all the minutes of the proceedings remained unanswered, and the President of the Court made the handing over of that documentation which was at the disposal of the court contingent upon the parties' consent, I had to content myself with the many documents I had accumulated during the preparations for the case, and the experience I gathered during the three days I stood at the witness stand, as an 'expert witness' on behalf of the District Attorney. So much for the transparency of the court system.

Raphael Israeli,
Jerusalem, Summer 2007

PREFACE

Explaining the Templar Metaphor[1]

LIKE THE ORDER of the Templars in the medieval Christian world, which combined religious zeal with soldiery to fight the infidels, and centred its world of symbols, loyalty and devotion around the Solomonic Temple in Jerusalem, so does today's Muslim movement of Sheikh Ra'id in Israel, that will be discussed below, except that the latter substitutes al-Aqsa Mosque for the ancient Jewish Temples that it does not recognize. Like the Templars, the Aqsa Foundation that was established by Sheikh Ra'id in his Muslim village of Umm al-Fahm in Israel soon gained international resonance and pursued fund-raising and recruitment for the cause, until banned by the authorities that felt subverted by the zealotry of these fighters. These external similarities and dissimilarities should not lead the reader to easy conclusions, however, for the two movements are of completely different roots, motivations and purposes, which led to the extinction of the former in medieval times and the continuing vitality of the latter in the modern world. More than anything else, the clinging of both movements to the symbolism of Temple Mount in Jerusalem, though under vastly divergent interpretations, has been the main justification for this rapprochement between the two. Their common sanctification of death for their cause is also strikingly reminiscent of each other, as one can deduce from the comparison between today's Islamikaze[2] and the following description of the Templars that is ascribed to St Bernard:

> The Knights of Christ kill without remorse and die in tranquillity; when they die, they do so for their own sake, but when they kill they do it for the sake of Christ . . . When they kill evil-doers this is not homicide but evil-cide, dare I say . . . But when they face the enemy, these gentle men who are sweeter than kids become more ferocious

than lions, to the point that I can no longer decide whether to call them monks or knights; maybe they should be called by both designations, because they combine with the sweetness of the monks the daring of the knights. They are the servants that God has chosen as guardians of the Holy Sepulchre . . .[3]

Certainly, neither the Islamikaze in particular nor members of the Islamic movement in general lay claim to or urge monastic asceticism and celibacy, nor were Templar knights who fought for Christ promised all the amenities and attractions of Paradise that Muslim martyrs die for. The Templars began in 1120 when two professional knights, who were assigned to guard the Holy Sepulchre in Crusader Jerusalem, persuaded fellow-fighters to put themselves at the service of Christ. They took solemn vows before the Patriarch of Jerusalem to protect Christian pilgrims in the land against bandits and to serve as knights to the king (at the time Baldwin II), embracing the triple slogan of 'poverty, chastity, obedience', and the growing of beards as an expression of their humility. Baldwin, who approved the move, gave them part of his palace as a base, namely al-Aqsa Mosque, which had been built on Temple Mount, the emplacement of the ancient Solomonic Temple. This permitted them to dub themselves 'The Poor Comrades-in-arms of Christ and the Solomonic Temple', eventually the 'Templars'. Their establishment at that critical moment came in the wake of the defeat of Roger of Antioch on the Orontes in 1119 and of the entrenchment of the remaining Frankish principalities in the Orient (Edessa, Acre, Tripoli, Jaffa and Jerusalem) after the first Crusader momentum was blunted and recruitment dwindled dangerously in Europe for reinforcement to the embattled Crusader enclaves. The urgent need for permanent units to defend Christendom in the Holy Land was what generated the birth of the Templars.

If one consults the platform of Hamas, a wing of the Muslim Brothers in Egypt – which combines religious indoctrination with military activity, recruits most of the prospective Islamikaze and other fighters of the Qassam Brigades, and with whose principles the Muslim movement in Israel has vowed to align itself – one would be struck by the parallel of their narrative with the Templars'. They too state in their platform[4] that since the 'Islamic world is burning', it becomes incumbent upon each Muslim individually to 'pour some water, little as it may be, with a view of extinguishing the fire as he can, without awaiting action by the others' (Preamble of the Charter); they declare their permanent state of preparedness and their 'readiness to sacrifice their souls and dearest in the Path of Allah' (Introduction); they vow to join hands with all jihad fighters to liberate Palestine (Introduction); they call upon 'successive battalions of the multifarious Arab and Islamic worlds to reinforce them until the enemies of Allah are defeated and Allah's victory prevails; and they proclaim the universal import of their movement, due to 'the clarity of its thinking, the nobility of its purpose and the loftiness of its objectives' (Article 7). Both Templars and Islamists pledged to fight the foreign 'invaders to their holy places in Palestine (Muslims and Zionists, respectively, see Article 7); both believed in the sanctity of the land, hence of the battle (Article 11 of the Charter); and both shunned peaceful negotiations to resolve differences with the enemy (Article 13 of the Charter). Exactly like the centrality of the Temple in the Templars' symbolism, Hamas determined in their Charter (Article 33) to confront and 'wage jihad against the enemy, in defence of the Muslim human being, of Islamic Civilization and the Islamic holy places, primarily the blessed Aqsa Mosque. Finally, much as the Templars drew lessons from the Crusaders that preceded them to learn about the enemy and face it, Hamas view the precedents of Muslim victories over the Crusaders as a guarantee that the Zionists will be defeated (Article 35).

The Templars and Hamas members would not have been the first pious people of their respective faiths who took vows to fight their enemies through a holy war. The novelty of the Templars was that regular monks, who were supposedly devoted to a life of peace and prayer, took upon themselves the audacious mission of killing, given that spilling blood for a devout monk was equivalent in its pollution of the soul to making money or engaging in sex. Between 1127 and 1129 Hugues de Payns, the Master of the order, and some of his colleagues travelled in the Christian West, and obtained legitimacy at the Troyes Council, thanks to the favourable intervention of Bernard de Clairvaux, one of the dominant figures of medieval Christianity. Shortly thereafter, a code of conduct for the Templars was worded which justified their violent means, and the white mantle with a red cross embroidered on it became their uniform. Hamas also had its Charter proclaimed together with the establishment of the movement that assembled together existing Muslim associations across the West Bank and Gaza. There, too, while preaching Islam as supposedly a 'religion of peace' (if the world should yield to their demands), they systematically recruited, trained, indoctrinated, financed and dispatched jihad fighters to blow up buses, restaurants and concentrations of civilians, with justifications for acts of terror by the founding leader, Sheikh Ahmed Yassin, and doctrinal back-up by such doctors of the Holy Law as Sheikh Qaradawi. Non-combatants could also become members of the Templars and Hamas, and they served in auxiliary, logistic and other supportive roles.

Both organizations launched vast and worldwide campaigns of information and propaganda (*da'wa* in the case of Hamas and the Muslim movement in Israel) in order to elicit donations from both rulers and private individuals, with some Templars, who took in only accomplished knights, yielding their property together with their persona to the order. But unlike some Templars who were at times of doubtful origin and integrity, the Islamists, who recruit and train their membership without any prior requirements, are usually common people from the crowd who show inclination for venturing into a life of piety and armed struggle. Only men were recruited into the Templar Order, and only those who vowed chastity and obedience, but the Order could also serve at times as a channel for laundering one's ill-reputed past. Members of Hamas – who pursue their normal and family lives, doubling up as jihad fighters, while also accepting new members who wished to erase their criminal past – undergo a rite of passage into the group which includes committing acts of terror in order to prove their mettle; they have had recourse to women and even teenage children in their recruiting effort. In these cases, more than the new recruits showing enthusiasm to join, they were either manipulated to volunteer or put under all sorts of pressure to 'cleanse their past misdeeds' or lured to gain immediate access to Paradise and thus short-circuit the misfortunes of this world. Exactly like the Templars, who escaped the jurisdiction of their regional bishops due to their direct submission to the Pope, Hamas, like other Muslim fundamentalists, are in opposition to the Muslim establishment in their countries, which they find subservient to the secular ruler, and follow almost blindly their own charismatic leaders like Yassin and Ra'id, declaring their loyalty to spiritual leaders, past and present, such as Hassan al-Banna, Sayyid Qut'b and Sheikh Qaradawi.

In an historical reversal of the role of the medieval Templars, who stood at the forefront of the battles of Christianity against Islam – its main challenger in the Orient and the Iberian Peninsula – the Islamists today see themselves as the avant-garde of the battle against infidels wherever Islamic dominion is challenged: in the Middle East, Kashmir, Chechnya and the embattled Muslim minorities in Europe and the rest of the West;

or in the domestic struggle against the regimes in their own countries, which they consider as subservient to the West, ungodly, illegitimate and traitors to their peoples. But unlike the leaders of the Templars – who throughout their bicentennial existence maintained their headquarters in the Holy Land, first in Jerusalem and then in Acre (finally in Cyprus), even in times of adversity, and made no distinction between the religious-political and military organizations which were one and the same – the present-day leadership of Hamas have devised such a differentiation between the two, hoping to shelter their supreme mentors and masters, who have found shelter beyond the Holy Land, from reprisals for the acts of terror they sponsor but take no responsibility for. To finance these vast operations and maintain the property that they control, donations are not sufficient and more grass-root fund-raising campaigns are needed. The Templars collected funds from whoever wished to contribute to them, but within the Christian world only; Islamists today have mounted front organizations which paradoxically draw contributions from generous non-Muslims in the West who are led to believe that they are giving charity to the poor and deprived in the Middle East and elsewhere, while in fact their money is often channelled to terrorist and violent operations against non-combatants. This is the niche that the Islamic movement in Israel found for itself worldwide, namely the collection of funds under the title of the al-Aqsa Charitable Foundation, which were diverted to aid Hamas terrorism. In fact, concurrently with the legal case that is the topic of this book, another case unfolded in Germany in the beginning of 2005 that ended up indicting and banning that foundation from the land due to its fund-raising activities.

The Templars never did much to substantiate their specific connection to the Temple which lent their organization its name, beyond the symbolic use of that name which under the medieval circumstances of the Crusades was powerfully attractive beyond their fight for the Holy Land and the preservation of its holy places in general. The Palestinian Islamists, by contrast, turned al-Aqsa from a mere mobilizing symbol to rally world Islam behind them, as the Mufti of Jerusalem had done during the 1930s and 1940s, into the focus of their activities. The physical refurbishing of al-Aqsa, and its expansion by the adherents of the movement, served the purpose of making that symbol a concrete, urgent and central duty in the life of Palestinian Muslims, on the one hand, and an obligation upon the believers to meet that duty on a continuing and escalating basis, on the other. The coming chapters will explain in detail the depth, scope and longevity of this obligation, which combined spiritual *da'wa*, financial commitment and personal involvement. Both organizations had made the Temple the scarecrow of their constituencies: the Christians by publicizing the 'horrors' committed by the Muslims in the Holy Land and its holy places for Christianity, thus prompting pious volunteers to join the ranks of the Christian defenders (that was after all the rationale for the creation of the Order of the Templars); the Muslim movement by making repetitive hysterical appeals to their constituencies to 'rescue' al-Aqsa from the Jews/Israelis who were allegedly 'undermining its foundations' in order to replace the monument with a revived Third Temple, of which they denied the legitimacy since in their belief no First or Second Temples had ever existed there. In other words, the Templars, in spite of their Christian zealotry and the ravages that the Crusaders had inflicted on Jewish communities in Europe and the Holy Land, did not disclaim the Judeo-Christian continuity, and their claims were based on the assumption that ancient Jewish sites were by definition also Christian by virtue of the biblical narrative which confirmed that sacred history. Paradoxically, in spite of the Islamic world's comparatively better treatment of the Jews both in Islamdom and in Palestine after the Crusades, their claim to al-Aqsa has assumed originality, David and Solomon being Prophets, not Kings of Judea, who did not build temples, and the Aqsa structure having descended from Heaven after Muhammad's ascension from that site on the night of the *mi'raj* and *isra'*.

The ostensible separation between the 'political' and 'spiritual' 'wings' of Hamas has permitted the leadership to spread propaganda, raise funds and train recruits, supposedly all volunteers, for acts of Islamikaze, or fighting members of the organization who would also gain martyrdom if they were to be killed in combat. Their leaders, whether the spiritual among them, like Sheikh Yassin, or the political like Rantisi in Gaza or Mash'al in Damascus, or for that matter Ra'id in Israel, have not been known for participating in combat themselves, nor have they sent their children as volunteers to blow themselves up or to fall in combat against their enemies. This is much unlike the Prophet himself and then the first Rashidun Caliphs (AD 632–661), who headed their troops in combat for the cause of Islam in the course of its expansion, and served as models of courage to their troops. Likewise, the Masters of the Templars, who united leadership in battle and in civilian affairs, were also famous fighters who headed their troops in war: five of them died in battles against Muslims; another was made prisoner of war and died in captivity.

Moreover, while Templars waged conventional warfare that was based on fortresses in Iberia and the Levant for defence and on large and far-flung campaigns for offence, in either case targeting the military power of the enemy, today's Islamists have been focusing exclusively either on terrorist attacks against defenceless civilians in the rival camp, or on guerrilla tactics in order to avoid an all-out military confrontation that they cannot sustain. Nevertheless, again paradoxically, the Templars who knew their rivals and the terrain they were defending due to the permanence of their stay, were also pragmatic and appreciated the constraints of local and temporary tactical truces and alliances in order to skirt unfavourable situations, while Hamas, like other Crusader chiefs, have usually been opposed to any ceasefires, let alone reconciliation or permanent peace with their enemies, total victory in Holy War being their goal and yardstick.

When the Templars were accused of heresy in Europe in 1307 and many of them were burned alive or otherwise executed by 1314, their last Master, Jacques de Molay, died courageously proclaiming his faith in the Order and in the Crusade enterprise. The organized army of 15,000 valiant monk-fighters which perished or dissolved, while not always behaving according to the standards set by the Church, were not heretical either, according to the judgement of modern historians. The Order was displaced by the French state authorities and finally disappeared because it was apparently too independent and was deemed an obstacle to the emergence of the pre-modern state, perhaps following their vain attempt to ally with the Mongols of Persia against the Mamluks in order to regain a foothold in the Holy Land (1299–1303). It was finally disposed of because others, like the Hospitallers, with whom the Templars refused to merge, were more docile and could take over some of their dwindling functions. In radical Islam, too, there are factions opposing each other, some being favoured by some Islamic states over others. Hamas, for example, which was the 'darling' of Saudi Arabia until recently, has now been receiving aid from intransigent Iran, which does not relent from its support to Islamic jihad across the world. As in the heyday of the Templars, when the knights of Europe scrambled to the service of those prestigious front-line fighters of the Cross, today's jihadist movements have no difficulty in recruiting new fighters from among the 1.3 billion Muslims who reside in 57 Muslim countries spanning the continents of Asia and Africa. Then, the front of combat against Islam extended only to Iberia and the Levant, but today the dissemination of Islam in its own countries and as minorities in the rest of the world, presents such a multifarious and vast frontline, that the demand for Islamist fighters can only keep growing. Israel and its Islamic movement are only one minor fraction of the emerging frontline that will be tackled in the present volume.

CHAPTER ONE

Religion and Politics: What are the Stakes?

ONE INSTINCTIVELY recoils before what seems a lethal (or troublesome at the very least) combination of religion, which is usually regarded as spiritual and supremely truthful, with politics, as a rule deprecated as this-worldly, brutal and tricky. For when politics, the dirty man-made rules of managing the world, interfere with the God-given purity of the spirit, the latter can be irretrievably distorted; conversely, if absolute notions and categories of religion are introduced into the political game, doctrinaire radicalism and the politics of the desirable take the place of the pursuit of the pragmatically possible. While politicians may be religiously inspired, or act as pious men themselves (e.g., in encouraging prayer in schools, opposing abortions, or manipulating religious symbolism), they are usually bound by larger and wider considerations of *realpolitik* both domestically and more so in the international arena. When they stand for re-election in democracies they also have to conform to the constraints around them and act as firemen who rush to extinguish fires with the explicit goal of being re-elected next time around.

Religious actors in politics are of a different stock, operating under given and set rules. They do not have to cater to their constituencies; their assumptions are universal and unchanging. They would rather ignite fires than put them out, their religious calling being supreme and unrelenting, and their faith uncompromising and exclusive of others. They may champion national, ethnic or political goals, within the establishment or in opposition to it, under the cloak of their religious authority, and they make use of their religious charisma to advance their agenda. A religious doctrine or political ideology motivate them to act on the sociopolitical scene, and/or they may simply be giving vent to their personal ambitions, as when Archbishop Makarios became the President of Cyprus, or when a Muslim scholar such as Ayatollah Khomeini in Iran, or Hassan Turabi in Sudan, became the supreme *éminence grise* in their countries. A religious actor may or may not have undergone official clerical training, taken on a religious title or filled a religious duty, but when acting in the sociopolitical arena he makes extensive use of religious terminology, symbols, beliefs, concepts and rituals. When part of the religious establishment he may deploy it for his advantage, or create alternative organizations and networks in pursuit of his goals when denied access to it.

The political role of the religious actor is especially manifested in areas and times of conflict, where he not only contends against others for leadership of his constituency *per se*, but can also manipulate religious symbols and vocabulary to sway his people against the enemy. In other words, the religious actor, just like his ethnonational counterpart, takes on the dual mantle of leadership inwards, in competition with others, but at the same time also focuses his appeal to the masses on the external threat, real or imagined, posed by the external enemy. Here we are not talking about theoretical and amorphous influences of religion, but about very concrete moulds of action, based on faith and ritual, symbols and terminology, creed and charisma, hierarchy and organization, a combination of the temporal and the sacred, that can shape the very destiny of the conflict and of the people involved. These elements are typically played out in Islam, where political theory is part of the Shari'a law and the separation between the secular and the religious is hard to ascertain. Furthermore, as the winds of Muslim radicalism that is often dubbed 'fundamentalism' continue to sweep the vast Islamic world, the involvement of religious actors in the political arena, both domestically and externally, seems to be increasing. In countries where Islam is the rule (such as Saudi Arabia, Iran, the Sudan and to a lesser extent Pakistan and much of the Arab world), the involvement of clerics in politics is taken as a fact of life and is almost irreversible. However, in some Arab countries and other 'moderate' Muslim lands, the trends of modernization and democratization may have had a mitigating effect on the role of religious politicians.

The unrest that has troubled Muslim lands in recent decades has drawn much world attention both to the domestic upheavals caused in those countries by local radical groups, such as Gama'at in Egypt, Laskar Jihad in Indonesia, Hizbollah in Lebanon and Hamas in the Palestinian territories; and the repercussions that such terrorist groups have generated internationally. Several jihadi movements, such as al-Qa'ida, have a priori been founded as supranational entities and designed so as to provide their worldwide networks with all the trappings of global organizations geared to intimidate their adversaries, notably the West and Israel. In all these varieties of Islamic radicalism–violence–terrorism the leaders, local and general, whether clerics by training and aspiration or executives on behalf of spiritual authorities, have played the role of religious actors par excellence, using their religious clout, or manipulating religious symbols to obtain political goals. These movements have been hardened by years of battle experience against the Soviets in Afghanistan, or against Israel in Palestine, or the Serbs in Bosnia and Kosovo, or the Indians in Kashmir. They have grown into sophisticated organizations whose recruits are carefully differentiated between spiritual leaders (such as Zawahiri for al-Qa'ida, Yassin for Hamas or Fadl'allah for Hizbollah), 'political' leaders (such as Khaled Mash'al for Hamas, or Nasrallah for Hizbollah), *da'wa* (mission) zealots who spread the message in the mosques and the media (such as Sheikh Qaradawi and his clones), operational masterminds (Mash'al or Bin Laden), financiers (like Bin Laden himself and any number of government and private donors) and the operatives themselves who blow themselves up in Islamikaze martyrdom operations or otherwise mount attacks against their targets.

All these participants in domestic and international violent operations are religious actors, whether they are the initiators of their acts or instigate others to perform them, whether they train themselves for 'martyrdom' or indoctrinate others to do so, whether they plan the attacks that are geared to sow terror among their victims or help finance them by collecting 'charity' moneys and channelling them to their operators. Sometimes they create conflicts which they can manipulate to achieve their goals (e.g., al-Qa'ida against the West), or enmesh themselves into an existing conflict (e.g., the Laskar Jihad into Christian–Muslim confrontation in the Moluccas, or Hamas and Hizbollah into the Israeli–Arab dispute), help fan its flames, expand its scope and turn it into a wide-ranging civilizational combat of apocalyptic proportions. Such organizations launch propaganda campaigns (*da'wa* in our case) not only in order to rally their constituencies around their project and encourage recruits and donors to join the cause, but in the fashion of the pre-Islamic oral poetry of the desert they derogate and demonize their prospective victims with a view of making them deserve the terror they design for them. In Islamic terms the targets are *kuffar* (infidels), or Crusaders who are to be countered by jihad until victory, and no room for compromise or negotiation is envisaged. To that end, either an active militia is cultivated wherever the state permits it (e.g., the Palestinian Authority, Iran, Lebanon) or is too weak to ban it (Indonesia, Lebanon), or in spite of the state war against it (Algeria, Egypt, Saudi Arabia). The militia is usually headed by a self-appointed charismatic leader/commander (Ja'far 'Amr Taleb in Indonesia, Abu Sayyef in the Philippines) who may or may not act on his own or get legitimacy and financing from a political or spiritual leadership within the boundaries of the country or outside it. This transnational networking is what lends to these movements a sense of solidarity with other Muslims, and to their leaders as religious actors the aura of acting for the *umma* of universal Islam in general.

The edge that the Muslim religious actor has on his secular/nationalist competitors is that he can at the very least pretend that he does not represent any particular political faction, and so persuade his constituents that he acts for the good of all Muslims. Furthermore, contrary to political movements and the established rulers (be they monarchies or authoritarian regimes of various types which lack legitimacy in the eye of the masses), religious actors can claim the legitimacy of the faith they profess and can justify or rationalize any of their acts by reference to Shari'a law or by issuing tailormade supportive *fatwas* (religious verdicts), or by asking a religious authority to promulgate one. Such a fatwa, being predicated on Islamic law, does not need the backing of a civilian authority to gain validity, for unlike national law it transcends the borders of the country where it is issued and places itself above and beyond time and space to embrace the entire Muslim community. Lending legitimacy to a particular act or threatening to withdraw it (for example the declaration of jihad or the justification of a certain policy) is a powerful tool whereby the religious actor can interfere in politics, sway his constituency for or against it, and coerce politicians to adopt it. For these reasons, Muslim political actors appeal to the Muslim masses in general (for example the Palestinian Hamas and the Lebanese Hizbollah address the entire Muslim world over the heads of their own national authorities). Individual Muslim religious actors who head those or similar groups develop worldwide networks of 'charities', personal relationships with other Muslim organizations, and make use of Muslim media to raise funds and channel them to finance their schemes. A case in point is Ra'id Salah who established such a fundraising foundation under the unifying universal symbol of Al-Aqsa, and has been focusing much of his activity as a religious actor on the mobilizing power of that symbol.

Relying on transnational constituencies affords the religious actor not only the sense of personal power and universal influence, but also the self-confidence that derives from the immense emotional, financial, and political hinterland that can be mobilized behind him when needed. It ensures that, even when faced with defeat or failure, he can try again elsewhere and at some other time, confident that the breakthrough can be achieved when the circumstances are right. For the religious actor will always be waiting for propitious events to converge and fall into his lap like a ripe fig. These may include social or economic deprivation, destitution, defeat in war, political crisis (such as government succession), frustration caused by unfulfilled expectations, the loss of a popular leader, government oppression, perceived undermining of the faith, or plain personal ambition to rule, to guide and to leave one's imprint on events. Admittedly, these very same elements can also be exploited by political leaders for their benefit, as when Saddam Hussein declared his war against Iran (1980–88) to be a repetition of the Qadisiyya battle of the seventh century, or when he added the Islamic war-cry *'Allah Akbar!'* to the existing Iraqi national flag in order to appeal to the world's Muslim audiences, or when he dubbed the Americans 'Crusaders' during the Gulf war of 1991. But no one would claim that Saddam was a religious actor. However, when religious figures such as Yassin, Nasrallah, Zawahiri or Salah use the same metaphors, terminology and symbols, they are less suspected of manipulation, because they do not obviously seek political power for themselves, and therefore would have many more followers among the Muslim masses who could be swayed by their apparent credibility and disinterest in politics.

Transnationalism of religious actors, be they individuals or organizations, carries yet another advantage in so far as since they are not necessarily political entities which can be held accountable for their deeds, and they are not always attached to a definable territory, they are by definition amorphous, evasive and almost immune to retribution. They can hide in the interstices of mountains from local and international authorities, law and order, gain popular support in lawless areas, and make their own law prevail. Their resilience in the face of the powers that persecute them, be they the United States in Iraq and Afghanistan, the Israeli military in the West Bank and Gaza or the Israeli legal system within Israel, or the Egyptian, Saudi, Jordanian, Pakistani, etc. governments, only adds to their charisma and popularity. Furthermore, their ability to resist major military powers, or their own governments which monopolize armed forces in their countries, is popularly interpreted as a sure sign of the justice of their cause. Their Muslim constituents admire the sacrifices of those persecuted religious leaders who often elect rags over riches, and generally live in pristine simplicity, and compare them favourably with the corrupt secular leaders who squander the people's resources. They would rather heed the sweat-iron-and-blood avenue envisaged for them by the religious actors than the rosy promises of prosperity, development and hope which seldom materialize. The hereafter, which is described for them in alluring detail by the religious actors, seems more attractive and attainable to the dispossessed than the gloomy existence which they are desperately locked into under the aegis of their hated and illegitimate rulers.

Religious actors in areas of conflict gain credit in the eyes of their followers not only because they are believed to intercede on behalf of their flock in the hereafter, but also because of their capacity to provide clear answers to the otherwise unresolved dilemmas of existence. This is a key issue because the question often arises: why would common people need a religious actor in an already complex situation where political actors fill the field? What is it that religious actors can offer which political actors cannot? What makes religious actors so salient, sometimes indispensable, especially in areas and eras rife with conflict? Religious actors who conveniently appear in periods of strife and despair do instil in their followers irrational expectations and convictions, not unlike the millenarian groups that Hobsbawm spoke about half a century ago in his classic *Primitive Rebels*, or the various *Mahdi* movements known in Islamic history, where the charismatic leaders at their centre are the driving force and the figureheads that will somehow usher in a new age of plenty and justice. No one else, certainly not corrupt and illegitimate political leaders, can produce such saviours. It is no wonder therefore that in Sunni Islam, unlike Twelver Shi'ism which is predicated on the permanent expectation for the return of the Hidden Imam, it is popular lore, not the established *'ulama*, that builds up the expectation for the appearance of a *Mahdi* as a saviour. It is popular Muslim clerics, not necessarily trained or ordained within the established hierarchy, who take the lead as religious actors of such Muslim 'revolutionary' movements (although established clerics also sometimes play this role).

'Revolution' is by definition an anti-establishment enterprise, often an anti-state in the making within the established order. Religious actors in politics, those we usually dub as 'fundamentalist' or 'radical' are then, by necessity, a threat to their own governments (Hamas to the Palestinian Authority, Hizbollah to Lebanon, the Muslim Brothers to Egypt and

Jordan), but they also accentuate their militantism against perceived outside enemies so as to outdo their governments which are often accused of 'soft policies' and 'sell-out' to the powers-that-be. In other words, religious actors who are competing for the souls of their societies must adopt more radical policies as a way to gaining more legitimacy than their governments in treating both the inner ills at home and the outside threats abroad, if they are to have any chance to survive in their environment and then to conquer it. Paradoxically, the 'revolutionary' message of these religious fundamentalist actors is anchored not in an innovative future-oriented utopia, but in a restorative nostalgia to an idealized past that is identified with the life of the Prophet of Islam. Far from writing the script for their 'revolution' and staging its performance with the religious actors at hand, they fanatically adhere to the ancient divine texts after cleansing them of interpretive accretions that are considered manmade, and they direct their show according to the precedents of the Prophet, his companions and the first Righteous Caliphs (*Rashidun*), while shunning innovation (*bid'a*) as abomination.

This vista of Muslim fundamentalist actors who have been rocking much of the world with their abuses that lead to revolution, fanaticism, violence and terror ought not, however, to overshadow the mitigating potential of other religious actors in situations of conflict. As against Laskar Jihad in Indonesia one could easily cite liberal Muslims such as Nahdat al-'ulama', or individual Muslim leaders in Lebanon, Jordan, the Palestinian Authority, North Africa, and even among the Muslim minorities in the United States, Europe and Israel who act to calm down the tempers and open their hearts to dialogue and tolerance. So do clerics of other faiths in other places, in the wake of the deep transformations undergone in the Catholic Church since the 1960s, as accusations against the Jews were toned down and the Vatican finally recognized the state of Israel which would have been anathema in previous years. At the same time one has to observe with sorrow that the mood in the Muslim world is not one of reconciliation and that for the most part Muslim religious actors play a role in exacerbating conflicts rather than attenuating them.

A distinction is called for at this point between the activity of religious actors in Islamic-majority countries and Muslim-minority ones. If we take it for granted that a certain convergence of events is what provides the religious actor with the opportunity to act, it goes without saying that in situations of Muslim-minority existence the field of friction between the Muslim guest-culture and the majority host-culture is usually wider and more thorny than in homogeneous Muslim countries. For, granted that within Muslim entities too there are wide-open possibilities for conflict, as aggression abounds on behalf of the Muslim majority towards non-Muslim minorities (Sudan, Iran, Nigeria, etc.), or between different Muslim sects and factions (Afghanistan, Pakistan, the Gulf states, Iraq, Egypt and the like), the situation is different where Muslim minorities are concerned. The reason is that within Muslim-majority states it is the official government which conducts the repression against other factions or minorities, and while the oppressed (e.g., the Gama'at or the Muslim Brothers in Egypt, Syria and Jordan) usually produce charismatic leaders who lead the resistance as religious actors, the latter seldom challenge the state's legitimacy. All they wish is to remove the regime, alter its policies, or gain a share of power within the state apparatus. However, since Muslims as a rule are required to live in Islamic lands, their presence under non-Islamic rule poses insoluble problems which end in crisis and unrest. Under such a convergence of events, where the plight of the Muslim minority is identified as 'religious', only recognized religious actors who arise to meet the challenge are capable of dealing with it.

There was a time when Muslim minorities were limited in numbers and scope of dispersion, usually as a result of interaction with the colonial powers who encouraged a certain amount of 'natives' to adopt their cultural ways in their own metropolitan centres, and some of them intermarried and stayed. However, the large waves of Muslim immigrants since the mid-twentieth century to the Americas, Australia and Europe, and more so the opening labour markets in the West to Muslim 'guest-workers', coupled with important movements of conversion to Islam as a result of intense Muslim *da'wa*, has dramatically increased the numbers of Muslim migrants to those countries. Moreover, the 'guests' have come to regard themselves as permanent residents with all the attendant privileges of citizenship and social benefits. In an interesting twist, not only do they no longer regard their presence outside the realm of Islam as temporary, embarrassing and calling for justification, but with the birth of the second and third generations (who grow to learn the languages, cultures and ways of their new habitats), the process of their acculturation into their new homelands has accelerated. As long as their rate in the general populations of their new countries was negligible, and the sociopolitical environment was liberal (as in the United States, Canada, Australia, Israel and Europe), then social pluralism and individual freedom of worship were advocated by the Muslim minorities. Under oppressive regimes such as the Soviets or the

Chinese, the Muslims were quick to adopt material acculturation into their host society, with all the trappings of language, dress, education and participation in the elites and social customs. The core of the faith was kept almost intact, however, with the Muslim calendar, festivals, dietary laws, worship and places of prayer preserved as far as possible. This was easier in areas where Muslim minorities were larger and commanded the critical mass necessary to sustain communal life, and far more difficult when the Muslim population was so sparse as to render any public display of Muslim identity impractical.

This state of affairs has changed radically in the past few decades due to the convergence of several factors: the deepening gap of the Western–Islamic divide following the Iran revolution and the subsequent Islamist takeover in the Sudan and Afghanistan; the growing unease among second- and third-generation Muslim immigrants in the West who felt excluded or marginalized; the outburst of unrest among those Muslim populations that had failed to integrate, which led to violence and terror; the general rise of Muslim fundamentalism and militancy in the world; the vast Saudi effort in cultivating Muslim radicalism of the Wahhabi type in many a Western capital; the exacerbation in the Arab-Israeli dispute, which gave many disaffected Muslims in the West a cause to rally around; the growing numbers of Muslim immigrants in Western countries, legal and illegal, which lent them the weight of a critical mass when they reached several percentage points of the general populations (up to 10 per cent in France and less in the rest; and the 11 September (2001) horror, which rendered many Muslims suspicious in their Western environment. This meant that Muslim visibility became greater, their *modus operandi* more violent and their *modus vivendi* with their adoptive countries less accommodating. These are precisely the interstices where fiery religious players, such as the immensely popular grandson of Hassan al-Banna, Swiss-born Tariq Ramadan, introduce themselves and take the lead of their communities, while the voices of reason and accommodation of moderate religious players such as Boubaker, the French government handpicked dean of the Paris mosque, are relegated to the margins. This is also the path that Muslim fundamentalists in Israel (and elsewhere) took by giving rise to Ra'id Salah, their recognized and vastly respected head.

These situations of rebellious guest cultures who no longer accept their minority status can give rise to violence that is aimed either at secession or various forms of autonomy, or can grow into an irredentist claim when the minority dwells in adjacent proximity/territorial continuity to their mother-country where the main bulk of their people is located (the Kurds in Turkey, Iran and Iraq; the Hungarians of Transylvania and Voivodina; the Sudeten Germans; the Arabs of Israel). Such claims, which may be bolstered especially when the minority becomes too large to govern, or becomes a local majority in its area of residence, gain currency when the demographic growth of the minority is so much faster than that of the host culture as to arouse hopes of a 'democratic' takeover by the one-man one-vote device that worked in Zimbabwe and South Africa. In other words, minorities of this sort, be they national or religious, do not seek to merge through integration as in Brazil and create a raceless society where no value is given to creed or original culture, but to dominate through victory and enslavement of the others when the numbers so allow. In these situations religious actors find a fertile ground to act, by advocating demographic growth in their communities, denigrating the majority culture so as to discourage acculturation into it, creating an atmosphere of separateness and strife, inventing irredentist claims and mobilizing their community to obey them in the pursuance of those ambitions.

When Muslim minorities become frustrated by the unworkability of a pluralistic society (e.g., in Cyprus, the Philippines, Israel and increasingly within European countries), either because they believe they are discriminated against or because their expectations are not met, they become antagonistic to their host society. So much more so when they perceive the majority as having transgressed the limits of previous coexistence and encroached upon their freedom of worship or conduct. In such cases, they use Western vocabulary (freedom, tolerance, democracy, human rights, etc.) to impress upon their hosts that while they wish to play by the rules of their adoptive countries, it is the latter that violate them. In more extreme cases, like some Muslim fundamentalist leaders (religious actors *par excellence*) in London, they claim that they came to Europe in order to change it, not to be reshaped by it, or they reject Western values lock, stock and barrel (like resisting the ban on the veil in French schools). This sets the Muslim minority, especially the fundamentalist elements in its midst, on a collision course with the host authorities. Militant elements among this disaffected minority may seek political or cultural autonomy (the London Muslim 'parliament', or various national or international Muslim associations, or organizations of Imams and mosque leaders, or the heads of the Arab local councils in Israel, or the demand for autonomy and for an 'Arab' or 'Muslim' university and other separate institutions. In India, Muslims had conquered the land and subjugated Hinduism, but when

Muslim power was eroded by the British, Islam sought and achieved separation from the Hindus for the most part, rather than submitting to the democratic rule of modern India that would have allowed the Hindus to exercise political domination over the Muslims. When the majority of Indian Muslims established their own state (Pakistan), their 'ulama spoke of the reinstitution of the Shari'a as their state law. There was no alternative to this arrangement if one bears in mind the fact that Islam is incompatible with other political ideologies. Maulana Mawdoodi, the prominent Indian Muslim modernist, has put it this way: 'To be a Muslim and adopt a non-Muslim viewpoint is only meaningless. "Muslim nationalist" and "Muslim Communist" are contradictory terms as "Communist Fascist" and "chaste prostitute".'[1]

Thus, as orthodox Muslims see it, and much more so the fundamentalists among them, Islam is ideally an either/or affair. Either Islamic law and institutions are given full expression and dominate state life or, failing that, if the state is non-Islamic, Muslims should try to reverse the situation or leave. In practice, however, things are not so clear-cut. As long as an appearance of peace and accommodation can be maintained, the minority Muslim community, although entertaining a vague hope for the fulfilment of its political aspirations at some future time, can contain the discrepancy between dream and reality, and the tension between the two can go unresolved. But if persecution of the minority is intensified, for example in non-democratic countries, to the point where no real Muslim life can be ensured, and when a practical opportunity arises, the minority Muslims are likely to seize it and proclaim either a separate Muslim entity or a Muslim state regardless of whether the Muslim population is a majority or a minority in the territory in question. For an Islamic state can encompass either. Muslims have experienced both a Muslim majority under non-Islamic rule, as in Christian Valencia where Muslims outnumbered the Christians four to one,[2] and a Muslim minority rule in Hindu-majority India and the Umayyad Christian-majority state in the Iberian Peninsula. It is Muslim rule, then, that defines the borders of the Abode of Islam, not Muslim majorities or minorities. In recent years the enhanced stature of Islam has led the Muslim centre to take a keener and deeper interest in the minorities on its periphery. This renewed interest has been manifested in the resolutions of the Islamic conferences which have been bringing under one roof delegates from some 55 Muslim-majority countries representing over 1.3 billion believers. More interest has been taken by remote Muslim communities in participating in the pilgrimage to Mecca, where two million people from all nationalities share their fellowship with their brothers and enhance the identity of the universal *umma*.

The Muslims of Israel (one million believers who constitute close to 20 per cent of the population in the Jewish state) have been allowed recently by Saudi Arabia to take part in the pilgrimage to Mecca, thus reinforcing their link to the Muslim world. They are not in direct conflict with their state, but they used for many years to be torn between their people (the Palestinians of whom they are part) and their country (Israel of which they are citizens). No longer, however, for since the outbreak of the first intifada in 1987, and more so after the breakdown of the Oslo peace process and the eruption of the al-Aqsa intifada in 2000, the Muslims of Israel (certainly the fundamentalists among them under Ra'id Salah's leadership) have totally embraced the Palestinian positions in the conflict, and steadfastly opposed their country's policies. If that were a mere expression of a political stance, the like of which we find among Jewish constituencies on the Right and the Left as well, there would be nothing abnormal about it. However, when the Muslim fundamentalists in Israel use Islamic vocabulary and symbols to express their views, they become religious actors according to the aforesaid definitions; all the more so when a Muslim spiritual leader, who doubles up as a political actor, takes their lead and champions their cause. Incidentally, Jewish religious actors also partake of political activity and enter into the boundaries of these definitions, and it would be interesting and instructive to draw comparisons between the two and try to depict their mutual contribution to the polarization of the parties in the conflict. It will be the task of the present volume to draw the contours of this religious activity on the Muslim side, in both the religious and political domains, to point out the link between them and to show how these generalizations about religious actors in areas of conflict are played out in this case-study. Moreover, since Ra'id Salah has also become something of a national leader among Israeli Arabs, though he does not play in the strictly political field, his activity also throws light on the grey areas between politics and religion and on the delicate texture of the relationship between religious and political actors among Israeli Arabs.

Even though no attempt will be made to force a given theoretical framework on this study, general questions cannot be avoided about the religious actor, his motivations, methods, interaction with other actors and with his environment. To what extent is religion the main engine behind him? When do personal ambition and lust for power prevail over piety and religiosity? The relationship between religious and political or ethnonational goals also demands investigation, as does the issue of the effect of the involvement of religious actors on the conflict, and what it takes to impact on it either way. When religious actors of different degrees of conviction and fanaticism act concurrently (though not in unison) in the same arena, what makes one trend prevail over the others? Is it solely the impact of the personality of the actor, his charisma, his oratory and his aggressiveness, or is the contents of his teachings the decisive factor in swaying the masses? Does that hinge upon his religious authority, reputation and mastery of the mass media, or on his capacity to act and to achieve visible results? Intriguingly, the same questions might be posed in a situation where religious actors of various faiths contend for the same constituencies, or vie for rival communities living together or in close proximity in a situation of conflict. In both cases, can the religious actor show adaptability and flexibility when acting in the political arena, or on unfamiliar grounds, and to what extent is he able to compromise the core of his belief in his quest to attain his goals, in which case he will be defeating his purpose? Finally, do the attitudes of the society in which he operates and of the establishment that he faces matter: are they propitious, open, neutral, indifferent, discouraging or hostile?

All these questions deserve investigation in any culture, religion or political system. However, since we are dealing here with Muslim religious actors, it is important to recall that there are traits of character and conduct that set them apart from Western tradition, because their ideology as religious actors is tinged with a Third World mood characterized by envy and anger *vis-à-vis* the West (and Israel) due to its power and high rate of development, its technological and military successes, as compared to their own impotence and backwardness, its democratic, legitimate and efficient regimes, compared to their illegitimate and corrupt systems, and its cultural dominance in the modern world. It is essential to detect and recognize these differences, because much of the anti-Western and anti-Israel vitriol and deeds of Muslim religious actors derives from them rather than from religion or religious activism. We have witnessed Muslim religious actors, such as Sheikhs Yassin, Nasrallah, Bin Laden, Zarqawi and the like who have taken great delight at the sight of Westerners and Israelis murdered *en masse*, while registering great shock and consternation in the face of the vigorous and resolute counterattacks launched against them which blunted their triumphalism and at times eroded their popular support. This means that while they regard their acts against the West, or against their domestic rivals (be they Christian or Muslim) as legitimate and called for, their victims are not supposed to retaliate or fight back. If they do they are 'aggressors', 'enemies of Allah', 'unbelievers', 'Crusaders', 'collaborators with the enemy', 'heretics' or 'turncoats' – all deserving of the wrath of Allah at the hands of those Islamic actors.

Muslim religious actors operate on the assumption of an unbridgeable gap between themselves and the Western world. Western culture, at least in theory, agrees to coexist with other cultures, even when they are weaker, and even as it tries to incorporate them into its global systems. The Muslim world, however, recognizing the power of the stronger West, also feels humiliated and frustrated by it. Frustration in a shame culture creates aggression. Several areas of comparison may be suggested which point out the differences between the two cultures and throw light on the thinking and *modus operandi* of Muslim religious actors. First among them is the apparent attitude towards human life, which has been epitomized by the current sayings of Muslim fundamentalists regarding their 'election of death with honour over life with humiliation', or by their executions live on television of Western hostages whom they capture, or the mass murders that they conduct in the name of Allah. Unlike Europeans who do not boast of their past cruelty, and Asians who still strive to hide their military massacres, Muslim fundamentalists boast in public of their murderous exploits and they cite the precedents of the Prophet and the jihad wars of the fathers of Islam, as well as the medieval *fida'iyun* and the martyrs of the Shi'ites in Iran and Lebanon to rationalize and justify their deeds.

The tool of Islamikaze[3] has been adopted by Muslim religious and political actors as the ultimate weapon of the weak to wreak havoc upon and instil terror into their enemies. It has further hardened their hearts in the belief that no mercy should be shown towards the enemy (the West or Israel) whom they accuse of terrorism, cruelty and mass murder. So much so that from a handful of fanatical volunteers, who became 'martyrs' on behalf of the Hizbollah and other Shi'ite causes, their circle has grown gradually to include the hundreds of Hamas, al-Qa'ida and Islamic Jihad members who volunteered for such acts against the West and Israel, the multitudes of non-Islamist movements such as the Palestinian Tanzim and al-Aqsa brigades who are ready to perform selfless martyrdom against the targets they are pitted against, and even women and children whose numbers have been increasing in the service of their operations. Such a mass operation, which could not succeed without the infrastructure of indoctrination and encouragement on the part of Muslim actors such as Yassin, Nasrallah, Bin Laden and Qaradawi, has become so widely accepted by mainstream Islam as to idealize it in the eyes of young people and to educate them in its light. The result is that since the operation involves a poignant self-sacrifice that is not incidental but conscious and rehearsed as in the case of the Japanese kamikaze (especially as it involves children, women and adolescents) the Muslim public focuses on its own grief caused by its own losses, not on the havoc and misery meted out to the victims.

Other harrowing aspects of Muslim fundamentalist attitudes to human life, often condoned by their religious actors, are manifest in the chopping-off of heads or the slashing of their enemies' throats. Those suspected of collaboration with the enemy (Palestinian collaborators with Israel, or simple defenceless civilians in the Algerian countryside), are similarly dealt with. Groups of Western tourists in Egypt, Tunisia or Algeria are massacred, buses and restaurants with all their occupants are blown up. Entire families are murdered or mutilated and their bodies dragged into the streets. Not only there is no concern for human life, nor for the families of the murdered, the maimed and the kidnapped, but the activists seem to be oblivious to the destructive impact of these acts on their own civilians and children who grow accustomed to this culture of mass murder. This is usually accompanied by masochistic displays of wounds and blood and the sadistic lynching of their enemies with their bare hands while the crowds look on and cheer, maddened by these orgies of cruelty, violence and inhumanity. Funerals of their own dead whom they consider martyrs are accompanied by shouting, shooting into the air: huge processions where the body of the dead person is seized by the crowd and tossed from hand to hand, with vows of violent revenge. Compare these with the silent and dignified funerals of the victims of terrorism in the West and Israel, and you have one of the keys to the difference between the two cultures. All these horrors, which are done in the open, often to the jubilation of the masses and with the support of mainstream media, are seldom if ever condemned by religious actors, and often condoned by them – something which lends them legitimacy in the eyes of the public.

This callousness in the attitudes towards human life is often supplemented by the horrendous re-enactment of scenes of murder as if they were sublime human experiences worth replaying and educating the masses to follow. This goes a long way to show how cold-bloodedly these murders are planned, often at the instigation of religious actors, rather than being a spur-of-the-moment act of 'frustration' by some ill-fated, 'desperate' or 'humiliated' Muslim. For when the scene of a café or a paper model of a bus are carefully and meticulously reconstructed in a public place at the heart of a Muslim city, mock flying limbs of the victims dripping with blood are hung around the scene, explosions are replayed and sounds emitted by the crying victims are amplified – and all this to the cries of joy of the assembled masses (including children and so-called 'innocent civilians'), then something is decidedly sick in the psyche of this society. If no amount of explanation and justification can excuse the horrible acts of murder themselves, how much more so the sheer madness of reproducing those acts, time and again, like a tape being replayed in slow motion to satisfy the sadism of its producers. We can understand that these re-enactments are the extension of the terrible *ta'zia* ceremonies widely celebrated by the Shi'ites during the Ashura Day, when believers relive the suffering of Hussein in Karbalah by inflicting pain and injury on their own bodies. But while the Shi'ites exhibit a masochistic sense of identification with their own kin, out of their own volition, as part of their ritual, and without inflicting pain or damage on others, the Hamas scenes sadistically reproduce sights of horror and terror that they caused to others, not as part of a ritual but as an expression of joy at the suffering of their enemies. In this light (or rather obscurity) the jubilation in the Muslim street following the trauma of 11 September can be understood.

Another gap between the West and the culture promoted by Muslim religious actors is their built-in intolerance towards other faiths. Although other monotheistic faiths are also exclusive of each other and regard themselves as the recipients of God's revelation to mankind, they have given up violence as a legitimate way of spreading their culture, whereas militant Islam and its supporters make ample use of force and hostility to promote theirs. The Western humanistic idea of tolerance of the other means that the other has come to be accepted, without value judgements. This approach has not only permitted the renouncing of the use of force, at least in principle, for spreading Christianity, democracy, free trade and other Western ideas, but has also allowed Islam and other creeds to compete on Western turf – without the Europeans or the Americans ever suspecting that the competition would ultimately end up over the turf itself. Moreover, since the West accepted the idea of separating the Church from the modern secular state, faith has become the domain of the private rather than public arena. In the Islamic world, practically all 'secular' governments, which for the most part lack legitimacy, must pay lip-service to the Islamists, at times by including them in their governments. Their presence as a threatening alternative to the existing rule forces the regimes to heed them and strike compromises with some of their demands, thus making it impossible for any Muslim territory to be neutral towards other faiths and open to anything other than Muslim activity. Furthermore, Muslim radicals, led by their religious actors, regard the defeat of their own illegitimate governments as a prelude to their restoration of the universal caliphate of all Muslims, and therefore treat the Western governments who protect, aid and sponsor the dictators in place as the direct enemy of Muslims. From their point of view, then, not only is Western culture despicable in its own 'right' and faulty due to its own deficiencies, but it has invaded their turf in order to subvert and undermine it from within, until it falls off like a ripe fig. It is the West that came to them, not they to it.

This creates a paradox, nevertheless: for while Muslim fundamentalists decry the Western cultural invasion (worse in their eyes than the medieval invasions of the Crusades), they and their less militant co-religionists at the same time queue to gain entry visas into those countries which are bastions of the Western values that they love to hate. Some explain their quest as a simple wish to study in the West, especially in value-free technical professions which are not 'soiled' by Western thinking, though they are the product of its genius. But they ignore the fact that by sojourning for protracted periods in the West they by necessity will be influenced by its spirit and might elect to stay there. Others wish from the start to improve their economic lot by migrating to the West, but once they get there they congregate around their kin and provide fertile ground for Muslim fundamentalist *da'wa*, led by religious actors. Still others, such as Sheikhs Bakri and Masri in Britain, have migrated to the West as 'refugees' from political or criminal persecution in their homelands, and the West was generous enough to accommodate them. Paradoxically, it is the latter who often place themselves at the forefront of the leaders of radical Islam in the West and who, while benefiting from the hospitality and social welfare arrangements in their host countries, recruit local converts or already naturalized Muslims for training abroad, for indoctrination at home and for activities in the path of Allah. It is those religious actors who are tolerated by societies against whom they are operating ideologically, who are the least tolerant towards their hosts. Their message is loud and clear: to Islamize their host societies and let Islam take them over. Until recently it was the integrationists – those who wished to integrate into society, fit into its political, social and economic institutions and become part of it culturally – who made an impact on their coreligionists, but the penetration of Muslim fundamentalism into the West has begun to turn these trends around. More and more Muslims rebel against their host culture and demand as fully-fledged citizens that their culture be recognized as a component of the national make-up: that state symbols (for example the cross on Scandinavian, Greek and Swiss flags) be altered to become inclusive, and that mosques, foreign Muslim languages and Muslim education should be subsidized by the state. In France, following the banning of veils in schools, young French Muslims who are the sons of immigrants from North Africa, frequently boo the 'Marseillaise' when it is played on football fields prior to matches.

Therefore, when Muslim religious actors speak of tolerance they mean, for the most part, a temporary measure of accommodation towards the Infidel, who clearly embraces an inferior creed, until Islam is strong enough to prevail. The miscalculation of al-Qa'ida on 11 September, and before and after that of Hamas and Islamic Jihad, was that Western societies were so ripe for their demise that a shocking trauma, or a series of smaller but frequent attacks, would promptly overwhelm the enemy. Thus, every time the enemy responds more forcefully than expected, like the United States in Afghanistan or the Israelis in the West Bank, the Muslim religious actors cry 'foul!', for this is not how the enemies of Islam are supposed to behave; their very resistance to their subjugation by Islam is regarded as 'blasphemous' for its failure to recognize the will of Allah, and their retaliatory strikes against aggression and terror are seen as 'signs of distress and despair', which augur their approaching end. Hence the increased activities of terrorism to speed up that process and bring it to its conclusion. This point of view does not recognize the right of the attacked 'for the sake of Allah' to self-defence. Muslims can attack, conquer, expand, kill, enslave, dominate and rule, for the universe is theirs to include in dar al-Islam, but woe to those who dare to resist that 'noble' process that is entrenched in the Will of Allah. Those who do are decried as 'aggressors', 'infidels', 'killers of civilians and children', 'arrogant' and performers of 'massacres'. Thus, any hideous attack against their enemies, even when it involves innocent lives as in the case of 11 September, is 'inevitable', 'blessed', 'well-deserved' and a 'great success', and causes masses to rejoice and writers to sing its praise throughout the Islamic world, while every retaliation is lamented, condemned and blasted as 'unjustified', 'out of proportion', 'cruel', 'wanton massacre' and 'proof' – if proof were needed – of the enemy's inherent evil.

The idea of fair play, of attack and counter-attack and, in consequence, of casualties inflicted on both parties to a conflict, is misunderstood in Muslim circles. Even the issue of aggressive and defensive warfare is foreign to them, because the Muslim definitions of warfare do not follow the accepted objective norms prevailing in the West, but abide strictly by the subjective rules drawn from Muslim jurists who have formulated Muslim political theory and international relations.[4] According to these rules, any attack by non-Muslims on Muslims is inherently illegal and immoral, and therefore it is incumbent upon all Muslims to assist their co-religionists, regardless of what they did to provoke the attack. Conversely, any Muslim attack, on the West for example, since it can be justified as a defensive war against the infidels, or as an act of self-defence against the spiritual invasion of the West, or as a battle to repulse the enemy from dar al-Islam (for example from Andalusia, Chechnya, southern France, Kosovo, Afghanistan or Palestine), is *eo ipso* a just war that all Muslims are called upon to support. In other words, once a war has been labelled 'jihad', and any of the latter examples justifies jihad, the arena is wide open for war. Guerrilla warfare or Islamikaze terrorism are means of warfare that are sanctified by Islam with all the attendant ideological and doctrinal elaborations. Intolerance that is based on the concept of superiority, whereby the superior does not have to conform like the inferior, is also apparent in the daily behaviour of the Muslim world towards other religions. Churches are burned throughout the Muslim world (Egypt, Indonesia, Nigeria) and Jewish synagogues have been burned by Muslims in the West Bank and most Western capitals, but rare are the occasions when Muslim mosques are attacked or set on fire. The Muslims do not take this and the fact that they can build their mosques anywhere in the West as an indication of Western tolerance and acceptance of the other, but as a sure sign that the others do not dare to resist Islamic expansion that is inherently right and justified, while they, in their countries, can curtail or totally prevent the construction of Christian and Jewish houses of prayer, and even destroy existing ones.

No country in the West retaliates systematically in kind to the scenes current in the Muslim world where US (and Israeli) flags and effigies of leaders are burned in public. Muslim inability to accept symbols of others' sovereignty as legitimate and equal to theirs is striking, while the West respects theirs as a matter of course. This has encouraged Muslim communities in the West, led by vocal religious actors, to demand the right to construct their mosques or perform their rituals in places known as holy sites to other faiths. Throughout their history Muslims have turned churches and synagogues into mosques and every occupied land into a *waqf* (holy endowment); but woe to anyone who dares to turn a mosque into a non-Muslim house of prayer or to take over land that is, or was, Islamic, for that is intolerable. They are implicitly declaring to Christianity and Judaism, in Bernard Lewis's memorable words: 'Your time has passed. Now we are here. Move over.'[5] This is not exactly tolerance. The Qur'anic inscription in the Dome of the Rock, 'He is God, He is One. He does not beget, He is not begotten', which was meant to reject the basic dogma of Christianity about God and His Son when the Muslims occupied Jerusalem in the seventh century, was also inscribed in the temporary tent-mosque in front of the Basilica of the Annunciation in Nazareth, when Muslims, led by their religious actors, attempted in vain to take over the plaza of the Basilica and erect a permanent mosque there. Coupled with the denial of Jewish rights on Temple Mount, this signifies that Muslims indeed view themselves as having superseded both Judaism and Christianity; hence their hatred of the construct 'Judaeo-Christian tradition' which they consider as having been relegated to a passing episode in history once the Seal of Prophets had dispensed to humanity the latest divine message.

Hardly consistent with these dreams of world dominion entertained by Muslims is their feeling that they are the victims of the West and specifically Israel, which they hate and wish to displace. However, they need the resources of the West. Most important for them is to explain to themselves and to the world why and how they, who had pioneered civilization and science in medieval times, and had caused Europe to tremble before their mighty empires, found themselves at the bottom of the hierarchy of world powers and the ladder of economic and social development as the modern era dawned. For a shame culture like theirs it is difficult, even impossible, to take responsibility for their deeds and to devise a policy of adaptation that could pull them out of that quagmire, for that would amount to admitting the deficiencies of their culture, the stifling restrictions of their faith, the pipe-dreams of their leaders, including their religious actors, and the insufficiencies of their social systems. Thus, rather than accept their drawbacks and seek succour elsewhere, it is easier for them to project their problems on others, to disguise their jealousies and bigotry as 'revivalism', and to accuse the West (and Israel) of imperialism and colonization. They do not want to recall that when they were the conquerors and occupiers, the powerful and colonizers, the imperialists and slave-drivers, they did not stop to ask themselves what they were doing with the people they conquered and the civilizations they decimated. It is in the rhetoric of Muslim religious actors that one finds the best evidence of self-aggrandizement and the most poignant expression of deprecation and condemnation of others.

Muslim nations have vast resources, human and mineral, a great tradition of learning and an immense ambition to restore themselves to their former glory. However, their self-inflicted deficiencies in government, economics and antiquated social structure do not permit them to develop. Uncontrollable population explosion and poverty are hardly the recipes to arrest these trends. While the Islamists and their religious actors boast their ability to make up lost ground and promise that return to Islam would bring salvation, their diagnosis of the situation is not much different from that of the rivals they seek to unseat: the West (and Israel) are to blame and Islam is the eternal victim. How else can they explain to themselves the continually growing gap that separates them from the West, and which they watch on television screens day in day out, but that the others are to blame, not they? This state of mind is aided in those societies by the dependence of the ordinary individual on his corrupt government for food subsidies, for employment, for education and faltering social services, for development and well-being in general. By heaping the blame on others, the rulers in place hope to escape their responsibility for the sorry condition of their citizenry. But the fundamentalist religious actors apportion the blame equally to the West and its allies among the Muslim authorities who combine their efforts to ban the Islamists from the corridors of power.

The eternal victim also believes not only that everyone owes him something, while he himself is exempted from any effort, but also that he is entitled to resort to violence to redress the ills done to him. Palestinian refugees, for example, led partly by their religious actors, have been living on handouts of flour from the UN for three generations. Thus they are mostly financed by the United States, which they love to hate. While their population has quadrupled, they still believe that the world ought to continue to feed them indefinitely. They produce children, but it is up to the West to take care of them. They have resisted all attempts at settlement in their host countries lest they lose their refugee status, and with it the 'benefits' of perpetuating their victimhood. They could have learned from others to absorb refugees and put them on the productive track, rather than encourage them in the mentality of eternal victim, with the attendant gains of eliminating the violence and terrorism that are engendered by bitterness and frustration. This is not only a matter of money or of economic development (watch Bin Laden and Saudi Arabia for example), but a matter of culture. If one is educated to take matters into one's hands, not to accept handouts, to stand on one's own feet and to help oneself, then dignity is restored, humiliation effaced or diminished, and the paralysing jealousy and stifling apathy replaced by aspiration, ambition, striving and achievement.

Being victims means that everyone ought to understand them. When they terrorize innocent civilians, that is merely retaliation for their humiliation. For every one of their orgies of death one must seek the 'roots' and comprehend the 'reasons' and address the 'causes'. Thus a reversal of roles is effected, whereby the West (and Israel) are the terrorists, while the Muslims simply act in self-defence. Hence the failure of Muslim countries to accede to the Western definition of terrorism which is, in essence, the 'use of violence against innocent civilians for political goals'. They refuse to relinquish the mantle of victimhood, therefore terrorism is only what is done to them, not what they do to others. They not only struggle on all international forums to show that their terrorists are in fact victims and martyrs, but their religious actors also provide the religious rationale that further encourages those acts and puts on them the stamp of 'in the path of Allah', with all the attendant rewards in Paradise. Other victims, such as the Americans killed on 11 September, or the Indians in Kashmir, or the Israelis in pizza parlours or buses, are not victims in the eyes of these Muslim fundamentalists. They deserve no compassion because they 'had brought that unto themselves', or better, 'had concocted that themselves', 'in conjunction with the CIA or Mossad', as on 11 September. The wide acceptance of conspiracy theories, including among intellectuals, opinion-makers and religious actors, adds to the universal sense of victimhood that is rampant in the Muslim world. Another important corollary of this attitude is that while in the Judaeo-Christian tradition martyrs are usually the victims of external aggression inflicted on them in the pursuit of their faith, in Islam it is the perpetrator of the aggression who also immolates himself in the process of becoming the Islamikaze martyr. In other words, the martyr is not he who suffers death or torture or misery on his way to martyrdom, since he chose that course; the martyr must kill in order to gain his place in the hierarchy of martyrs.

This aspect of Islamic culture is also closely tied in with the world of fantasy and self-delusion that they often sink into to avoid the shame or the harshness of reality. Religious actors are often the instigators, shapers and promoters of such illusory narratives. In that culture the ability of the word to move people and to incite them to action (a key element used by religious actors in the training of the Islamikaze) is supplemented by a rich world of fantasy in which wishful thinking replaces fact, mantra-like slogans supersede policy and the unpleasant is denied as if did not exist (Muslims did not commit the 11 September horrors, the Israelis did). Slogans are coined and repeated (the Israelis have injected HIV into the Palestinians, or Israel perpetrated a massacre in Jenin). They boast of their own exploits (Egyptian democracy is exemplary) and denigrate their enemy (Jews are cowardly, the descendants of apes and pigs). Lies are made up to cover deficiencies (economic difficulties are caused by Israel, not by the intifada and terror); and denial is exercised when one is faced with facts (no Twin Towers, no Karine A). History is invented (Palestinians are descendants of Canaanites), false analogies are made (Palestinian leaders are like the American founding fathers), and facts are denied (the Holocaust and Palestinian involvement in terrorism). Self-embellishment and self-aggrandizement are sought (the future belongs to Islam, the West's demise is imminent). Self-delusion operates on other levels as well. Convinced of the righteousness and exclusivity of their Islamic universal message, Muslim fundamentalists cannot understand why the West and Israel pursue them, and why they do not allow them to follow the path of Allah. For the message of Allah is clear and unambiguous: it declares the Jews as monkeys who have drawn upon themselves the wrath of Allah; it forbids Muslims to befriend Jews and Christians, enjoins Muslims to kill unbelievers wherever they find them, to fight and slay pagans, seize them and beleaguer them. So why do the infidels act in denial of these words of Allah?

The hard-core Islamists are therefore shocked that the West fights back and resists them, instead of submitting to them and recognizing that Islam is their only salvation. We have seen appeals on behalf of Muslim religious actors to President Bush to convert to Islam and astonishment at his procrastination about doing so. They cannot comprehend how and why Westerners are failing to see the light and do not hurry into the fold of Islam. In their world of delusion they already see 'thousands of

Americans' repenting for their previous obtuse misunderstanding of Islam, and their being 'reduced to tears' when they listen to the words of the Qur'an recited to them. Their world view, which cannot accept a plurality of creeds, also cannot understand why they, the disseminators of the good of Allah and his message should be held in low esteem and feared and persecuted by the West. After a fabrication of stories is achieved which bears no relation to fact, it is repeated often enough until throughout the Muslim world it becomes a reality ('the Jews were responsible for 11 September'). Then the denial stage sets in, when Muslims in question realize (as with Karine A or the Twin Towers) the havoc they have caused in the world, and paradoxically, at the same time that they deny their deeds they exhibit public jubilation about them. In other words, they wish to dissociate themselves from the atrocities they have committed (lest they face intimidation and punishment) and to 'enjoy' their result at the same time. In the aftermath of 11 September, in spite of their displays of uncontainable joy, Muslims from Pakistan to America, from Egypt to Afghanistan, denied that 'any Muslim could commit such horror', because it was patently against 'the compassion and tolerance of Islam', and verses were cited in support of this contention. For example, Islam 'was opposed to compulsion in faith', or to the execution of 'innocent civilians', unless they challenged Islam or 'humiliated it'. And anyone who displeased them for one reason or another could always be accused of either offence.

Another current claim among the Muslim populace was that an act of terror of such proportions as 11 September could not possibly have been planned, let alone executed, by any Muslim state or organization, thus exonerating themselves in advance, even if that implied an admission of their incompetence in carrying out operations on such a scale. Even as the evidence was being gathered and divulged of al-Qa'ida involvement, and demands were mounting for the group's indictment, Muslims continued to insist that 'unless America provided decisive and undisputed evidence for Muslim involvement', it was wrong on the part of the West to 'smear the entire Muslim world' which 'was opposed to terrorism', on account of the 'yet unproven' deeds of a few. The roles were therefore reversed once again: the Muslims, who needed no evidence for their delusions, and never stopped to reflect on the irrationality of their accusations against the West (and Israel), suddenly found themselves being scrupulous about 'evidence' when the indictments were laid at their door. They also found themselves pledging that should any evidence emerge of Muslim involvement, the culprits ought to be prosecuted by 'Muslim justice' and dealt with according to Muslim procedures, which in effect meant exonerating Muslims altogether. But the facts kept pressing at the door, and the Muslim claims of innocence had become so ludicrous that the stage of projection set in, namely throwing upon others the blame for the deeds that could no longer be denied. Becoming suddenly meticulous about data-gathering and the provision of 'conclusive evidence', they began to fabricate piecemeal stories about Israelis and Jews who had been 'forewarned by their kin' and who evacuated the premises of the Twin Towers prior to the blast; or about the 'takeover of the control towers by suspect elements' (also presumably Jewish) who 'collaborated with the hijackers', or about other hoaxes.

Similarly, when the Americans opened up their counter-attack against the Taliban, and attempted not to harm civilians unnecessarily in the process, even dropping significant quantities of food to sustain them during the fighting, it was the stories of 'massacres of innocent civilians', 'poisoning of the dropped food parcels', the 'intentional bombings of schools and food depots' and the 'cruel arrest of Taliban POWs and their transport to Guantanamo Bay, where they were treated 'inhumanely', that dominated the Arab and Muslim reporting of the operation, and not the intentional atrocities committed by the Taliban and their supporters. For the Arab and Muslim audiences the purpose was not to report a balanced truth, where the evils and motivations of both parties were recounted, and where the sequence of cause and effect had to be explained concerning the horrendous terrorist attacks against civilians which had to be rooted out and punished; only the senseless and callous 'American attacks against civilians', committed without reason or cause, to satisfy the evil instincts of the Americans, were reported, and repeatedly so, *ad nauseam*. For Arab and Muslim audiences, vilifying, debasing and libelling their enemies was the only way to recast them as inhuman predators, so as to pave the way for additional terrorist attacks against them. This sort of projection onto the enemy not only permits his delegitimization and encourages more attacks against him but also, more significantly, exposes the hidden dreams of what Muslim fundamentalists would do to the Westerners if they could.

Finally, Muslim fundamentalists have been plagued by a pathological anti-Semitism that is promoted chiefly by their religious actors and which affects and conditions every act of theirs on the international arena, either when they mount attacks against the Jews or when they justify their actions by some Jewish conspiracy. The old and stale anti-Jewish stereotypes that appear in classic European anti-Semitism, and which have been copiously replicated in Arab and Muslim anti-Semitic writings, have of late effected some new twists, concurrent with the enhanced anti-Semitic mood in the West. The main founts of inspiration have not changed dramatically, and are drawn from Muslim sources (e.g., dubbing the Jews the 'descendants of apes and swine'), and borrowing from old Christian themes such as Blood Libel, the *Protocols of the Elders of Zion*, the world Jewish conspiracy and the idea of 'poisoning' in various forms. Anti-Semitism is also paraded, in a new twist, as anti-Zionism or anti-Israelism.

The areas where this new operationalization of anti-Semitism works are varied and widespread. Here we shall briefly address some five or six of them, before we reach some tentative conclusions. They are: (1) using Christians, both in the Middle East and in Europe, where many have succumbed to the *dhimmi* state of mind, to denigrate Jews and Zionism; (2) expanding the range of Jew-haters and hate-mongers from obscurantist clerics to vast strata of mainstream intellectuals and professionals; (3) encouraging anti-Semitism as a legitimate tool to combat Israel; (4) adding to the old Christian themes a denial of the Holocaust; (5) 'perfecting' the theme of poisoning to new heights (in line with the world of hallucination where many Muslims dwell); and (6) vilifying the Jews to such an extent as to fill Muslims with a paranoiac contempt and disgust of Zionists and Israelis.

CHRISTIANS AS A TOOL

In an article published in the establishment *al-Ahram* in Cairo, an enlightened Coptic scholar, Dr Babawi, lambasted the American Congress for not stopping 'Israel's artillery attacks on the Nativity and the Aqsa Mosque', and he urged American Muslims and Copts to demonstrate against 'crazy Sharon, who began behaving like a madman after he was hit in his sensitive place by a bullet during the 1948 war, which left him with only one testicle, something that has affected him psychologically, and he has become a crazy psychopath, using power to hide his weakness . . .'[6] This broadside, which in Arab tradition demeans the man by pointing to his sexual weakness, sought to twist the Nativity event, where Palestinians invaded the Holy Church at gun-point, by imputing the moral wrong to Israel who tried to dislodge them. But no one could have missed the point:

a Copt in Egypt, a member of a persecuted and dispossessed minority in an Islamic country, must be more Arab than his compatriots to evince his loyalty, and there was evidently no better grounds for that exercise than an anti-Jewish attack. The Bishop of the Assyrian Church in Lebanon followed suit by asserting that though the heads of the Church today are not Jewish, they are 'led by Jews, whose faith is inimical to God, to the people and to Christianity'. He cites Jesus as having said to the Jews: 'you are the sons of Satan, and you practise the will of Satan your father', to which they supposedly answered: 'No, we are not the sons of Satan, we are the sons of Abraham.' But he insisted: 'Had you been the sons of Abraham, you would be acting in accordance with the precepts of Abraham . . . You are the sons of Satan.'[7] This wholesale discrediting of the Jews, to gain favour with the thugs of Hizbollah, defies logic in so far as the dwindling Christian minorities in the Islamic world should have made common cause with the Jews, but it is evident that Muslims exploit the persecuted and intimidated Christians to 'prove' the universal disgust that they sense towards Jews.

EXPANDING THE SCOPE OF HATRED

When one peruses Arab and Muslim publications and media, one cannot help but notice that the scope of anti-Semitism has been expanding beyond obscurantist clerics or fanatically nationalistic elements in those societies, and has come to embrace also supposedly liberal, enlightened and professional mainstream milieus. In that discourse, the interchangeability between Jews, Zionists and Israelis is unmistakable when all three are alternately threatened with outright extermination. An Egyptian, Dr Adel Sadeq, a senior psychiatrist by profession, who often castigates President Bush and the West for their ignorance of the Arab psyche, has no qualms about fighting Israel to the finish, more than two decades after his country signed peace with it. He writes:

> What is happening now indicates that Israel will not exist for ever. We as Arabs must know that this war will not end . . . and anyone who deludes himself that that there will be peace must understand that Israel did not come to this region to love the Arabs or to normalize relations with them . . . Either the Israelis or the Palestinians, there is no third option . . . There are no Israeli civilians,

they are all plunderers, for history teaches this. I am completely convinced that the psychological effect [of the Islamikaze] on the Israeli usurper will be his realizing that his existence is temporary . . . Remove the Apache from the equation, leave them one on one with the Palestinian people with the only weapon being dynamite, then you will see all Israelis leave, because there is not even one Israeli among them willing to don a belt of explosives . . . We will throw Israel into the sea, there is no middle ground. Coexistence is total nonsense . . . The real means of dealing with Israel directly is those who blow themselves up. According to what I see in the battle arena, there is no other way but the pure, noble Palestinian bodies. This is the only Arab weapon there is, and anyone who says otherwise is a conspirator.[8]

And so on and so forth, *ad nauseam*. The Jews apparently ordered the start of World War I, and got the United States to participate by spreading the rumour that an American ship (the *Lusitania*) had been sunk by the Germans. During that war, they prepared the grounds for both communism and Nazism, as a follow-up to the work done by the Jews Marx and Engels half a century earlier when they circulated the *Communist Manifesto* in London. Eventually, communism and Nazism gained power and came to confront each other, 'exactly as the Jews had planned'. The Second World War erupted due to the limitations imposed by the Allies on the Germans at Versailles by order of the Jews, thus pushing the Germans to revolution and enabling the rise of Hitler. The Jews also brought about the fall of the Ottoman Empire, and they planned to reap the fruit thereof by concentrating all wealth in their hands.[9]

ANTI-SEMITISM AS A TOOL TO COMBAT ISRAEL

This bizarre retelling of history is aimed primarily at discrediting the Jews and pointing to the dangers they pose to the world. It is implied that the Jewish state is dangerous to world peace and therefore illegitimate. These calumnies, part of which have been concocted for centuries in Europe, were imported to the Middle East and then re-exported to the West. They are not believed to be a tool of propaganda, because they are so much replicated and repeated that their forgers end up believing them as conventional wisdom and documented history. Thus, forged citations, made-up 'facts', fake sources, trumped-up accusations and all manner of other hoaxes, for which one can be prosecuted in civilized countries and serve prison terms, become widespread currency in Islamic countries, for the most part with impunity (scholarly or criminal). The innocent and misguided masses, who have neither interest in the facts, nor any way to learn them beyond the propaganda they are exposed to, take that nonsense as a legitimate way to battle Israel and the Jews.

Islamikaze bombings by Palestinians against Israel, have often been couched in Zionist terms and encouraged against the background of the pathologically vilified Jews, who have 'earned' the onslaughts against them due to their schemings and the dangers they pose to the world. An Egyptian columnist, for example, preceded and followed by many others, specifically urged the Islamikaze to step up their operations against the Jews, and called upon more Muslim volunteers to join the murderers. His imagination is gruesome in its detail and inhumanity:

> with every blow struck by al-Aqsa intifada, my conviction grows stronger that I, and those like-minded, have been right all along, and I am still right in my belief that the despised racist Jewish entity will be annihilated. Contrary to others, however, I am not ashamed to speak about driving them into the sea, to hell or to the trash heap where they belong . . . I maintain, and Allah is my witness, that the annihilation and defeat of the Israelis, after which there will be no resurrection, does not require all those things. All that is required is to concentrate on acts of martyrdom, or what is known as the 'strategy of the balance of fear' . . .
>
> Let us do some mathematical calculations: 250 Palestinians have signed up for martyrdom operations, and it is not impossible to raise their number to 1,000 throughout the Arab world . . . i.e., one fida'i out of every 250,000 Arabs. The average harvest of each act of martyrdom is 10 dead and 50 wounded. Thus, 1000 acts of martyrdom would leave the Zionists with at least 10,000 dead and 50,000 wounded. This is double the Israeli casualties in all their wars with the Arabs since 1948 [sic].[10] They cannot bear this. There is also the added advantage, not noted by many, of the negative Jewish emigration, which as a result of 1,000 martyrdom operations, will come to at least one million Jews, followed by the return of every Jew to the place whence he came . . .
>
> I am signing myself up as the first martyr from Egypt and declare

that I am ready to commit an act of martyrdom at any moment. I will place myself under the command of Hassan Nasrallah, the Hamas, Islamic Jihad and any other Jihad movement... Never in my life have I asked Allah for money, honour or power. All I have asked, all I ask, all I will ask, is that Allah allow me to become a *shahid* and grant me the honour of reaping as great a harvest as possible of Israeli lives....[11]

This rabid anti-Semitism, which proclaims its genocidal aims in a mainstream journal without encountering the least resistance or objection from fellow-writers, the authorities, the media, or human rights groups anywhere – and in a country which had signed a peace treaty with Israel more than two decades earlier – was unsurprisingly echoed in other Islamic media. In Iran, the hub of Islamic terrorism and support for terrorism against Israel, reports came of funds raised to support Palestinian 'suicide operations' against Israel, and of promises from Tehran to Islamic Jihad that its financial sustenance would no longer be channelled through Hizbollah but disbursed directly to it.[12] Israel is perceived as a danger to the entire region, and not only to the Palestinians. Imam Khomeini was cited as determining that 'the goal of this virus [Israel], that was planted in the heart of the Muslim world, is not only to annihilate the Arab nation, therefore the solution is to annihilate this virus, for there is no other treatment ... The Islamic states and the Muslims should initiate the annihilation of this den of corruption in every possible way. It is permitted to use charity money for that purpose...'[13] Similar calls to 'annihilate the Jews' have become routine in Muslim mosques, as well as in the writings of Saudi and other Muslim writers.[14]

HOLOCAUST DENIAL

Even though Holocaust denial is not new in Muslim countries, and sponsoring lecture tours by infamous 'revisionist historians' has been going in tandem with the banning of *Schindler's List* within their boundaries, it seems that recently (especially since the eruption of the al-Aqsa intifada) this has become one of their favourite pastimes. They do it not out of concern for 'historical truth', but simply to sustain their long-standing accusations against the Jews and to turn the blame of terrorism on the Jews for 'using organized terrorism to cultivate that legend and turn it into a fact which ties the hands of historians'.[15] The Jews are also condemned for 'forging history' (an accusation dating from the inception of Islam) despite the 'constant refutation by scientific articles which have proven the non-existence of gas chambers, or that the numbers of the dead were significantly lower'.[16] Some Muslim media even claimed that, far from being hurt by World War II, they on the contrary profited from it, for had Japan and Germany won the war, the Jews 'could not have continued to blackmail the Gentiles with their lies'.[17] Abu Mazen, the 'moderate' successor of Arafat in the Palestinian leadership, also joined this cacophony of Holocaust denial in his infamous doctoral thesis, published as a book in 1984.[18]

From denying the Holocaust, or diminishing its horrors, to accusing the Jewish victims of Nazism of having conspired with it against their own people (as Abu Mazen did), it is a short step to defending Hitler against the 'offences' caused him by the Jews and their supporters. Following Western and Israeli protests to the Egyptian government regarding the unbridled sympathy for Hitler that is current in the Egyptian and Arab press in general,[19] the government daily *al-Akhbar* relented for a while but could not contain its irresistible fascination with Hitler for long and soon reverted to it with vengeance. This time a cleric from al-Azhar, Mahmud Khadr, entitled his contribution 'In Defence of Hitler', attacking not only Israel and the Jews but also the hated West.[20]

POISONING AS THE ULTIMATE JEWISH CONSPIRACY

The repetitive use of the *Protocols* and the Blood Libel in the Arab media (especially the manufacturing of new popular soap operas and other 'documentary' series on television during the peak watching month of Ramadan) create the ambience in which any calumny against the Jews is readily believed and repeated in other media as well, not least in countries such as Jordan and Egypt which have supposedly made peace with Israel. In this atmosphere lies spread about the Jews are picked-up and diffused, and the masses are only too eager to absorb them, and further spread them around as 'facts', without investigation or critique. The most virulent kind of hoax of this sort are the stories of poisoning that are attributed to the Jews, which originate from the well-poisoning calumnies inherent in European anti-Semitism. One could often hear Yasser Arafat attributing to Israel the distribution of poisoned sweets among Palestinian children in order to maim them, or the use of depleted uranium in bullets used to quell the intifada in order to incapacitate sexually Palestinian fighters and thus contribute to diminishing their numbers. At the height of this campaign, the Palestinian representative at the Human Rights Commission in Geneva, a Dr Abdallah Ramlawi, accused Israel of injecting HIV into 300 Palestinian children in order to impair their reproductive organs.

When Israel sent its experts to Egypt to develop high-tech agriculture in the Nile delta area, with astounding results, reports abounded in the press that the Jews had no other purpose in coming to Egypt (who did not need them and could itself teach them what agriculture was all about) than to poison the soil of Egypt and destroy its age-old and advanced farming. Papers also recycled *ad nauseam* the allegation that Israel distributed throughout the Arab world an aphrodisiac chewing-gum geared to raise the sexual desire of Muslim women in order to lead them astray. But perhaps the greatest hoax in this regard, which was constructed by Palestinians and then built on by other Arabs, Muslims, the UN, the European press and even the Red Cross, and which became a *cause célèbre* during the months of March–April 1983, was the story of the poisoning of schoolgirls in the Jenin district, which was then under Israeli rule. Against all available evidence, and in spite of the fact that a number of official investigations were launched by Israel and international bodies which produced no incriminating findings, the story reverberated across the world, until proven false.[21] But even then, no one outside Israel found it necessary to castigate the fabricators of the hoax. The end result was that the Palestinians, and other Arabs and Muslims for that matter, discovered that splashing mud on Israel could go on with impunity, and they pursued the practice wholeheartedly. It is interesting to note that the depleted uranium story and the AIDS injection hoax followed the girl-poisoning episode.

After the 11 September horror and the onset of the anthrax panic in the United States, the scientific Egyptian journal *al-'Ilm* turned the tables on America and Israel, accusing them of the most hideous war-crimes, including the use of non-conventional weapons of mass destruction. With regard to Israel and the Jews, this is what this scientific publication had to say:

> In the summer of 1949 cholera spread throughout Egypt, following the establishment of Israel in 1948. Egyptian documents indicate that the disease originated from Israel . . . The US used germs in Vietnam

and against North Korea and China . . . Biological weapons research is being conducted by Israeli universities. Prior to the October War (1973) they injected birds with germs and released them above Jordan, Palestine and the Suez Canal . . . The US and Israel keep biological weapons at American bases; if they were to be used, they would destroy half the population of the area under attack. Some of this weaponry makes women miscarry . . .

Also, Jewish tourists infected with AIDS are traveling around Asian and African countries with the aim of spreading the disease . . . It is no coincidence that the US is the only member of the UN that has not signed the agreement on punishment for the collective annihilation of people . . . Israel continues to use germ warfare to destroy the Palestinian people on its occupied land, thus challenging the international community . . .[22]

CONCLUSION

These materials are so repetitive, prevalent and widely diffused in all strata of Arab and Islamic society that they are regarded as true. Children are 'educated' in their light, educated adults read or write about them in the press, clerics preach them in mosques, politicians occasionally refer to them in their public addresses, and the media, written and electronic, abound with them. They have become part of the infrastructure of education and socialization in those countries. The hierarchies, including those who have signed peace treaties with Israel, do nothing to criticize the writers, still less to prosecute or punish them. On the contrary: the authorities turn a blind eye, which is interpreted as official backing. Thus these writings, especially those emanating from Egypt, which is considered the cultural hub of the Arab world, are widely read, cited and appreciated.

These are the themes that recur in the discourse of Muslim religious actors, some of whom may see eye to eye on them with other Third World leaders with whom they find themselves in solidarity, though not necessarily for the same religious reasons. In any case, since religious actors do not operate alone in the political arena, their adaptation to the circumstances and to other actors of necessity conditions their own deeds. For example, while conditions of deprivation, conflict and oppression may facilitate the task of the religious actor inasmuch as desperate people tend to gravitate towards them, a situation of plenty and tranquillity may produce reverse results, but not necessarily (see the cases of Saudi Arabia, Kuwait or the Gulf states). Also of importance is whether the religious actor operates within a Muslim majority that is more conducive to his success, or a Muslim minority in a strong non-Muslim state where the chances of headway are a priori limited. Connected to this is the idea of Islam as the state religion, in which case it has legitimacy, as compared with a tolerated minority faith. A religious actor can exacerbate the divide between his followers and the sociopolitical environment, or he may on the contrary try to bridge it. The religious actor may insist on playing in the two rival arenas of politics and religion separately, as a way to reduce the tensions by diminishing the cumulative effect of politics-cum-religion, or may on the contrary take them in the aggregate, thus inflating them beyond measure. One cannot overlook the built-in connection between the institutionalized religious actor who represents the policies of his authorities (the Jerusalem Mufti under Arafat, or the Al-Azhar Sheikh) and the changing import of those policies: he can exacerbate or tone them down according to the whim of the ruler. Conversely, the popular/populist and anti-establishment religious actor will always stand outside the ruler's fiat and challenge it if necessary, usually to take it to new extremes of radicalism (the Muslim Brothers, Gama'at, Hamas, Hizbollah). Usually Muslim religious actors, especially the radical among them, would rather resort to extremism in order to appeal to worldwide Muslim audiences (see Bin Laden, Zarqawi or Nasrallah), than to reconciliation and moderation in an attempt (hope?) to elicit support and sympathy from international public opinion. For radicalism is a mobilizing agent while moderation is not. Muslim actors (Sheikhs Ra'id, Zawahiri, Abdallah Azzam) know that their acts and speeches will reverberate throughout the Muslim world, while any words of conciliation would marginalize and condemn them to oblivion (Sheikh Palazzi of Rome, Sheikh Boubaker of Paris and to an extent Sheikh Darwish from Kafr Qassem in Israel).

What seems to differentiate a political actor from a religious one is that while the former wishes to attain political goals and may manipulate religious vocabulary and symbols in so doing, the latter may use political means but strives to attain religious objectives. Given that in Islam religion and politics are intertwined, as political rule ideally acts in defence of the faith while religion provides the ideological underpinnings of government, the boundaries between the two domains are often blurred. It goes without saying that a strictly 'secular' ruler could never claim to play a religious role, while a purely religious actor could not lay claim to political empowerment or legitimacy. But it is the seam-line between the two which is problematic and may defy definition, except in the case of Muslim fundamentalist rulers such as Khomeini and his successors in Iran, where the religious-spiritual leader is also the supreme guide of government who retains a veto power, or the Taliban regime in Kabul, where Mullah Omar was also the superior arbitrator in government business. This is not much different to the role of Muhammed, the prophet-statesman, or the traditional Muslim Caliph who combined his spiritual mantle with his executive title of *Amir al-Mu'minin* (Commander of the Faithful), down to the twentieth century. It is no coincidence that Muslim fundamentalists, who seek power in their countries as a step towards unification of the Muslim world, hark back to the Caliphate as an ideal of Muslim rule. Except for these attempts to revive unified rule, new compromises have been worked out in modern Islam whereby spiritual leaders strike alliances with military powers domestically (Sudan, Saudi Arabia), thus bringing together religious and political actors to act in unison to make up in a corporate fashion for the unified leadership that is no more.

CHAPTER TWO

The Arab Minority in Israel

ISRAELIS WHO ARE NOT aware of the existence of a large Arab minority in Israel (20 per cent in 2005 and growing: 1.3 out of about seven million), and more so outsiders who are even less aware of that demographic datum, are repeatedly stunned by recurring eruptions of Arab self-assertion in the country. The most recent were the violent riots by Israeli Arabs in support of the outbreak of the Aqsa intifada (September 2000) of the Palestinians against Israel, which tragically ended in human casualties. These outbursts, which express rejection of Israeli domination no less than a positive assertion of identity, have been epitomized by slogans such as the Islamic 'Long live Khomeini' in the early 1980s, or the irredentist '[With our souls and blood] we shall liberate you, O Galilee!', or the perennial: 'We are part of the Palestinian People!', realizing full well that to identify with one's country's enemies can have very grave consequences. On closer examination, however, one should hardly be surprised at these developments, if one takes into consideration the rise of Palestinian nationalism and Islamic fundamentalism among the Arab citizens of Israel and the general prevalence of support and sympathy for the Palestinians in Western Europe.

By the same token, many Israelis and outsiders have been clinging to some important examples of Arabs who have become established enough and interested enough to find their place within the Israeli system, to draw the unwarranted conclusion that Arabs in Israel can be 'Israeli Arabs', as if this were not a contradiction in terms. The wishful thinking that accompanies the vision of a liberal democratic Israel where the Arab minority can achieve parity with the Jewish majority, simply runs counter to the fact that most Israeli Arabs find it impossible to become fully-fledged Israelis. Admittedly, a number of Druze, Bedouin, Christian and even Muslim Arabs have attained the higher echelons of government, academe, army, police and business, and more than a few of them are active in national politics. However, most perpetuate their hostility and opposition to the state in response to their constituencies, and those who serve the establishment are shunned by the majority of their Muslim co-religionists and pressed to conform to the hostile attitude of the majority towards the Jewish state. Israeli and other observers of all sorts have been talking of late about the process of 'radicalization' that has taken place among the Arab minority in Israel. By this they usually mean the claims for 'national rights' that are being advanced by this population. But seen from another perspective, there is no radicalization involved, because this is actually a return to the norm, or a revival of the old cravings in an era that is propitious to raising such demands after the removal of military government over the Arabs of Israel in the early 1960s and the general trends of liberalization and democratization of the system from which all Israelis, including the Arabs, have benefited.

What we are witnessing, then, is a growing self-confidence, born of the open regime that allows it, of the now critical mass of Palestinians in Israel. Along with this has gone the rise of Muslim fundamentalism which has been providing under some charismatic leaders (including Sheikh Ra'id) renewed religious underpinnings for the Palestinian struggle with the Jewish majority. This struggle is for the most part political and in the political arena is led by legitimate means; however, it sometimes transgresses into the realm of violence and lends salience to the polarized positions of the majority and the minority. For the struggle is not over civil equality, as it sometimes purports to be, but over the very soul and identity of the country, its national goals, ethos, and destiny. Given that Muslim fundamentalists press for the realization of their dreams in all Palestine here and now, most Arabs in Israel embrace a more pragmatic approach of wait-and-see, of gaining territory, self-rule, areas of authority, rights without duties, and a state of mind which entitles them to a nobility status whereby they may draw all the benefits they can from the welfare state while in practice contributing little to the accumulation of wealth and success that would enable it to disburse those benefits. This matter has grown so acute that it is no longer of concern only to Friday-night 'salon' discussions, but has become the primary topic of debate and soul-searching among the ordinary Jews of Israel.

Among the more than 1.3 million Arabs (as of 2005) holding Israeli citizenship, there seem to coexist four different, sometimes contending and sometimes complementary, foci of identity: Israeli, Palestinian, Arab and Islamic (for the 80 per cent among them who are Muslims, the others are roughly 10 per cent Christian and 10 per cent Druze). In their constant search for identity, they have crystallized an 'incremental' compound whereby they are both 'Israeli' and 'Arab', 'Palestinian' and 'Muslim', and any other combination thereof. They seem unwilling to wear a single tag, always embracing two or more choices and sometimes emphasizing the one, at times insisting upon another. We may describe the complexity of this compound in four concentric circles that coincide with those four foci.

The innermost circle of identity is the Israeli. Ever since the 1948 war a minority of Palestinian Arabs has remained under Israeli rule, either by accident or by design, rather than embracing the status of refugee in one of the surrounding Arab countries. But due to the continuing conflict between Israel and its Arab neighbours, Arabs in the Jewish state soon realized that they were torn between their new country, whose citizenship they possessed and whose rights and laws they enjoyed, and their people across the border, who continued to exhort them to shed their loyalty to hateful Israel and subscribe to its demise. Until the 1967 (Six-Day) War, which generated a profound soul-searching among the Arabs, as a result of what some of them bitterly termed their 'glorious defeat', the Arabs in Israel were well on their way to accepting the idea of the Jewish state and adjusting to their existence as a minority within its confines. Even after the trauma of that war, the growth of the Arab minority in Israel was not impeded despite the increasing dilemma inherent in the insolubility of the contradiction between rising national strivings among the Palestinians on the one hand, and Israel's Zionist aspirations and Jewish identity on the other.

The impressive growth of the Arab community in Israel, from a poor peasant society whose leaders had deserted her in 1948, into a predominantly urban and modern society, is in itself an indication of the pace of acculturation of this minority into the Israeli system. At present, 95 per cent of all Arab children attend school, from kindergarten to university. The younger generation of Arabs who were born and raised within the Jewish state has produced a new elite of university graduates, some of whom are employed in the state bureaucracy, or have launched their own businesses, or have embraced professional careers. From two municipalities that existed in 1948 there are now dozens of city and village councils, where elections run freely according to Israeli standards of democracy. The process of urbanization notwithstanding, the amount of Arab land under cultivation has greatly increased since the establishment of Israel. Much of the land is under irrigation and yielding good crops thanks to the mechanization and modern agricultural techniques introduced by Israel. While in 1950 more than half the Arab manpower was employed in agriculture, in the 1980s only 15 per cent depended for their livelihood on farming, despite the great increase in cultivated areas and productivity. By 2000, dependence on farming in the Arab economy had decreased still further, approaching the Jewish rate of 3–4 per cent, which is the conventional rate in the developed world. The balance of manpower turned to typically urban occupations such as construction, services, industry, tourism and other branches of the economy. By 1976 only half the manpower of the Arab sector was employed locally, while the remainder sought and obtained work outside their localities: a trend that has continued to send more and more manpower to the job market. The impact on the Arab villages has been tremendous: many backwater villages have become towns and cities. A great boom in construction, modern furnishings, electric appliances, roads, electricity, running water, telephones, health and education services and banks has turned the rural Arab population of yesterday into an ambitious community. Paradoxically, the more it resembled the Jewish majority, the more strident its demand that it be recognized as different. The more Arab individuals feel liberated, advanced and close to attaining their personal ambitions, the more they insist that their communal–national needs must be addressed.

This seemingly smooth integration of the Arab community into Israeli society was nevertheless marked by a growing sense of alienation on the part of individual Arabs severally and of their corporate whole jointly. The liberal policy of the Israeli government which was devised to keep the Arabs happy and quiet, far from contributing to Arab integration into the host society, simply perpetuates the gulf between them. For example, a separate Arab educational system militates against the inculcation of Israeli values into the Arab population. The fact that Arabs enjoy civil rights, such as the right to vote and to be elected, does not in the least alleviate their frustration at their inability to obtain full acceptance into the Israeli bureaucratic and political elites. A built-in 'Catch 22' has developed whereby the more liberal Israeli policies are towards its Arab citizenry, the more vocal is the latter in its demands and protests for more liberalism. More and more Arab youths who are educated in Israel rise up against what they view as discriminatory attitudes and policies of the Israeli government. One of them stated in a recent public symposium: 'now that we have attained material satisfaction, it is time for us to seek spiritual fulfilment'. There is a double claim, of discrimination and the need for fulfilment, and both are problematic. The claim of discrimination hinges on the criteria of definition: is it moral, material, or legal? For example, is it ethical to allocate the same rights equally to citizens who fulfil their duties to the state and to those who do not, or should there be a differentiation between those two categories of citizens in terms of allocations and benefits on the part of the state? Do we gauge discrimination by comparing one's contribution to the state versus the benefits one has drawn from it? As to fulfilment, the yardsticks are even more difficult: is recognition of the Arabs as a national minority (in which case Israel would become bi-national) the prerequisite for their fulfilment, or ought Israel to alter its state symbols and shed its Zionist ideals as a condition of satisfying its Arab population? In short, can the Arabs become equal citizens to the Jews in Israel under the present circumstances, and pending that, can 'discrimination' be eliminated without tearing the country apart at the seams?

Because of the lack of common values between Jews and Arabs in Israel, children from different ethnic groups grow up internalizing different modes of thinking and contradictory ideals. For example, Israel is nurtured on Zionism, which encourages Jewish immigration, and strives for settling the land under the Israeli defence forces, where universal conscription obliges every young man and woman to serve his country. The Arabs on the whole negate those national goals, struggle against them and would not lift a finger to defend their country. No wonder then that the Day of Independence, the most hallowed in the secular calendar in Israel, where Jews proudly hoist their national flag, is marked in the Arab street as the *Nakbah* (Disaster) Day, with the Israeli flag often burned in their villages. What is then left in common for both communities to share? Rather than spell out 'bi-nationalism', which would put an end to Jewish nationalism and Jewish self-determination, the Arabs of Israel mitigate that bitter pill for the Israeli majority by calling it the 'state of all its citizens', a smooth and seemingly innocent formula like the racist-in-reverse 'one man, one vote', which meant not only an end to white rule in Africa but also to the democratic possibility that a white citizen of an African country could be elected to lead that country. Similarly, the 'state of its citizens' means not only the end of the Jewish state but also that in yet another Arab-majority state (the 23rd) the Arabs would ultimately preclude any manifestation of Jewish rule in Israel. This formula has been unpopular with Israeli Jews due to its pitfalls, because it signifies for them the potential elimination of the state which they have toiled so long and so hard to obtain. Some Jews suggest a compromise which would encompass the attributes of the Jewish state together with the 'state of its citizens'. However, this would only complicate matters further, because this contradictory proposition would then be given endless interpretations and would be unlikely to be the focus of consensus. Various forms of autonomy for the Arabs as part of the Israeli state have also been scrutinized and have so far been discarded.

If one sums up the issue of Arab existence in Israel as part of its citizenry, one comes to the conclusion that it is a no-win solution. For even though the Arabs in Israel are not the only group that cares for its own sectional interests (cf. the ultra-Orthodox, or groups of new immigrants), none of the others has utterly and publicly shed its responsibility for the welfare of Israeli society in general, and none is so thoroughly divorced from the basic aspirations of the state. They may express their views from their own biased ideological or practical angles, but they are nevertheless for the general public benefit. Conversely, one can hardly find an Arab in Israel who is concerned about the major issues of existence that are at the root of national consensus in the country. For example, national security, the buzz-word for anything of importance relating to the defence of the state, is totally ignored or even resisted, resented and attacked by the Arabs of Israel, as are the questions of settlement and development of arid areas, reforestation and the like. In any peace negotiation between Israel and other Arabs, the Israeli Arabs would align themselves automatically with Arab demands, and would never consider the possibility that their own country might be right in the debate. In questions of national security or development, the Arabs would not lift a finger: they could not care less if their country were defeated by other Arabs or by any other enemy; they would not approve any military expenditure; would not yield anything for the country's general welfare; would not rejoice in its successes; nor expend any effort to spare its image or defend it from attackers. Young Arabs who volunteer for military service in the Israeli armed forces come under unbearable pressure, as if they were fighting for their enemies, and every act that is defined as a national imperative by the authorities is vigorously and unrelentingly opposed. For example, in order for the military to train, they need firing-ranges and fields for manoeuvres, which occasionally necessitates confiscation of lands for public benefit. The Jews accept that situation, albeit reluctantly, but no one questions the need for the army to train. The Arabs raise all the reasons in the world to attack the military as 'oppressive robbers', and will not advance any alternative course of action to have the army, which also defends them, adequately trained. So it goes for land-confiscation for the purpose of building roads or strategic outposts, airports and other facilities in Arab-populated areas, which are always sure to create havoc as if a foreign power had invaded them.

The second circle of identity is the Palestinian one. There was a time when it was anathema for the Arabs in Israel to identify as Palestinians, not only because that was considered a contradiction in terms (an Israeli could not be a Palestinian), but there also prevailed a systematic denial by Israel of Palestinian nationality. However, since the 1967 war, when the West Bank of the River Jordan was seized by Israel, and the reconnection that was effected as a consequence between the Palestinian populations on both sides of the Israeli borders, the notion that an Israeli Arab could be, indeed was, Palestinian, began to gain currency. Moreover, following the first Land Day of 31 March 1976, in which Israeli Arabs started to commemorate annually the confiscation of their lands by Israel, the first shot was fired towards expressing their grievances against the Jewish state in national terms, and no longer in linguistic, ethnic or religious terms. Since then Israeli Arabs have assumed a Palestinian identity; even their Knesset members cry out their Palestinian affiliation at every opportunity and seem to delight in the controversy that the present state of war between Israelis and Palestinians arouses. For when Israel has differences with its Palestinian neighbours, the Israeli Arabs can be counted unfailingly on the Palestinian side, and thus by necessity find themselves in a state of conflict with Israel. The identification of the Arabs in Israel is not only formal and emotional, but it embraces the domains of Palestinian culture, folklore, history, mythology, hero-worship, aspirations and political programmes. There is hardly any domain of human and political activity between the two neighbouring nations where friction and contention do not compel the Israeli Arabs to take a position against their country, no matter how hard they try to escape the choice or to plaster over the differences.

Since then, irredentist slogans vowing to 'liberate Galilee' from Israel have been heard at public demonstrations by Israeli Arabs, who make common cause with the demands of their Palestinian brethren. These trends reached their peak during the October 2000 intifada, when Israeli Arabs erupted in a spree of violence and extremist sloganeering that cost them 13 lives. The recurrence of pro-Palestinian demonstrations, coupled with growing instances of squads of young Israeli Arabs who were recruited to mount acts of sabotage against their country, brought the relations between the Arab minority and the host society to boiling-point, especially against the background of the growing political, economic, ideological and at times operational support that Israeli Arabs bring to the Palestinian enemies of their country. Politically this has been expressed by the declarations on record of practically all Israeli Arab leaders that they were in support of the Palestinian 'Right of Return', namely an uncontrolled repatriation of the descendants of the 700,000 refugees of 1948 (now numbering millions), which would so inundate Israel demographically as to eliminate its Jewish national status. Israeli Arabs have closely learned the counter-example of Israel absorbing its own Jewish refugees from the Arab world and elsewhere, and they understand full well that refugee status is not inherited from generation to generation, and that had their Arab compatriots wished to absorb them the way Israel did, there would have been no Palestinian refugees today. The fact that they subscribe to the Arab demand for the 'Right of Return' means that they wish to harass Israel and force it into submitting to the Arab demand for dissolution. This is hardly a 'patriotic' stance in the face of Palestinian demands.

These trends were manifest already in the 1976 West Bank elections and the Israeli elections in 1977. In the former, a new and young leadership arose which swept aside the traditional patriarchal notables and announced its sympathy for the PLO. In the Israeli elections pro-PLO elements either gave their votes to the communist Rakah Party or boycotted the elections altogether, as even Rakah seemed too moderate to their tastes and not nationalist enough to reflect the mood of the times. Thus, while in the previous elections of 1973 some 80 per cent of the Arabs in Israel cast their vote, this time only 72 per cent went to the polls, the balance being attributed to the boycott by extremist elements. Rakah won more votes than in the previous elections – nearly enough to win them a sixth seat in the Knesset. This surging Palestinian identity, now openly proclaimed by most Arabs in Israel, made the compound 'Israeli Arab' almost a contradiction in terms. For not only has the Israeli–Palestinian segment of the Middle Eastern conflict escalated and made it intolerable for the Arabs to identify as Israelis, but even on the symbolic level the common grounds of Arabs and Israelis have shrunk considerably. Since the Israeli colours have come to symbolize for the Arabs oppression, expropriation and occupation, the latter naturally identify the Palestinian flag as their national symbol. This neatly connects with the separatistic trends that are rife among some Arab circles in Israel, pending the implementation of the Right of Return which would turn the country into another Palestine in the long-run. Though for the time being separatism can only be expressed culturally (Palestinian literature and folklore, a separate educational system, an Arab university, the cultivation of Palestinian–Arab values and heritage and the like), it is evident that the long-term goal is an overthrow of the Zionist state and reunion with other Palestinians. Hence Palestinianism among Israeli Arabs consists of supporting the 2½ state thesis – the already existing Palestinian majority in Jordan, another state in the West Bank and Gaza and autonomy in Israel, all to be merged ultimately in a greater Palestine to be established on the ruins of Israel. Nationalism does not need to be recognized by anyone in order to exist. Whether Israel likes it or not, admits it or not, it is there. All Israel can do is to devise ways to defend itself from dissolution, but it can no longer ignore or deny it.

Then comes the third circle of identity – the Israeli Arabs consider themselves Arab no less than Palestinian. In fact, the Palestinian nexus for them is their link to the Arab world, apart from the fact that they share with the rest of the Arabs their language, patrimony, history, customs and religion. Palestinians and other Arabs alike are fond of repeating that Palestine is the core of the Arab–Israeli dispute, the pivotal point in the Middle Eastern conflict, thus assigning to the Palestinians the veto power over its resolution. If until 1967 Arabs in Israel were deprecated by other Arabs as 'collaborators', their image and worth as potential allies of the Arab world in their war against Israel has been on the rise ever since. Although outside summons to Israeli Arabs to revolt against their authorities during the 1973 (Yom Kippur) war remained unheeded, Arab propaganda channels never relent in their hope of reversing this situation. During the 1976 Land Day the Arab leaders acclaimed the 'heroic Arab stand within occupied Palestine', and this certainly fuelled the Arab-Israeli hope of a pan-Arab national struggle against Israel. Moreover, Zionism being in Arab eyes antithetical to Arab nationalism, the Arabs in Israel whose national loyalty to their people is now beyond doubt, stand in the frontline of the pan-Arab effort to overwhelm the Zionist polity. In consequence, it has become a political reality that the Arab-Israeli leaders, including members of the Knesset, are on record as automatically supporting all the Arab views against Israel, regardless of who provoked whom or who did wrong to whom. One rule of thumb has been established by them: Arabs can do no wrong and Israel can do no right. If Israel acts against Syrian or Hizbollah aggression against their country they would justify their country's enemies and express condolences to them, and if their Israeli compatriots fall victim to Arab terrorism, they would send aid to the families of the terrorists, not to their victims. This approach has been epitomized in the name of one of their parties (The National Democratic List) where the adjective 'national' refers to the Arabs, not to Israel. It would be as if German or Japanese citizens of the United States or Britain established a national German, or Japanese Party and ran for elections in the midst of the Second World War.

The peace that Israel signed with Egypt (1979) and then Jordan (1994) has further complicated the dilemmas of the Arabs in Israel. On the one hand, suspicion, scepticism and sometimes hostility were evinced by Palestinians, including some Israeli Arabs, towards the Arab signatories of peace with their country; but on the other hand, new hopes seemed to arise for some Palestinians, including Israeli Arabs, who contacted the Egyptian and then the Jordanian authorities, regarding them as channels of negotiation and sponsors and protectors in their dealings with Israel. All the same, Israeli Arabs have for the most part succumbed to the anti-Israel and anti-Jewish stereotypes and abuses used by their other Arab brethren, as for example the charge of 'racism' (at times dubbed 'Nazism'), knowing full well the sensitivity of Jews on such an issue. This sort of abuse is not only unfounded, but it also increases the tensions between the parties. The frequent charge of 'racism' by Arab parties at every instance when Israel's policies are not to their liking also makes any criticism of Arab misdeeds impossible, lest the accusation of 'racism' be levelled. For example, if Arabs build illegally against the rules of urban planning (and they do regularly, usually with impunity), any attempt to call them to order would be countered by that charge of racism.

The peace accords that have been concluded thus far between Israel and the Arabs, and which should have facilitated the peace between Jews and Arabs in Israel proper, have remained so problematic as to act otherwise. For the populations of those countries that made formal peace with Israel continue to be educated to hate Israel and the Jews, and to cultivate the old anti-Semitic stereotypes, peace notwithstanding, under the ruling elites. Judging by the amount and intensity of the claims advanced by Israeli Arab organizations against their own country at various international forums, not only is there no attempt made by Israeli Arabs to act as bridges between their country and the Arab world, but there prevails, with few exceptions, an all-out attempt to revile Israel. The Arabs in Israel understand that the higher the value of Arab positions in the Israeli–Arab peace negotiations, the better their own chances to cut an advantageous deal with Israel. Their need to be part of the Arab world not only improves their negotiating positions but also reinforces psychologically their stance in the Middle East, inasmuch as they sense once again that they belong to the winning and powerful majority of the Arabs and no longer have to yield to their minority status. For them the Arab world holds the promise of space and resources, in contrast to the confines of Israel where they lead their daily lives. The hopes that they entertain for the Arab world are those of the mythic unity that, when accomplished, will enable them to attain all their wishes and dreams. Occasionally, they cling to an emerging figure of a great unifier, such as Saladin in medieval times, who would bring all of them together and beat the enemies of the Arabs. In the 1950s and 1960s it was Abdul Nasser of Egypt who provided that mythical unifying figure; later on Saddam Hussein of Iraq played that role until he lost popularity during the second Gulf war (1991). From the Israeli point of view, the combined onslaughts of Arabs from the inside and the outside are always to be feared, hence the lumping together of Arab threats all around with the menace of the 'fifth column'.

The fourth circle of identity – the Islamic one – is directly concerned with religious actors in general and Sheikh Ra'id Salah in particular. It will be the subject of the next chapter and indeed of those that follow.

CHAPTER THREE

The Islamic Movement in Israel: Ideology and Organization

THE FOURTH CIRCLE of identity, and the most relevant to our narrative here, is the Islamic one. In Israel, 80 per cent of all Arabs are Muslim, of the Sunni–Hanafite rite. They are conscious of belonging to a vast world of 1.3 billion believers spread across 56 Muslim-majority countries and some two dozen more states where they constitute sizeable minorities: notably in India (some 130 million), Russia and China (some 25 million in each), Europe (*c.* 25 million) and many other American and Asian countries. Thus, if the Arabs of Israel feel comforted by the backing of the millions of other Arabs in 22 Arab countries, so much more so can they sense the immense weight of their worldwide Muslim *umma* that lends them support, sustenance and limitless resources. These basic data gained more prominence in the past few decades as the profile of Islam has risen worldwide, and the phenomenon of Islamic radicalism or fundamentalism has come to the fore.

The genesis of Islamic fundamentalism in Israel cannot be divorced from the surge of militant Islam the world over. Indeed, the victory of Islam in such states as Iran, Sudan and Afghanistan, and its significant inroads in other Muslim countries such as Algeria, Lebanon, Jordan, Egypt and Pakistan, have come to identify militant Islam in terms of religious nationalism.[1] Thus, many Muslim Arabs in Israel have come to cling to their Islamic identity, more markedly than to their Arab or Palestinian stock, as a divide separating them from non-Muslims and as a common denominator attaching them to other Muslims. Therefore, while the differences between the Jewish majority and the Arab minority in Israel are often bridgeable by common language, economic interest and neighbourly relations, the Muslim radicals have injected massive doses of Islamic symbolism into the Arab–Israeli conflict and given it a religiocultural nature, thus rendering it virtually insoluble. In turn, Muslim fundamentalists in Israel, who would perhaps otherwise accept their minority status and adjust to life under a Jewish authority, once imbued with the general mode of thinking of other Muslim radicals, tend also to exacerbate their anti-Israeli and anti-Christian rhetoric and attitudes. Their anti-Jewish posture has impelled them to rebel against the Jewish state, and their historical anti-Christian bitterness is pushing them to remove the rule of Christians over Muslim communities when they can.

The Muslims of Israel, even more than other Muslims worldwide, feel resentment and frustration at their inability to retrieve the rule over their Holy Land and holy places. For they experience in an immediate fashion the humiliation of being ruled by an erstwhile *dhimmi* people which had itself, for long centuries, submitted to Islamic rule and which had projected a questionable reputation in Islamic tradition. The pious among them cannot overlook the vehement anti-Jewish and anti-Israeli arguments advanced by masters of radical Islam all around them.[2] Add to that the general feeling of discrimination among these Muslims, their uphill battle to gain equality in the rights and services extended to them by the state, and their impossible emotional cleavage between their country of citizenship and their co-religionists in the Arab and Islamic camps, and you have a recipe for upheaval and radicalism. Some of these tensions are tapped by radical Muslim leaders among Israeli Arabs and directed towards the revival of the Muslim faith. Indeed, more mosques have been built in Israel during the past decades than ever before, and more expressions of Muslim radicalism in politics, in social organizations and in local government have come to the fore than at any time. Islamic associations, which had handled local *waqf* affairs or dealt with social welfare, suddenly took to election campaigns and became involved in local and national politics. Not unlike the Muslim Brothers of Egypt, they have accumulated enough reserves of goodwill among the population through their caring leadership, devoted work for the community and networks of charity and educational and health services, to expect political support from their constituencies.

The process of Islamization seemed to many Muslims the way out of their crisis of identity. They could not identify with the country from which they felt alienated, and they did identify with their Muslim brethren who were in a state of war with Israel. They felt that, together with other Muslims, they constituted the wave of the future, and therefore they sought links to their Islamized Palestinian kin in the Territories occupied by Israel in 1967, and beyond them to Jordan, Egypt and other Arab and

Islamic countries where fundamentalist movements were active. After 1967 Muslims in Israel began inviting renowned Palestinian clerics from the West Bank and Gaza to deliver sermons in mosques, schools and social gatherings. In consequence, the ideologies and doctrines of the Islamic Liberation Party of old, and of the Muslim Brothers, were propagated and became household words among the Muslim Arabs of Israel. Conversely, the Muslims of Israel who attended Islamic institutions of higher learning in those territories returned to their communities in Israel imbued with the new Islamic revivalist spirit.

These developments had an immediate impact on the Muslims in Israel: a massive return to Islam among the young, in tandem with a similar trend in the West Bank and Gaza. The Islamic movement gained further impetus in those years following the Iranian revolution and the emergence of extremists in Egypt and Syria who attempted to topple the regimes of those countries. As a result, some Muslim fundamentalists in Israel, like their counterparts in neighbouring Arab countries, decided to effect the transition from quietist ideology and rhetoric into action and violence. A tiny group among them, Usrat al-Jihad (The Family of Jihad) set out to launch a war against Israel and targeted some economic projects until it was apprehended in its entirety and imprisoned, including the founder and leader – Sheikh Abdallah Nimr Darwish.[3] This outburst of Islamic violence understandably put the Muslim community in Israel on the defensive. For while some of them were conceivably in favour of an Islamic revival, they did not intend to turn violently against Israel and to endanger the very existence of their entire community. Thus, the Muslim leadership condemned the group and temporarily put a lid on the entire revivalist movement. However, the radical part of the movement survived in Israeli prisons where discussions continued between the inmates who were attempting to chart together a post-gaol future. After their release from gaol, following their pledge that they would no longer engage in violence, they formed, together with others, what came to be known as the Muslim Youth Movement. This organization has dominated the revivalist movement in Israel since the early 1980s, and has been avowedly more quietist in its approach, observing the strictures of law.

Sheikh Abdallah of Kafr Qassem became a guru for many frustrated Muslims in Israel, gaining credence from his well-earned reputation as a devoted leader who cared for his community. Indeed, he was credited with helping drug-addicts and organizing a vast network of charity and welfare services for his constituents. Soon Muslim believers began flocking to him from towns and villages in Galilee and central Israel to enlighten themselves with his teachings. Outwardly, he and his disciples adopted the slogan of activity and change by peaceful means within the law. But judging from the infrastructure they were preparing in some of their villages, one suspects that the more fanatical among them were dedicated to building their own Islamic enclaves and dissociating themselves gradually from the Jewish state. This trend gathered momentum in the towns and villages ruled by radical Islamists, led by Sheikh Ra'id Salah of Umm al-Fahm, who in the late 1990s split from the mainstream (which remains under the aegis of Sheikh Abdallah), thereby signalling a two-pronged Islamic movement: a pragmatic versus a radical group. The circumstances under which the split occurred will be discussed below; first let us examine the 1980s and early 1990s when the pre-schism Islamic movement was taking shape.[4]

Umm al-Fahm, which has become undeniably the hub of Muslim fundamentalism in Israel, owes its status to Sheikh Ra'id, a local youth who attended the Islamic College in Hebron in 1976. After graduating in 1979, he began roaming the country and professing a return to Islamic values. An Islamic association was set up locally, as in other places, to step into the social and cultural vacuum left by the lack of socio-economic involvement of the Israeli government in the township. The Islamic message had a tremendous appeal to unskilled labourers who worked in Tel Aviv and other Israeli urban centres, and who underwent daily humiliation in their encounter with Israeli prosperity and cultural assertiveness. It also appealed to the youth who were seeking new avenues and new answers, and to professionals who were in search of new channels for their nationalism and new definitions for their identity. The movement also attracted the rank and file who observed and partook, with admiration and pride, of the welfare projects that the local Muslim movement, led by the young sheikh, was undertaking in the township.

The municipal elections of February 1989 signalled to the Israeli public in general, and the Arab–Islamic sector in particular, that the Muslim movement had turned from a religiocultural pursuit for born-again Muslims, into a religiopolitical organization intent on seeking power as a way to implement its programme. Indeed, while in 1983 only one mayor of the Islamic movement had been returned by the polls in the small village of Kafr Bara, 1989 saw five Islamist mayors, including Sheikh Ra'id, elected together with another 45 councillors in various municipalities and local councils. Hence the watershed mood among the Muslim population in Israel, born out of the euphoria of that success which had been expressed during the election campaign by the slogans: 'Islam is the Solution!', 'Islam is the Alternative!' and 'Islam is the Truth!' One of the Arab villages most affected by this upsurge of Islam was Kafr Kanna (the biblical Cana-in-Galilee, known for the miracles performed by Jesus Christ),[5] in close proximity to Nazareth. An otherwise unobtrusive township, 75 per cent Muslim and the rest Christian, this is where another young, talented and charismatic Islamist leader, Sheikh Kamal Khatib, made his debut. In the 1989 elections, the Sheikh got 38 per cent of the vote, but because a second round was needed to gain the majority, he was defeated by a coalition of his opponents. Nevertheless, his Islamic list won one-third of the seats in the town council (six out of eighteen), much to the displeasure of the local Christians who formed a coalition with the others to defeat him.[6]

In neighbouring Nazareth, the largest Arab city in Israel, the Islamists' show was less spectacular, due mainly to the grip that the vastly popular Tufiq Zyad had on local politics. There too an Islamist, 'Umar Shararah, ran for election as a candidate for the Islamic movement, but unlike his Kafr Kanna neighbour, Sheikh Khatib, he had no record of public and welfare service. In Nazareth, it was Zyad's communists and the local churches who were running the summer camps and the educational and charitable organizations in the city. Nevertheless, Shararah swept a majority of the vote in the Muslim neighbourhoods, and the absolute majority of all Muslims who participated in the 1989 election. Tufiq Zyad, the head of the communist Hadash list and the incumbent mayor, was re-elected in a test of his personal popularity. Perhaps only the fact that he was a Muslim (though not an observant one) permitted his victory in that atmosphere of Islamic euphoria. In 1984 he had won 70 per cent of the vote, but now only the strengthening of the communist vote in the Christian neighbourhoods (an apparent reaction to the menacing ascendance of the Islamic movement) allowed Zyad to be re-elected for a fourth term.

What happened in Kafr Kanna and Nazareth heralded a political break between the Muslim and Christian communities in the towns and villages, the former rallying around the Muslim movement while the latter closed ranks, in self-defence, around the communists. But that was not to last, due to the shrinkage of the communist appeal after the demise of communism elsewhere. Henceforth, the Christians would face other choices, such as lending their support to all-Israeli parties, rather than succumb to the pressures of the Muslim fundamentalists. During the 1989 elections the Islamists attempted to persuade the Christians to join them, employing anti-communist arguments and suggesting that Christian candidates might appear on Muslim fundamentalist lists. But the Christians elected to form coalitions with other political parties, which for the time being arrested the Islamists' candidates. But they did not miss the alarm signal. They still constituted the majority in eight towns and villages, and the minority in eight others, including Nazareth and Kafr Kanna in Galilee, and they had to find a way of preventing their identity from being swept under the new wave of Islamism. All the more so since Nazareth and Kafr Kanna had been both fundamentally Christian places, with holy places and houses of prayer and institutions harking back to the life of Jesus and to the history of the Church in the Holy Land.

The victory of the Muslim fundamentalists in the local elections of 1989, coupled with the continuation of the intifada which had broken out in 1987, and in which the Hamas Muslim fundamentalists had been scoring points, certainly strengthened the hands of the adepts of the Muslim movement in Israel. The anti-Jewish, anti-Zionist and anti-Israeli propaganda of the Islamic movement[7] extended also to the Christian Arabs, even those who championed most vociferously the Arab and Palestinian causes. In fact Muslim fundamentalists in Israel are no different from their co-religionists elsewhere who accuse Christianity and the Christian world of seeking to undermine the Islamic world and to corrupt its youth. Sheikh Khatib of Kafr Kanna wrote thus:

> My words may sound harsh to proponents of Arab nationalism who regard the solution of the problem in national terms, while I regard it in Islamic, and only in Islamic, terms . . . Jerusalem and Palestine, which had warmly embraced 'Umar [ibn al-Khattab], Khaled [ibn al-Walid], Abu 'Ubaydah and Saladin, cannot embrace [Archbishop] Capucci or George [Habash], because she is a loyal spouse . . . The absence of her true spouse does not mean that he has died . . . He will return with passion and longing . . .[8]

In other articles in the journal of the Islamists in Israel, Hanna Seniora, one of the spokesmen of Palestinian nationalism in the West Bank, was charged with having warned America against the rise of Islamic fundamentalism and with having maintained contacts with personalities in the 'Jewish entity'. It was also claimed that the 'new Crusade' in Palestine had been fostered by people such as Boutros Boutros-Ghali, a Copt and then

Minister of State for Foreign Affairs in Egypt (and later the Secretary-General of the UN) and Clovis Maqsud, a Christian and delegate of the Arab League to the UN, who 'pretended to speak in the name of the Muslims'.[9]

Al-Sirat, the main mouthpiece of the Islamic movement in those years, spread its revivalist messages on matters ranging from return to the faith, women and youth, to matters of state, jihad and incitement against Jews and Christians alike. It soon bifurcated into a monthly and a weekly, and became the main platform for support to the Palestinians in the territories. At the end of 1989 it was closed by the authorities due to its abuses against the Jews, which went as far as the denial of the Holocaust, and was immediately supplanted by the new *Sawt al-Haqq wal-Huriyya* (The Voice of Truth and Liberty), also a weekly. But the Islamic movement also expounded its positions and publicized its views in posters, leaflets and audio and video tapes which became very popular with the young. The movement could look with pride on its achievements in a relatively short span of time and periodize its history as follows:

1. The period of infancy, referring to the 1979–80 Usrat-al-Jihad venture which ended in disaster when most members of the group found themselves in gaol;

2. The time of growth, beginning in 1983, when the movement based itself on local voluntary associations which operated within the confines of law, especially in extending religious and welfare services;

3. The coming of age in 1989, when the movement established itself as the leading and fastest-growing political force among Israeli Arabs, with mayors and city councillors exercising actual power in many towns and villages.

If they were to continue that periodization, the Muslim fundamentalists would probably mark 1991 as the beginning of the split in their ranks. That year saw deep divisions among the Arabs in Israel as a result of the peace process sponsored by the United States, following Saddam's defeat in the second Gulf war. Most Arab parties in Israel, together with the moderate trends of the Islamic movement, were in favour of that *démarche*, while the more doctrinal part of the movement was opposed to it.[10] In consequence, the pragmatists, headed by Sheikh Abdallah, were in favour of participating in the 1992 elections in Israel, but the more extremist minority maintained its boycott of the Israeli political system. To have embraced it would have implied recognition of the Jewish–Zionist political entity. For, unlike the local elections in which the Islamic movement came to take up several mayoralties, thus contributing to self-reliance and to reinforcing the trend of separateness from the Israeli mainstream, running in national elections would entail three major doctrinal breaches:

1. Participation would mean an acceptance of the rule of the non-Muslim majority.
2. Respect for the laws of Israel, which every elected member of the Knesset states in his inaugural oath, would mean Israeli law overriding Islamic Shari'a law.
3. The sovereignty of Israel would, as a consequence, be implicitly recognized over lands that the Muslims consider *waqf*.

The elections of 1992, in which for the first time more Arabs voted for general Israeli parties than for particularistic Arab lists, also signalled the sharp decrease in the communists' appeal all over the country. Since on the one hand the Islamists did not participate in the vote and on the other the rate of voters among the Arabs shrunk from about 73 per cent in the previous elections in 1988 to about 70 per cent this time,[11] one might speculate that Islamists who shunned participation in the elections continued to abstain from voting. Tufiq Zyad of Nazareth was re-elected to the Knesset, this time as the head of the Hadash list, and his party got about 50 per cent of the local vote (9,448 out of a total of 21,000) in spite of the general losses of his party both locally and countrywide.[12] These and other processes came to full maturity in the local elections of 1993 where

- unlike the national elections a year earlier where only 70 per cent of the Arab voters went to the polls, 90 per cent of the Arabs participated in their local elections, evidence enough of their emphasis on their local authorities through which they could vent their concerns;
- the Hadash Party continued to lead in local Arab politics in spite of its sharp losses in the national elections: this time, the party won only 12 mayorships compared with 15 in 1989, but in Nazareth it registered gains, mainly due to Zyad's stature;
- the Islamic movement maintained its strength, having five mayorships and 50 councillors on local councils.[13]

But the Christians of Israel in general, and those of Nazareth in particular, could not help seeing the writing on the wall: their political status was slipping, and the rise of the fundamentalists was beginning to pose a direct threat to them. This generated a loss of confidence in their future as a minority within the Arab minority in the country. Even though the more moderate elements within the Islamic movement in Israel support the 'links of fraternity between Muslim and Christian Arabs', the Christians know what awaits them as *dhimmis* if the Islamic entity ruled by Shari'a law were to materialize in Palestine. In 1992 the organ of the Islamic movement, *Sawt al-Haqq wal-Huriyya*, carried an outright attack on a respected Christian journalist, Atallah Mansur, for a series of articles he had published criticizing the moral conduct of some Islamist leaders. He was accused of harming Islam, diffusing lies and damaging the integrity of Muslim fundamentalists and Muslim women. He was condemned as a racist and as a warmonger who sowed discord among the Arabs of Israel. Mansur sued in court and was compensated for the libel, but the Christians in general continued to sense that the state of Israel ought, as a democratic state, prohibit by law incitement against them.[14]

Attacks and condemnations against Christians are also often heard in mosques, in sermons and in publications of the Muslim movement. On the eve of Al-Ad'ha festival in 1996, a leaflet was distributed in Umm al-Fahm, which accused local youth of improper behaviour 'mimicking that of Jewish and Christian Unbelievers'. The manifesto reached Nazareth and caused outrage there, which was reflected in the local press that is owned and edited by Christians, such as *al-Sinara* and *Kul-al-'Arab*.[15] In response, the Christians, far from counterattacking, on the contrary reacted like a *dhimmi* people, which sings the praise of the ruler while being beaten by him. They protested that they were as Arab as all the others, and they pointed to their contributions to Arab culture and history, something that only encouraged further attacks on them. In June 1996 an Arab Christian scholar ran a survey among high school students in Nazareth, as part of his thesis in psychology, on the question of the identity of the Christians in Israel. The questionnaire that he circulated among the students in the Baptist school in Nazareth, which had been filled by other Christians in other towns in Israel without a hitch, now occasioned a storm that could neither be foreseen nor justified and was widely echoed in the Arab and national media in the country, including the Islamic *Sawt al-Haqq*. Again, in a sycophantic fashion worthy of *dhimmis*, even the Christian writers who tried to fend off the Muslim (and some Christian) attacks on that unfortunate scholar, whose only offence was to search for the truth, heaped blame on their co-religionist. He was accused of 'sowing the poison of racism and division between Arab Christians and Arab Muslims'. The school authorities were also blamed for permitting the circulation of the questionnaire.[16]

Another case in point was a conflict around land-ownership in Nazareth, which was to become the antecedent of the much larger dispute that erupted into the open in 1997–99. During the years of Zyad as mayor, a mosque was built without the required city permit on the site of the tomb of a local Muslim saint – Nabi Sa'in – which dominates the city from the surrounding heights, in close proximity to a Christian monastery. The illegal construction of the mosque later received a post-factum permit, when the city leaders realized that their intervention would mean a clash with the Muslim majority. The growing Muslim movement in the town later came up with the claim that the adjoining terrain, on an area of 213 *dunam*, was a *waqf* land, while the municipality confirmed its ownership of the grounds. This issue became a bone of contention between Christians and Muslims, and the Islamic mouthpiece *Sawt-al-Haqq* devoted an entire article to it (22 November 1996). The local Christians feared that the Muslim claims, followed by acts of encroachment upon properties that were not theirs under the pretext of their being *waqf* land, were a stratagem to pursue the takeover by Muslims of the erstwhile Christian city of Nazareth.[17] Conversely, this Muslim success was evidence enough that neither the Christian minority nor the Israeli authorities were able to challenge the Muslim movement: the former due to their fear of further raising the Muslims' wrath; the latter due to a general unwillingness to clash with the Muslims of Israel.

On the eve of the 1996 national elections in Israel the question of the Muslim movement's participation once again came to the fore, coupled with other issues of contention and national ambition. Most of the membership, together with the organs of the group, controlled by Sheikh Abdallah, overwhelmingly supported the resolution to run for the Knesset, albeit in tandem with another Arab partner so as not to appear (Allah Forbid!) to have joined the Israeli party system. But Sheikh Ra'id and his fellow radicals, such as Kamal Khatib of Kafr Kanna, rejected this resolution and – taking advantage of Abdallah's absence abroad – published a communiqué which stated that the resolution did not apply to them. Many attempts to reconcile the two contending parties were made, but in vain. Then, Ra'id gathered his forces and declared the establishment of his own 'Islamic movement', seemingly much more radical and clear-cut on the main issues than the original; however, it was difficult sometimes to discern the fault-lines between the two, since the ideologies and the ultimate goals were not as much at variance as the tactics and the daily practicalities. Thus, while there was no disagreement on the need to establish segregated environments where members of the two groups could carry on their lives, their statements about the need for coexistence with the Jewish state or with the Christian minority therein have been more ambivalent. Among the more radical group, there were threats of open revolt against the Jewish state, coupled with the vision of establishing a Muslim state over the entire expanse of Palestine to replace the Jewish state, and where Jews and Christians would take up their Shari'a-allocated status of *dhimmis*.

To the pragmatists this sort of coexistence permits their movement to organize, to participate in elections (local and national), to inculcate its norms into its constituencies, to champion Islamic causes, and at the same time to maintain Muslim separateness in order to implement their agenda. By exploiting the means afforded to them by open and democratic Israel, they are willing to play by the rules of democracy as long as their purposes are served. Ultimately, at some undefined future, they entertain the hope of replacing the existing system by a new Islamic order. Those among them who speak about an Islamic state in Palestine seldom specify its boundaries, or the circumstances under which it may come into being, leaving open the possibility that it might encompass the entire territory, including Israel, which at any rate is considered a *waqf* land by them. The pragmatists specifically prescribe a Palestinian state alongside Israel and accept the Oslo Accords. But when asked they say that if this materialized they would continue to dwell in Israel rather than in the Palestinian state, as they realize that they are much better off and much freer than they would be in any Arab country (despite their protestations to the contrary). In most Arab countries indeed, including the most 'moderate' among them such as Jordan and Egypt, Islamists cannot stand for 'election' as such, while in Israel they can and do. Either way, a nationalist Palestinian element is implicit in their demand for a Palestinian state, although the Islamic movement, in Israel and elsewhere, negates nationalism as a matter of principle and opts for the revival of the unified universal Caliphate. In Jewish Israel, nationalism for the Arab minority does not of course mean a Jewish identity, but an Arab–Muslim one, thereby underlining yet another dimension of the unresolved contradictions of identity discussed above.

Sheikh Abdallah, the founder and leader of the Muslim movement, has distanced himself from the daily management of the group, but continues to command the respect of his followers as their supreme spiritual guide. But after the split in the movement, his political stature was undermined by his radical rivals. His town of Kafr Qassem, as well as neighbouring Kafr Bara, the Bedouin settlement of the Negev, the towns of Jaljulya and Karf Qara, and the mixed cities of Jaffa, Acre, Lod, Ramlah and Nazareth, continue to be counted among his constituencies. The ranks of his supporters include the two Knesset members who represented the movement, one from Kafr Kanna and the other from Jaljulya, as well as the member of the Nazareth city council, Salman Abu Ahmed, who headed the Muslim majority in the council in competition with the Christian mayor. On the other hand, the more radical group led by Sheikh Ra'id enjoyed the support of Umm al-Fahm, the largest Muslim town in Israel, of which he was mayor until he resigned to devote himself to Islamic politics, some satellite villages around his town, and part of Kafr Kanna under his fellow radical, Kamal Khatib. Nothing is more indicative of the thinking and ambitions of the two groups than their respective *modus operandi*. Sheikh Abdallah focused on parliamentary activity via the Muslim movement's Knesset members, and tirelessly laboured for *rapprochement* between Arabs and Jews in Israel. He also mediated in local rifts and conflicts between Israeli Arabs and won himself a reputation as a man of peace and reconciliation. He was, however, crippled by the schism as the two young and promising talents – Ra'id and Khatib – were left out, and he was deprived of the hub of the movement that was Umm al-Fahm where the printing house, the editorial set-up of *Sawt al-Haqq*, the Islamic college, the Islamic sports association, the Zakat board, etc. were located. He had to set up his own parallel organizations in order to make up for the lost ones, and founded a new journal, *Al-Mithaq* (The Covenant) which, unlike *Sawt al-Haqq*, reflected the new directions of the parliamentary activities of the movement in collaboration with the Israeli establishment. The group led by Ra'id took over all the institutions based in Umm al-Fahm, from which he pursued his brand of activism outside the establishment, and often in collision with it.

Ideologically, though the two Islamic movements are acknowledged outgrowths of the Muslim Brotherhood in Egypt, the Sheikh Ra'id group, which is our concern here, is the more direct descendant. In fact the two movements reflect the history of the Brotherhood inasmuch as it too always knew how to adapt itself to circumstances in order to survive. On its inception it was more militant and strove to take over the political order in Egypt and then the rest of the Arab world. In so doing it did not hesitate to kill politicians and even to plot against the powerful Nasser and then Anwar el-Sadat, whom it assassinated in 1981. It did not wish to operate within the establishment but rather to supersede it, compete with it and convert the masses to its cause. But in the past few decades, having felt the heavy hand of the regime and feared for its survival, it has been happy enough to maintain a low profile, to shun politics and to engage more in social, cultural and welfare activities which increase its fund of goodwill. To the extent that it runs for office, it does so only in conjunction with other political parties, so as not to appear to contend for power. In many Arab countries, and not only in Egypt, the Muslim Brotherhood is not permitted to act as a separate political agent. In this regard one can compare the genesis of the united Islamic movement in Israel to the early militant phase of the Brotherhood: its routinization and joining the political system to the current 'moderation' of the Brothers, and the split that severed Sheikh Ra'id's group from the 'moderated' mainstream to the splinter elements who remained true to the ideology of the founders and evolved into the breakaway Gama'at, Takfir wal-Hijra and the various jihad groups which the regime has been systematically eliminating.

When Hasan al-Banna founded the Brotherhood at the end of the 1920s in Egypt, it represented a rejection of the Western colonial powers and their value systems, including democracy, multiparty politics, elections and the like, as well as science and technology, which had begun penetrating the Arab world, as epitomized by the Wafd in Egypt. He taught a return to the fundaments of Islam (hence *fundamentalism* in our parlance), which implies the institution of a Shari'a state as of old, in the form of a universal Caliphate. The Brothers, like the puritanical Wahhabi-Hanbali school of Sunni Islam, and unlike the predominant and more lenient Hanafi school that the clerical establishment in most of the Arab world follow, leaned more on the Allah-given foundations of Islam (the Qur'an and Sunna of the Prophet) and less on the human interpretations that tend to flexibility if not permissiveness. The rationale was clear: only a return to the Prophet's purity and strictness could purge Islam from the catastrophic accretions which have bastardized it over the generations and turned it from a victorious faith into a subordinate one. Outwardly, the application of the Shari'a has also implied a return to the ancient terminology which had divided the world between *dar al-Islam* (that is, the abode of Islam), or the territories it controlled regardless of the composition of their populations; and *dar al-Harb*, or the abode of war, namely the lands which lie beyond the rule of Islam which must be engaged in war until they submit to Islamic rule. In the abode of war, special urgency is allocated to former lands of Islam such as Palestine, Andalusia and Kashmir which had been snatched away from Islamic rule and need to be retrieved by political and missionary effort if possible, or by force and jihad if necessary.

This view has engendered the attitude of regarding Muslims who presently dwell under non-Muslim rule in those lands as *murabitun* (stationed or garrisoned) on the frontiers of Islam, and those territories as *ribat* (lands of garrison), that is, they are not just Muslim citizens in non-Islamic lands, but a sort of pioneering *avant-garde* who will ultimately restore to Islamic rule the lands in which they are stationed. Sometimes that appellation can also refer to Muslim minorities in non-Muslim lands in general, such as in Europe, where demographically they have attained the critical mass that drives them closer to an eventual Muslim takeover. In the interim, the Muslim population is bound to establish Muslim enclaves which will ultimately serve as the launching-pads for Muslim conquest via jihad. This approach has also led to turning the tenet of jihad from a communal obligation (*fard kifaya*) into an individual commitment (*fard 'ayn*), so that every Muslim must participate personally in the enlargement of dar al-Islam, or use the *da'wa* (missionary or propaganda work) to spread the word of Islam in the world, in preparation for that takeover. Domestically, Muslim movements dispense a wide array of social services to attract Muslims into their fold and increase the circle of 'born again' believers; externally, they use the *da'wa* either to encourage conversion to Islam in foreign countries, or to render religious and social services to Muslims abroad in mosques and Islamic cultural centres that are usually financed by the Saudis and cultivate its Hanbali style of Islam. *Da'wa* is a unilateral affair, namely that while other faiths are prohibited by law or fiat from proselytizing in Islamic lands, Muslims take full advantage of Western tolerance and openness to indulge in propaganda, conversions and spreading of Islamic culture and faith. For these purposes they establish networks of propaganda and fund-raising under the guise of front charity associations, which deploy a wide array of volunteers and activities, part of which is legal and legitimate, but part of which is channelled to terrorist groups or illicit activities such as arms, ammunition, intelligence or recruiting for training and terrorism.

The Brothers, as epitomized in Sayyid Qut'b, their most prominent guide in the 1950s and indeed until he was executed by Nasser's regime in 1966, developed the thesis that modern Muslim society has been led astray by Western values of modernity, until it has become comparable to the early medieval *jahili* society of pre-Islamic Arabia. Therefore, as the Prophet of Islam had to effect the *hijra* (migration) from his native Mecca to Yathrib (Medina), where he built his Islamic base and whence he launched the final assault on Mecca, so believers today must detach themselves from their renegade societies until they can reconquer them from within. And if it is physically impossible to detach oneself from one's community, one might as well effect a spiritual migration by creating those Muslim enclaves inside Jahili society, either among other Muslims (as in Egypt) or among non-Muslims (as in Israel, Spain and Europe in general), until conditions allow the establishment of Islamic rule. Islamic movements usually reject Western values and ways of life; hence some of their spiritual heads, such as Sheikh Yussuf Qaradawi (an Egyptian who lives in golden exile in Qatar), and more so the heads of al-Qa'ida and other jihadist movements, have sanctioned the use of violence against westerners to intimidate and make them conform to their ideas. If some spiritual leaders, such as Qaradawi, are sometimes publicly ambivalent with regard to the physical elimination of innocent Western civilians, they mostly seem to be unanimous concerning Jews and Israelis. Bin Laden and Zawahiri explicitly sanction the battle against Jews and Crusaders, and their ideas have rubbed off on many Islamic movements throughout the Muslim world, such as Hamas, which does not always openly acknowledge its affiliation to the parent organization of the Brothers, but nonetheless reflects their anti-Western and anti-Jewish convictions.

Hamas, which is a branch of the Brotherhood, is its most obvious, declared and open manifestation among Palestinian Arabs (including Israelis), and it states overtly its intentions and ambitions. Israeli Arabs who toe its line are more careful not to appear or sound overtly hostile to their country. Moreover, the processes of acculturation that the Arab population in general has been undergoing in Israel, notably in the domains of liberty, freedom of expression, democracy, etc., are so complicated and diversified, that no blanket statement can be justifiably applied to all of them. For while Israelization is proceeding apace as regards the values of human rights (and indeed awareness of them), technology, education, social services and the substitution of meritocratic and personal politics for the old machinations of the traditional patriarchal hierarchies, other elements of alienation, Islamization and

Arab nationalism remain deeply entrenched. Spurred on by the success story of Muslim fundamentalism in the world today, it is conceivable that many more Muslims in Israel will regroup around their religiocultural heritage in years to come. If they do so, and regardless of the Islamic faction they will elect to follow, their common doctrinal and cultural patrimony and the joint ideological infrastructure they have cultivated over the years will provide them with a common denominator to rally around. This common denominator is made up of two components: one negative, regarding the Jews and Christians amongst whom they live; the other positive, reflecting their vision of the future Islamic state they wish to achieve.

The first element is rationalized and reinforced in the writings of leaders such as Sayyid Qut'b (see above), who is worshipped by the two rival groups alike. He built upon other Islamists' accusations and condemnations of Jews and Christians to such a degree as to turn them from a vehicle of irrational hatred into a rational and systematic 'scientific' discourse. He did so in the process of 'proving' that the only divine truth left to mankind was Islam, while all the others, including Islam's predecessors – Judaism and Christianity – were repositories of falsehood and distortion. Therefore Islam, as the only truth, must assume its role of universal leadership in order to liberate mankind from its errors. Moreover, Jews and Christians, being the purveyors of false revelations, were for that reason an insidious threat to Islam, as the current Judaeo-Christian 'conspiracy' proves. Not only are Jews and Christians detested in their own right, but being the long arm of the West in the Islamic world, they are considered as its agents in its endeavour to subvert Islam, alienate its youth through permissiveness and immoral conduct, and penetrate its educational systems under the pretext of reform, technological advances, modernization and democratization, in order to ultimately destroy them. At the outset of this battle, the Islamists had made their goals clear:

> Our programme has clear stages and well-defined steps. We know what we want and we know how to get there . . . Our goal is the Muslim people and the Muslim person, therefore we act so that our message may reach everywhere to every home. We want the banner of Allah to flutter again proudly over the lands that used to constitute Islamdom at any time in the past, and where the voice of the *mu'azzin* could be heard praising Allah . . . We want our call to reach everywhere and to be heard by all people in the universe. Every one

of our stages has its means and ramifications, but we are reluctant at this point to elaborate any further.[18]

Israel is a democracy and freedom of expression prevails. One can incite, libel and pour scorn on entire communities and groups with impunity, all in the name of the sacred freedom of the individual which is protected by the courts. Theoretically, incitement and libel can bring indictment, prosecution and punishment, but the state of Israel has usually refrained from pursuing this course and elected to avoid scandals, sensations and counter-accusations of discrimination and oppression which might generate friction and conflict within the delicate intercommunal balance. Only personal cases of libel can be settled in court, via civil suits which take for ever to reach judgment and verdict. Therefore, the Islamists have learned to sail close to the wind, and the rate of criminality among Israeli Arabs is about double that of the general population. A large part of it is 'ideological',[19] namely acts of violence or sabotage carried out particularly by Islamists, not for personal gain as are 'normal' crimes, but for the purpose of harming the state of Israel or scaring off their Jewish or Christian neighbours.

However, the regular and customary means for the Islamists to attain their ends, especially the moderates who accepted the Oslo Peace Accords, is to play by the rules of Israeli society and pursue their goals through the ballot-box. Therefore, beyond the national elections where the Islamists gained their two parliamentary seats in 1999 in conjunction with another Arab faction, so as to escape the accusation that they are running an Islamic Party under the aegis of the Jewish state, they have tended to focus on local elections in Arab towns and villages where it is easier to bring their strength to bear. In the local elections of 1998, both splinter groups of the Islamic movement sharpened their messages and updated their views. Sheikh Rai'd rejected the Wye Agreement between Israel and the Palestinians on account of what he considered to be too many concessions extracted from the Palestinian side. He also virulently opposed the subsequent 'abrogation' of the Palestinian national charter that the Israelis demanded as an indispensable condition for implementing this agreement. Sheikh Abdallah, on the other hand, lent his support to both *démarches*. The end result was that the two groups in fact aligned themselves along the Hamas–Palestinian Authority divide. While in the local elections of 1998 Sheikh Ra'id got 70 per cent of the vote in his third straight bid for the mayoralty, the communists sustained a severe blow in the national elections of 1999, where their constituency among the Arabs went down from 37 per cent in 1996, thus moving from a five Knesset-member faction (the largest among Arabs in Israel), to 22 per cent with only three members. The largest faction henceforth would be the Islamist-led United Arab list, where the more moderate group of Sheikh Abdallah gained two seats and others three.

CHAPTER FOUR

Sheikh Ra'id Salah: The Shepherd and his Flock

SHEIKH RA'ID'S JOURNEY from his first steps in the Islamic movement to his acknowledged leadership of its militant pro-Hamas faction, and his ideological and practical break with the state of Israel, evolved during the decade of the 1990s. Under his leadership, the Islamic movement turned from a sociocultural pursuit for 'born-again' Muslims into a religiopolitical organization which sought power as a way to implement its programme. Indeed, while in 1983 only one mayor of the Islamic movement had been returned in the polls with six councillors in four different Arab villages, February 1989 saw five mayors elected together with 45 other councillors in various municipalities and local councils, the most formidable of whom was Sheikh Ra'id, and the councillors who clustered around him, in the city of Umm al-Fahm, the largest Muslim township in Israel (some 30,000 population). Hence the 'watershed' mood in many Arab local governments in Israel where, depending on one's political loyalties, there prevailed either a sense of confidence and euphoria about the upward Islamic trend, or fear about that same process. That feeling was reinforced by the general success of the Islamic movement in the Triangle in central Israel, one of the three major concentrations of Arabs in the country (the others are in Galilee and the Negev Bedouin region). In that area the Islamists won about 30 per cent of the total vote (25 out of 81 councillors), compared to 15 per cent in Galilee (eight out of 52 councillors) and 23 per cent in the south (three out of 13 councillors in the Bedouin townships). Though the national average of Islamist councillors remained low (less than 10 per cent), the movement was able to return 25 out of the 116 total number of all elected councillors in the Triangle, i.e. 21.5 per cent, and that was a stunning victory by the rather conservative standards of Arabs in Israel.

The comparatively high results won by the Islamists in the Triangle can be accounted for by the fact that, unlike Galilee where many Christians reside, the Triangle Arab villages are almost exclusively Muslim. However, Sheikh Ra'id's personal victory, a landslide of 75 per cent of the vote and eleven of the fifteen councillors, considerably increased the Islamist average of the entire Triangle area. And so, at the age of 30, he became the key figure in the Islamic movement's storming of the political scene among Israel's Arabs. His aim was not to join the various Arab parties contending for seats in the Knesset in Israel's national elections, so as to conquer a majority of them, but, on the contrary, to signal that his Arab–Muslim constituency ought not to participate in the Israeli democratic process at all. In other words, his was a statement of defiance to the Israeli system that heralded a new policy of alienation from the Israeli state. He is a member of the Mahajneh clan, formerly a Druze family from Syria that had converted to Islam, moved to Palestine and helped found the village of Umm al-Fahm. After graduating from the local high school he studied at the Islamic college in Hebron where he was ordained as Sheikh. In 1988 he also gained the prestigious title of *Hajj*, following his pilgrimage to Mecca, but throughout the 1980s he had become the central figure of Islamic revivalism in Umm al-Fahm, the leader of the local Muslim association and the enthusiastic recruiter of the young to the movement. As a result of the opening of the borders between Israel and the West Bank, many young people travelled to Muslim institutions there and Palestinian preachers came to speak and teach in mosques in Israel. Thus the mood of return to Islam began to prevail among Muslim youth in Arab villages, and Ra'id was quick to capitalize on that mood and lend to it the organizational shape it needed.

Due to the backwardness of local services and the physical degradation of the township, Sheikh Ra'id was one of the first who took the initiative in order to demonstrate that he and his followers could do what the Israeli establishment had failed to achieve in terms of development and services. He organized volunteer groups who collected garbage from the streets as an example to fellow townsmen, and announced that he was contributing part of his salary to the bankrupted local treasury. His opponents claimed that he was swept into office not only by an aggressive election campaign designed by the Islamists in town, but also because of the preceding twelve years of persistent *da'wa* (propaganda) that had been disseminated among the population. By spreading the slogans 'Islam is the alternative', 'Islam is the truth' and 'Islam is the solution', Ra'id and his followers depicted their opponents in the Communist Party, which had ruled the city for decades, as anti-religious. Just prior to the elections, Ra'id was taken to court by his opponents in the Rakah Communist Party who contended that instead of printing his full name on the voting-tickets, as required by law,[1] he contented himself with his first name Ra'id and his father's name Salah. Actually the young sheikh belonged to the Abu Shaqrah clan which happened to have settled in the Mahajneh clan neighbourhood, one of four in the township. Thus, in spite of a quirky local custom which made one's identity contingent on one's quarter in town, Ra'id rebelled against convention because he wished to identify himself as a candidate representing a transclan constituency and not only the Mahajneh to which he belonged only technically. However, he lost his case and was ordered to add the borrowed clan name to his voting slips.

Nevertheless, Ra'id's success was a landslide, almost unprecedented in that town. For except for the incumbent mayor's clan, the Mahamid, which closed ranks behind their candidate as was customary, an overwhelming majority of the village's overall constituency voted for him. This was quite a feat as it showed that not only could the traditional shackles of clan politics be broken and circumvented, but also that Islam was a strong enough mobilizing factor to pull together rival clans, given a charismatic and popular religious actor to command loyalty and raise enthusiasm. On election night, when the first returns were announced and predictions were made heralding Ra'id's success, he was so overwhelmed that he retreated to his home, even cancelling a live television interview. His supporters and followers were swept off their feet with joy and cries of victory echoed throughout the small alleys of the village. The Sheikh's house was invaded by a jubilant crowd of hundreds who broke in to see the triumphant but still diffident and incredulous young mayor-elect. Soon the courtyard of the house overflowed with thousands more who came to greet him for his/their unexpectedly magnificent victory. The Sheikh had ultimately to appear before the multitudes of his admirers and speak to them in his soft but clear voice, quoting, as is his wont, from the Qur'an and the Hadith.

Ra'id is a preacher at heart. Whenever you ask a question he replies with a speech. Aware of the bad experiences of the 1970s when his fellow townsmen were incarcerated because of their acts of sabotage (burning woods and crops in nearby Jewish settlements), he became extremely cautious not to play up his political views, preferring at first to devote all his attention to the municipality that he was elected to lead, and then to the spread of Islam and to his international activities in raising funds in order to advance his cause. But even during those heady days, Ra'id's imprint on the ideological issues of the Islamic movement could not escape unnoticed. *Al-Sirat*, the mouthpiece of the movement that was formally headed by its chief, Sheikh Darwish, came under Ra'id's influence not only due to his imposing personality and the immense authority he acquired after his election, but simply due to the physical presence of the editorial and printing facilities of that journal in Umm al-Fahm of which he was the elected mayor. Many editorials, which began as early as 1988 to evince support to the Palestinian intifada (1987–92), could conceivably have been written by Ra'id, though rarely was that stated openly. In one case in 1988 harsh words of criticism were put in the mouth of an 8-year old Palestinian boy, who stated to his Israeli captors that he was 'acting under the orders of 'Umar the Caliph, Khalid ibn al-Walid the famous warrior of early Islam, and Saladin who defeated the Crusaders'.[2] Since 8-year-olds cannot be prosecuted, that was a convenient way to air accusations against Israel without running any risk. As identification with Hamas became more open and defiant among the Islamists, their journal became more audacious in declaring war against Israel and the Jews, though on such statements the leaders of the movement did not dare to sign as yet. By the end of 1989 *Al-Sirat*, which had attained a distribution of 10,000 copies (compared to 1,500 in 1986), was supplanted by the new weekly *Sawt al-Haqq wal-Huriyya* (The Voice of Truth and Freedom) which continues to this day to expound the views of the militant Islamists in Israel, even after the split in their movement in 1996.

After the Islamists' victory in the elections of 1989, which resulted on the one hand in their growing self-confidence, and on the other in the Israeli government's reluctance to confront them head-on, open declarations of jihad against Israel became routine.[3] The *Sirat* of November 1989 went even further when it reproduced a picture of al-Aqsa Mosque on its cover with the caption: 'O Fighter of Jihad! Wake up! Acre and its shores are calling upon you! Don't fall asleep! Come and defend our rivers!!' A statement worthy of Hamas, which surely could not have been made without the knowledge and approval of Ra'id. It became then a matter of course for the *Sirat* to hail the Palestinian participants of the intifada as heroes and the Israelis who fought them as 'maddened dogs',[4] a process which culminated in an editorial denying the right of Israel to exist and anticipating its destruction:

The politicians of this country pursue their vain ideas regarding the frontiers of their state from the Nile to the Euphrates. We will not be surprised if some of them will lay claim to the Hijaz . . . for this has been the pattern of the Zionist invasion on the model of the Crusades. Their venomous arguments and their forgeries of history, far from serving their goals, contribute, on the contrary, to the rule of aggression and oppression . . . Those lies and forgeries will not convince us to accept the *fait accompli*. All political solutions that have been proposed all around will not persuade us to renounce our ideological justice . . . For no one who behaved for a few years as a peasant can prove *eo ipso* that the land is his, because his parents may have usurped it. They forget that it was the Balfour Declaration which granted them in 1917 a National Home in Palestine . . . That expedient measure cannot suddenly be transformed into a national right . . .

You should content yourself with the fact that for the time being the world has recognized you as a nation, but you should not delude yourself any further lest you wake up to a horrible reality . . . Your very existence, which is founded on arrogance and high-handedness, is but delusion and vanity, and therefore it is void by definition, because it is not predicated on legitimate rights and accepted truths, but upon vain premises and means of usurpation, killing, expulsions, domination of others' lands by force . . . and a society of ingathered from all parts of the globe, whose inner contradictions are evident . . .

The laws of the universe will bring upon them [Israelis/Jews] a decisive rout, the like of which they had suffered at the hands of the Romans and others. They will always be parasites in other nations' civilizations, due to their obduracy and defiance of history and its laws. Their arrogance can only lead them from one defeat to another . . .[5]

Gradually, Sheikh Ra'id shed his caution as he was catapulted to the forefront of the political concerns of his movement, though at first he committed himself to the affairs of his Umm al Fahm fief. In no small measure his involvement stemmed from the centrality of his town in the Islamic movement in general. At first, many editorials and articles of *Al-Sirat* and then *Sawt al-Haqq* cited his sayings or doings, but soon he not only became a main source of information and inspiration for those publications but also contributed directly by writing editorials and articles himself, either under his own name or at times under pen-names. This was particularly so in matters relating to al-Aqsa Mosque, which he perceived, like the Mufti of Jerusalem since the late 1920s (Hajj Amin al-Husseini) as the most potent mobilizing factor of the Muslims in the country and the most promising launch-pad for any claim of leadership of that constituency. So, while he was taking his first steps as the mayor of his town, he had already set his sights on the symbol of al-Aqsa to rally around him Palestinian, pan-Arab and possibly pan-Islamic support. Following an incident in which a group of Israeli fanatics was arrested by the Israeli police for trying to 'lay down the cornerstone of the Third Temple', Ra'id was cited in an editorial as saying that

> Al-Aqsa Mosque is the heart which gives us life and it stands above all political decisions which may be taken day in day out . . . The Temple cornerstone affair is but one expression of the larger scheme which has preceded it. We read in the *Protocols of the Elders of Zion* that the Third Temple will be built on the ruins of the Aqsa Mosque. The schemes are multiple: first, tourists were allowed to enter the Mosque, then Jews were permitted to pray there, and then excavations were undertaken around it and tunnels were dug underneath it in order to facilitate the demolition of the Mosque.[6] And let us not forget the arson of the Mosque.[7] Therefore we should transcend resolutions and proposals and go over to acts and deeds.[8]

Sheikh Ra'id never reneged on his promise, and as we shall see, in total disregard of history, fact and reason, he continued for years to deny Jewish links to Temple Mount, accusing Israel of arson and trying to delegitimize its historical claim to the site. He maintained that Israeli excavations were acts of sabotage against the mosque, lest archaeological findings would refute his fantasies about the place (as indeed they did). Therefore, during most of his mayorship his preoccupation with al-Aqsa would take much of his time, and when he resigned after being elected for a third term, he dedicated himself to the al-Aqsa Foundation, an organization that was to bring him to clash openly with the authorities, leading to his arrest and trial during 2004–05. A tenth-grader from the Umm al-Fahm school system was quoted as having written a poem for the journal in which he said: 'carry your weapons for the days are coming when Islam will win and the rascals will be defeated'.[9] And so, under Ra'id's aegis, blunt irredentist statements against Israel (which finances that school system), as well as outrageous anti-Semitic slurs, were ingrained within the Islamist population of that town. It became abundantly clear, the year Ra'id took over power in town (1989) was only the beginning of a long process of indoctrination (inadvertently sponsored by the state of Israel itself) that was bound in the long run, as that generation came of age, to escalate the crisis he was planning.

Ra'id's tremendous success in education, social welfare and *da'wa* practice had made him popular during the decade of his activity in Umm al-Fahm, well before he was elected mayor. But after he was elected, his new authority and prestige added much clout to his deeds as a religious actor. Perhaps nothing symbolized his victory more than the impressive Islamic centre he built at the top of the hill overlooking the village. In contrast to the battered, neglected and decrepit town that the Islamists found when they took power, the luxury of the Islamic centre looks out of place. It is an enclave within the society that they laboured to convert to their cause. It dramatically illustrated what the Islamists could do, and the heights, spiritual and material, to which they were capable of lifting their constituents. Ra'id began the long, arduous and frustrating task of shifting the interest of the youth from matter to spirit, from the here-and-now to the hereafter. He firmly believed, as he does now, and as his followers are convinced, that 'everything comes from Allah', that 'neither Marx nor Sartre' could provide the answers to existence or to man's place or mission in the world. He said that the return to Islam was part of a universal trend which came to the fore with the collapse of communism and the rebuilding of churches in former Eastern Bloc countries. In his early days he liked to couch his remarks, especially those to the press, in universal terms so as to make them acceptable to a foreign audience. He did not emphasize then the uniqueness and exclusivity of Islam or the truth intrinsic to it, as he was to do later, and stridently so, preferring to dwell instead on the phenomenon of religious revival everywhere.

In Umm al-Fahm there were as yet no industrial parks to provide jobs, no leisure centres, no police station, no fire station; and the muddy alleys bore no names. There were no playgrounds, no youth clubs, no swimming-pool, no market-place and no bus-stations. The lack of public facilities was so staggering that it took imagination, resources, enthusiasm and persistence to achieve all that, and it was incumbent upon the inexperienced young mayor to meet those challenges. Even the cafés had closed down because of the banning of alcohol and the return of many of their customers to Islam. The local soccer team, dressed in track-suits, kneeled to pray before each game to invoke the support of Allah, and when friends visited, women were herded into separate rooms while men clustered together in the large living-room. Many of the inhabitants prayed five times a day and those employed in Jewish factories requested prayer-breaks in respect of their rite. So, once Sheikh Ra'id's personal example of self-reliance had installed correct Muslim behaviour and decency, he turned his attention to reforming the administration of his town. Material gains, which were the object of his contempt, were at the top of his agenda for reform. In an interview with a foreign correspondent he explained: 'Islamic thought does not differentiate between the secular and the religious. We consider service a form of worshipping and obeying Allah'.[10] He obtained funds from Muslim associations and used them to build kindergartens, day-care centres and institutes to train religious cadres. An Islamic College was built in Umm al-Fahm in 1989, joining two others in the Triangle villages of Taybeh and Baqa. So, though the permits to open those schools were granted by the Israeli government on the assumption that young Muslims would no longer need to go to Nablus, Hebron or Gaza to pursue religious studies, the point of no return had been already crossed, and the close relationship had been established between the Islamists in Israel and their Hamas brethren in the West Bank and Gaza. The colleges were founded with assistance from the World Islamic Association, operating from Saudi Arabia, whose representative in the area was the East Jerusalem Mufti, who sought the advice of the head of the committee of Arab mayors in Israel.[11]

In 1989 (the year of his triumph) Ra'id argued that 'even if Umm al-Fahm were located in Switzerland, the Islamic Movement would have won there',[12] meaning that he imputed much greater significance to doctrinal, regional and global affairs than to the Israeli government's actions or omissions so far as his rise to power was concerned. That countered the conventional wisdom that was repeated *ad nauseam* by nationalist Arabs, and the press and academia in the country, to the effect that under-development was at the root of Arab dissatisfaction. This meant – again, contrary to conventional wisdom – that it was ideology and not poverty or the dearth of material resources which channelled Muslims to the radical groups, the best examples being Iran and Saudi Arabia as states, Bin Laden and other major donors to that cause as individuals. And in fact, Ra'id and his colleagues in other Muslim townships in Israel have shown that by mobilizing available resources, volunteers and the informal tithe (*zakat*) in their communities, and by re-ordering priorities within their villages, they have succeeded in eliminating underdevelopment and in embarking on large self-financed projects to promote social and educational development. The consequences of this realization may be staggering: that religiously motivated Muslims are likely to act far more boldly and with more self-sacrifice than politically oriented activists. When this transcends into guerrilla/terrorist activity, it is evident that the *fida'i* tradition in Islam which today translates into the phenomenon of Islamikaze[13] may push Muslim activists to the furthest limits of violence and terror. Paradoxically, though, Islamic fundamentalist circles in Israel and Lebanon have been playing up the theme of deprivation and oppression as their chief motives for engaging in terrorism, either justified as a pan-Islamic jihad, or as a personal jihad by Muslim individuals.

A case in point emerged in 1986, when the local committee for the Islamic work camp in Umm al-Fahm announced that it was raising funds to build a mosque in the town, which was still under communist rule, with the stated purpose of 'raising the ideological, political, social and religious awareness of our youth'.[14] But the committee soon discovered that they were in competition with the incumbent communist authorities in City Hall, which tried to block that initiative, for the very building of a public institution by a volunteer body of citizens exposed the municipal authorities as incompetent and careless. The mosque and library were begun, but it turned out that they were illegally sited on government land. Orders were served by the authorities to halt construction and destroy what had been built illegally. The Muslim movement appealed to public opinion and organized a sunset service at the incomplete skeleton of the mosque in order to consecrate it as a 'holy place', immune from dismantlement.[15] Islamists blamed the mayor specifically for 'having joined hands with the Israeli authorities' to undermine this project that would have benefited the Islamists – a fear that was fully justified three years later when the Islamists took over power. Ultimately, much to the mayor's dismay, the religious complex continued to stand, following the interference of the Muslim religious authorities in Israel who were appalled at the prospect of a mosque being destroyed.[16] This pattern of creating a *fait accompli*, and then banking on the Israeli authorities' reluctance to be accused as 'racist' or 'anti-Muslim', especially during election year, was established and became a very effective *modus operandi* of the Muslim movement. Thus the communists, who had ruled Umm al-Fahm and many of the other local Arab councils for many years, had to watch the emergence and growth of a dense network of sociocultural and religiopolitical activities which were the Muslim movement's best means of defeating the communists. The multitude of organizations and associations dealing with all aspects of life meant that no stone was left unturned to lure away their would-be constituents from the rival camp. Clearly beaten on the level of action, the communists mounted abominable charges and rumours against the Muslim fundamentalists, such as the levying of the Zakat using Mafia methods and suggesting that the new recruits joined the movement to fulfil their 'greed and personal ambitions'. The communists also accused the Muslim movement of aspiring to take over the entire land of Palestine, in this way constituting the Israeli branch of the Muslim Brotherhood,[17] hoping to deter some Arabs from that 'extremist' position, which in fact constituted a compliment to the Islamists.

Free from the 'moderating' shackles of the Abdallah Darwish group and of the authority of its leader, Sheikh Ra'id now felt ready to embark on his more actively militant course in order to implement his agenda which was far more ambitious and required greater effort and risk-taking than anything the unified Islamic movement had hitherto envisaged. First, he undertook to restore to Islamic tenure, and to refurbish physically, old *waqf* assets and Muslim holy places, especially the ruined mosques and cemeteries in the multitude of Arab villages that had been ravaged and abandoned during the 1948 war, and which no one had cared to tend to. This is particularly significant given the mood prevailing among Israeli Arabs of commemorating the *Nakbah* (the 'disaster' of the loss of Palestine when Israel was established), at the same time that Israelis were celebrating with great pomp their jubilee in 1998. The signal was clear: while other Arabs in Israel commemorated, lamented or demonstrated, Ra'id's group was bent on rehabilitating, constructing, claiming ownership and taking the lead in reclaiming the lost patrimony. They began to scan and monitor all Israeli national construction projects, such as roads, infrastructure, major housing projects or new settlements, in order to stage physical opposition and raise the level of awareness among Israeli Arabs against any attempt to run over or desecrate what they considered to be a religious site. A case in point is the Istiqlal cemetery near Haifa where the Islamic hero of the 1930s, Izz a-Din al-Qassam, was buried after he was killed in battle by the British in Samaria in 1935. This old burial ground had been neglected and forgotten for decades until it regained prominence when Hamas called its military arm 'the Qassam

Fighters'. When the municipality planned to widen the highway on the fringe of the cemetery, the Islamists put up a round-the-clock watch on the newly spruced-up tomb and advised the authorities that they would prevent any attempt to encroach on these grounds.

The Ra'id group also strives to restore Islamic control over old mosques which had been either destroyed or put to entertainment, tourist, commercial or other use; and they demand that the revenues from the *waqf* assets in the country be put under their direct management. Their activities are so well publicized that they have won acclaim from Muslims in Israel and elsewhere. So much so that other more moderate Muslims have adopted the technique of reclaiming, or simply invading and taking over any premises they covet, that may or may not have been linked in the past to Islamic ownership. They declare the property w*aqf*, thereby imputing holiness to it, and squat there until the authorities give in in order to 'avoid bloodshed'. This pattern has been followed, for example, by the Muslims of Nazareth who for the most part are moderates but in several instances acted just like the radicals. This raises several questions:

- Are there really moderates and radicals among these Muslim fundamentalists, or is this simply a matter of opportunism, tactics and strategy as regards the best and most expedient means to attain the Islamic goals shared by both wings of the Islamic movement?
- Where was 'moderate' Sheikh Abdallah – the reputed mediator and intermediary, the 'man of peace and reconciliation' to whose directives the Islamists of Nazareth yield, when the Muslims there repeatedly and over a long period of time invaded public property, squatted and threatened bloodshed if they were forcibly removed?
- Does not the pattern of action of both groups suggest a common strategy of expanding at the expense of their Christian and Jewish neighbours when they can, under the dubious pretext of reclaiming *waqf* property?

The radicals also use other themes to mobilize and increase their grassroots support in Israel and in the international Muslim community for their activities of reclaiming their patrimony – foremost of which is Jerusalem in general and the Aqsa mosque in particular. As we have already seen, when the Islamic movement in Israel was united under 'moderate' Sheikh Abdallah, its mouthpiece *Sawt al-Haqq* annually blamed the Israeli authorities for the arson of the Mosque perpetrated by an

Australian Christian tourist in 1969. Since the split in the movement, it has been principally the radical group which has taken on the responsibility for that campaign against Israel, as part of its routinely sustained charges against it; and it is Sheikh Ra'id who has become the standard-bearer of the struggle for Arab and Islamic Jerusalem. He constantly warns against the 'impending menace to al-Aqsa' and attempts to rally world Islamic public opinion around him in order to 'rescue' the mosque. He virulently condemns the Israeli excavations around the site, flatly denies any link between Jews and their ancient Temple on the site, and has invited Muslim delegations from Israel and Islamic countries to see for themselves the works that are calculated, in his opinion, to undermine the foundations of al-Aqsa on the compound. Sometimes a contradiction is introduced into the debate, as when Jews are accused of destroying the mosque in order to restore their Temple – an edifice supposed to never have existed in the first place. To counter this perceived threat, Ra'id has initiated and led the takeover and refurbishing of the underground floor of the mosque known by the Israelis as 'King Solomon Stables', but to Muslims as the Musallah al-Marwani – a prayer-place named after Marwan, one of the Umayyad kings – thus adding considerably to the prayer space during the peak month of Ramadan. Ra'id also initiated a gathering of Islamists in Israel in which he lamented the state of al-Aqsa Mosque under 'Jewish occupation' and ran a Jerusalem festival, which attracted some 40,000 believers, for the same purpose.

Ra'id has intensified his material and moral support to the families of Hamas casualties, even when a terrorist act had been performed by the deceased which has led to loss of life among Israeli civilians. The excuse is 'humanitarian' aid, though it is clearly an act of encouragement to Hamas. Similarly, in 1992, when 415 Hamas leaders were captured by Israel and exiled for a year to southern Lebanon, Ra'id organized truck-loads of food, medicine and clothing for the exiles, and personally attempted to cross the border and deliver his aid, before his zeal was contained by Israeli police. Ra'id also travelled extensively to Islamic countries, especially Egypt and Turkey. The latter was at the top of his priorities and hopes during the brief tenure of the Erbakan government in the 1990s which championed world Islamic causes. He sought recognition for his Islamic College in Umm al-Fahm by the Turkish Muslim authorities, hoping thereby not only to attract Muslim youth in Israel but also to exact subsidies from Turkish and other Muslim donors. He also maintained a close relationship with the so-called 'political leadership' of

Hamas in order to show his sympathy with them and to escape sanction for supporting a terrorist organization. When Sheikh Yassin, the founder and leader of that group was jailed in Israel at the beginning of the 1990s, Ra'id built up a close partnership with Dr al-Zahar, the No. 2 man in Hamas, and when Yassin was released in 1997 he was on hand to greet him and celebrate his freedom. So much so, that he gained adulation among wide audiences in the Islamic world. All this activity was doubled when Ra'id resigned his post as mayor after he was overwhelmingly re-elected for a third term in 1999 in order to devote himself totally to his Islamic work, mainly through his al-Aqsa Foundation, the tentacles of which reach all over the Muslim world. Ra'id had obviously had enough of the petty politics of Umm al-Fahm. He was evidently convinced that a greater calling awaited him in the world of Islam as a dominant religious actor.

But Ra'id, however charismatic, energetic and hard-working, could not achieve his goals singlehandedly. There is no leader without the led, no chiefs without Indians and no king without subjects. One of the most fascinating aspects of this study is the relationship between his enthusiastic followers and their leader. What is the discourse that holds them together? Are the rank and file aware of the intricacies of the Muslim fundamentalist doctrines that he expounds, or are they motivated by simple symbols, slogans, impressions and emotions that he well knows how to arouse and mobilize? In other words, is it enough to expound the rational or material elements that push fundamentalists to action, or should one also try to understand the heart and soul of the phenomenon? On a personal note, I happened to be appointed member of a governmental commission of inquiry to deal with unrest in the city of Nazareth. The Pope had pledged his presence in the city for the celebration of the Millennium in the year 2000. Members of the commission who were searching for a way to calm the city, met with its Muslim leaders, some of whom were prominent businessmen. However, the head of the Islamic faction in the municipality insisted that Islamic symbols should be conspicuous in the city (which had become majority Muslim) and would not let Christianity take centre stage during the celebrations, in spite of the fact that business might suffer as a result. This admirable position, which gives precedence to principle and belief over material gain, is yet another indication of how emotional shooting from the hip can overshadow rational, pragmatic and measured evaluations of situations. Or take the Bin Laden model of a wealthy man who could have pursued in tranquillity the corrupt, decadent and wasteful living style of his peers in Saudi Arabia, but elected instead to live in caves on the Pakistani border with Afghanistan, persecuted and under constant threats and bombings, in the hope of beating the West from his hidden redoubts.

Such patterns of behaviour evoke very strong emotional adulation on the part of the masses, as did the tremendously popular Ayatollah Khomeini when he returned from exile to Tehran in early 1979 after the Islamic revolution. He could have easily settled in the deposed Shah's palace, which would have also made sense in terms of the transfer of symbols of power. But he elected instead to settle down in his modest two-bedroom apartment in Qom, thereby signalling to his followers that he attended to the people's needs by being one of them and by shedding the symbols of corruption of the previous regime. The emotional response of the populace was overwhelming. The rank and file of fundamentalists react similarly to the modest, materially ascetic and impeccably pristine lifestyle of Bin Laden, Sheikh Yassin of Gaza, Sheikh Ra'id and other fundamentalist leaders who are involved in religious politics. There are examples of glamorous, globe-trotting and mediatized fundamentalist clerics, such as Sheikh Yussuf Qaradawi, who pursues his luxurious life with the aid of Western-made airplanes, microphones, and air-conditioned cars, all the while heralding the demise of the West. But in spite of his tremendously popular *fatwas* he commands no congregation, and his exile in Qatar, far away from his beloved home in Egypt, which he was forced to leave long ago, does not allow him to lead a constituency. When leaders are watched by their followers, and closely and constantly so in the era of the media revolution, they become models to emulate; they are loved and not only respected and heeded due to their wisdom and knowledge. This inevitably creates an emotional commitment to the leader who then is followed almost blindly, regardless of what turn he might take or of the errors he might make, or of the misfortune he might bring to his flock.

In a Muslim fundamentalist group, due to the undisputed authority of the leader, and the adulation which puts him at its apex, reality is not perceived in practical terms based on data and rational analysis, but through the filters that are manufactured to fit the leader's purposes. Moreover, through repetition and auto-suggestion, by way of mantras and slogans that are imprinted in minds and etched in souls via posters, road-signs and audio- and video-cassettes, leaders themselves end up believing in the virtual reality that they have created. One way of creating the virtual world that the followers obey without question is the elaboration of a vocabulary and consensual commentary on existing terminology which end up shaping a very peculiar and uniform world view that sanctifies the imagined world created by the leader as the sole truthful reality. In the context of Israel the Muslim fundamentalists are so imbued with hatred towards the West for its decadent values, its support of corrupt and un-Islamic governments in the Muslim world and its endorsement of Israel, and towards the Jews, Zionism and Israel for their own sake, that they constructed this sort of virulent terminology to indoctrinate their followers. It is no different from what Hamas teaches. While they are convinced that Islam ought to be respected by everyone, they do not believe that they owe the same respect to other revealed faiths, not even those that share their monotheistic convictions.

One day in January 2001, at the height of the Aqsa intifada, the Israeli press carried the picture of a procession in Ramallah, which paraded a donkey wearing a Jewish prayer shawl and sporting on its forehead the Star of David in the shape of a swastika, with a large crowd on both sides of the road applauding and roaring in laughter, under the watchful eye of the Palestinian police which joined in the 'celebration'. The Israeli public was thoroughly shaken, regarding this act of profanation and abuse as a continuation of the torching by Palestinian mobs of the Jewish synagogue in Jericho and Joseph's tomb in Nablus in the initial stages of the upheaval. In all those cases what transpired was a Palestinian–Muslim determination, born out of frustration, hatred and a deepseated intolerance towards other faiths, which prompted them to take revenge on Jewish religious symbols, knowing full well the hurt and anguish they would cause among the Israeli public. The angered and disappointed readership of the papers was reminded that when in 1997 an Israeli settler in Hebron held a poster where the Prophet Muhammad was reviled by the drawing of a pig, she was arrested, tried for anti-religious incitement and duly incarcerated for three years. That event, which rightly caused Muslim outrage, was condemned across the board by Israeli politicians and religious leaders who understood the sensitivity of such provocations. Naïve Israelis therefore expected to see a similar reaction on the part of the Palestinian authorities and their religious hierarchies, but in vain. Worse, following the example of Hamas, the Islamic movement in Israel, while vociferously but justly denouncing the Hebron affront, had nothing to say when Israeli sentiments, faith and symbols were trampled upon. Similarly, while it has become customary for Muslims everywhere to burn Israeli flags and effigies of Israeli leaders (usually coupled with the same abuse of American symbols) as part of any demonstration against the Jews or their state, or to burn down Jewish synagogues around the globe, no condemnation of those acts have been forthcoming from any Muslim movement, least of all in Israel, though one could imagine what wild reaction a comparable act against Muslim symbols would have provoked.

The intifada erupted during the Jewish High Holidays of 2000, and no respect was paid to the sanctity of the season either by the Palestinians or the Islamists in Israel who joined them in the massive disturbances of October of that year. Violence was perpetrated against Israelis across the breadth and length of the West Bank and Gaza; Jewish worshippers at the Western Wall were pelted with rocks, and police were compelled to take them into custody for their own safety. But when Ramadan set in, it was the same Israeli police who protected the right of Muslims to worship freely on Temple Mount, and it was taken as a matter of course that Israeli authorities should handle Arab disturbances with extra care so as not to trigger further antagonism. The result is that Muslims under Israeli rule, both inside Israel proper and in the Territories, have become accustomed to believing that their faith deserves respect while other religions, notably Judaism, must absorb without protest all the scorn, abuse and calumny they might care to offer. Thus we find the Palestinian Mufti, as well as Sheikh Ra'id and his peers, denying any historical link between Jews and Temple Mount, deriding all Jewish historical and archaeological claims to it, and insisting on Muslim exclusivity for that holy site. It is no coincidence that Ra'id has emphasized and succeeded in his endeavour, the threat that the Jews were posing to the al-Aqsa holy place, by the very fact of their presence there and by their excavations which 'menace the foundations of the mosque'. The experiment of sharing holy sites, which had been imposed by Israel in the Hebron Tomb of the Patriarchs, far from teaching a model of tolerance, on the contrary has been decried by Muslims as a 'desecration', under the yoke of occupation, of Muslim holy places.

The mantra that calls upon Muslims to rally around the cause of al-Aqsa, the Aqsa foundation, the Aqsa festivals and the like, have gone a long way to crystallize it as the symbol of the Islamists' struggle against Israel, which by its very nature can also ensure the endorsement of that struggle by Muslims worldwide. The appeal to 'rescue al-Aqsa from the depravity of the Jews' has gone so far as to claim that since Israeli occupation in 1967, the men and women soldiers of Israel have taken part in drunken sexual orgies within the mosque compound, and that it was an Israeli conspiracy to burn the mosque in 1969 by the hand of an Australian Christian tourist – something that makes this enterprise all the more urgent. This view upholds the fallacy that it was the visit of Ariel Sharon on Temple Mount that triggered the intifada in the first place. But all the same, that act serves as a warning that no official Israeli personality can claim any right on Temple Mount without incurring the wrath of Muslims. For anything Israel does which is not to the Muslims' liking is provocation and aggression, but anything Muslims do, even the most murderous attacks, are commendable acts of bravery for which they earn the title of *shahid* (martyr). For the sake of attaining that goal they would resort not only to repetition *ad nauseam* of jihad mantras, but they would send children in their hundreds to pelt rocks or bombs at Israelis and against the forces of order. However, when the latter respond with force then they become the cruel enemy who shoots indiscriminately at innocent Arab kids. It does not occur to them that if they do not dispatch children to scenes of confrontation but rather keep them at home, none of them would be hurt, or indeed that the entire intifada and its ensuing casualties could have been averted had they contained their anger.

The outbursts of rage, which are usually translated into violence and terror, under the label of jihad in the path of Allah, are justified by religious leaders to the crowds of their followers in terms of the humiliation, injustice and oppression that are meted out to them by their enemies. We have heard heads of Muslim terrorist movements such as al-Qa'ida and Hamas thus rationalize their acts against the West and the Jews. This mantra, which repeats that those two intertwined entities are inherently inimical to Islam and are undermining it, is presented, rehearsed and exemplified by the humiliation, injustice and oppression that they sense is being caused to them, by Israel with regard to Palestinians and the rest of the Arabs, and by the United States concerning world Islam. Humiliation, due to the counter-example of successful societies and regimes which the Muslims have attempted to emulate for the last three or four generations, but in vain. Frustration, since Muslims can neither lift themselves to Western heights, nor failing that bring down the successful and counter-examples which stand as the epitome of their own impotence. Injustice, because as long as Islamic justice is not done, and lands that they consider Muslim (such as Palestine, Andalusia, Chechnya, Kashmir, etc.) do not revert to their just ownership, injustice will persist. Muslims cannot operate in such an unjust world, and cannot turn to dealing with their domestic problems as long as injustice is not addressed. Hence the attribution of all their ills – corruption, poverty, overpopulation and backwardness – to the injustices done to them by the imperialist and colonialist West, which now owes them reparation: to provide for their refugees and destitute; to exert pressure on Israel; to adopt policies in their favour and to desist from exercising pressures on them to conform. Oppression, because the enemies of Islam, instead of plying to the just demands of Muslims, facilitating their spread into the Western world and helping them to retrieve their lost lands, on the contrary are standing up to them, accusing them of terrorism in which they have no part, checking their unbridled expansion into the West and expecting them to introduce reforms into their systems. These are the messages that are reiterated almost verbatim by Islamist leaders from one end of the Islamic world to the other.

The Islamist leaders often demonize their enemies, particularly Israel and Zionism, in order to make them easy prey for retribution. Demonization is expressed either in terms of the 'atrocities' (real or more often imagined) committed by the West in Chechnya, Iraq, Afghanistan or Jenin, or of dubbing them 'Nazi' or 'Nazi-like', so as to delegitimize them, in total disregard of the real horrors they commit in their mass murders and terrorist activities. One would assume that Muslim leaders, including the popular sheikhs among them, would not only understand the difference between what the Nazis did in Europe and the 'massacres' they attribute to the West and Israel, but that they would refrain from using that comparison which in addition to doing injustice to the truth, serves only to inject more hatred into this already complex situation. Things reach absurd levels: not only is Israel falsely accused of 'poisoning' Arab schoolchildren and injecting them with the AIDs virus, but even when the West went to Kosovo to rescue Muslims from the Christian Serbs, their troops were condemned by Muslim media for using depleted uranium ammunition in order to cause cancer to the Kosovars. (That claim was soon thereafter transplanted to Palestine and laid at Israel's door, with equal invalidity.) Deprecation of the enemy can also be served by calling them 'Crusaders' or 'new Crusaders', a symbolic appellation which not only counters Bush's 'crusade' to eradicate terror but also evokes the memories of the all-out victory that Saladin had brought Islam in medieval times when he routed the original Crusaders. Victory, not an agreement or a settlement or a compromise, is sought by the Islamist leaders, and this is one of the slogans they reiterate.

Internally too the mantra system is hard at work in the Islamist milieus. First of all, the triple slogan of 'Islam is the Truth, Islam is the Solution and Islam is the Alternative' appears at all rallies, is cited on posters, video- and audio-cassettes and in speeches of the leaders. The qualities of the martyrs (*shahids*) are hailed by the leaders and their publications, with the recorded messages of would-be Islamikaze distributed as models of emulation to encourage recruitment of volunteers to their missions of mass murder. In Gaza, tiny children are encouraged to say they will become *shahids*, while their teenage relatives are sent on Islamikaze missions in Israel where they perish, with not only their sheikhs and preachers but also some professionals, writers and journalists singing their praises. Worried parents who question the practice are silenced by the voices of proud mothers who, after sacrificing their sons (and lately also daughters) in response to the prompting of religious leaders, also vow that their other children will follow. The rewards in Paradise, where the *shahids* will gain a prominent place in the vicinity of Allah and be entitled to 72 beautiful black-eyed virgins, also play no small part in the picture drawn by the preachers to attract Muslim youth to those murderous missions. Jihad, which was traditionally waged by the Muslim state or community, by authority of its political or religious leaders, has acquired a more immediate and concrete interpretation, to the effect that when the house is burning every individual is bound to pick up a bucket of water and extinguish the flames. In other words, individual Muslims are encouraged by these repetitive messages to take action and not wait for the community to act. When all this is relentlessly repeated in the media, in mosques and schools, and enjoys the support of writers and the general public, it ultimately numbs the capacity of individuals to reason and think for themselves, and they are carried along in the general frenzy of violence which makes outsiders wonder how it could happen at all in the civilized world.

CHAPTER FIVE

Indictment and Evidence

IT WAS AGAINST this background, in conjunction with the raging intifada of the previous three years, which was publicly supported by the northern faction of the Islamic movement in Israel (headed by Ra'id Salah), that the Israeli authorities decided to act. They decided to move, after many years of hesitation, due to the concern among the security apparatus of the Israeli government that the linkage that had been established for years by Bin Laden and other master terrorists, between the Islamist war on the West and Israel ('the Jews' in Bin Laden's parlance), might prompt Israeli Islamists to join the fray. These fears were founded not only on the growing numbers of Israeli Muslims who were caught red-handed committing acts of terror against their country, or helping Palestinians from the West Bank and Gaza to infiltrate into Israeli territory and perform some horrific acts of terror, but also by new developments in the world jihadist activities. After Israel withdrew unilaterally from Lebanon in 2000, Hizbollah cadres who were convinced that it was their relentless pressure on Israel that had caused its retreat, were dispatched into the Palestinian territories where they professed the same strategy and began organizing clandestine cells to escalate the pace and scope of terror against Israeli targets. Moreover, there was fear that those cells had entertained links with al-Qa'ida, which would have constituted a formidable new threat to Israel's security, in view of the anti-Israel commitment of both Hizbollah and Bin Laden. Sheikh Ra'id's intensified activities, which were monitored by the security apparatuses, appeared to be fitting into this worldwide network that was closing on Israel, and it became imperative to break it.

In 2003, after a long and intensive investigation by the police and other Israeli security bodies, which included wiretapping that was permitted by the court of law, Ra'id and four of his colleagues were arrested and legal proceedings were opened against them. A team consisting of the Haifa

District Attorney who headed it and another five young lawyers with some experience in the Arab domain, undertook to put the indictment together, based on thousands of documents that had been assembled in dozens of dossiers during the investigation. But to make the case credible to the district court, headed by Micha Lindenstrauss, who co-opted Judges Y. Dar and A. Schieff, it was necessary to appeal to many experts in the fields of security, Arab affairs, finance, intelligence, terrorism and the like, who were prepared either to write expert statements and/or to appear before the court on behalf of the claimants and to undergo lengthy interrogations by the battery of lawyers that the Islamic movement had hired to defend the five indicted individuals and their two front organizations. Predictably, chief among them was Attorney Avigdor Feldman, the criminal lawyer who regularly defended Arabs or other anti-establishment figures in high-profile legal cases that attracted both domestic and foreign attention. Having published three books on the Arab minority in Israel, I was asked by the District Attorney to stand at the court as an academic 'expert', to write an 'expert opinion', which was also distributed to the judges and to the defendants, to be prepared to give a deposition in court, under oath, and to undergo a cross-examination by the defendants, which might take several days. But let us first examine what the indictment was all about.

While Sheikh Ra'id, as the founder, leader, and chief player of the northern branch of the Islamic movement, was the main target of the indictment, the identity of his co-defendants and the nature of the front organizations (also of Ra'id's making) that were put on the defendants' bench, is indicative of the turn the trial would take. By alphabetical order on the indictment sheet Ra'id Mahajneh, born in 1959, came only second to Mahmud bin Muhammad Mahajneh, born in 1968, and was followed by Tawfiq Mahajneh, born in 1973, all from Umm al-Fahm and from the same clan. Then came two family members from the Agbariyyeh clan: Nasser, born in 1972 and Suleiman, born in 1957. They were all connected with the two indicted front organizations: the Humanitarian Relief Society (HRS) and the Humanitarian Salvation Committee for the cause of Orphans and the Needy (HSC). Both organizations, like the individual defendants, were based in Umm al-Fahm. While the former appeared as a company (limited), the latter was registered as a non-profit-making organization. But as will transpire from the indictment, a whole gamut of other front organizations, some of them illegal, and an entire array of other people, all belonging to the Islamic movement, and obviously from among Ra'id's disciples, appointees and protégés, constitute an intricate organizational web, with some activities legal and some illegal, some overt, and others concealed. This made the investigation, and in consequence the trial, one of the longest in Israel's legal history. The fact that it also remained inconclusive when the parties 'agreed' on a plea-bargain, where the considerations, the motives, the pressures and counter-pressures prevented a real and definitive airing in public of the serious charges involved on the one hand, and of their total and unqualified rejection by the defendants who claimed innocence and accused the police of 'framing' them on the other, is indicative of the political and ethnic sensitivities which aborted a show-down and a definitive decision in this instance.

According to the indictment, Ra'id Salah founded HRS on 12 October 2000, and for a few months managed it. He also held shares of his institution and served as its president until he was indicted. However, Mahmud Mahajneh (defendant No. 1 on the indictment sheet and a relative of Ra'id) was the principal manager, except for the first few months when Ra'id filled the position, and Ra'id deputized him to be in charge of contacts with other organizations abroad, with Tawfiq Mahajneh (No. 3 on the list) as his main assistant. It was Nasser Agbariyyeh (No. 4 on the list) who together with Mahmud Mahajneh opened and managed the institution's bank accounts, held some of its shares and was involved in the daily administration of its affairs. Both were authorized to sign cheques and documents on behalf of HRS. So far so good. The problem was that the indicted group was also found to have been involved with other foundations and institutions linked to Hamas, which had been outlawed as a terrorist group, not only in Israel but also internationally. The major link was led by Ra'id and his underlings with the Aqsa Foundation, of which he was the titular head in Israel and which was connected with other Islamic fund-raising and 'charitable' front organizations which channelled money to terrorist activities. The web of such institutions, some of which are virtual and existed only on paper for the purpose of laundering money for illegal purposes, generated the two indictment counts of which Ra'id and his group were accused. The Aqsa Foundation that is based in Germany, where it was also declared illegal, has been recognized as part of the Hamas organization and also maintains branches in Belgium and the Netherlands. Mahmud 'Amr who resides in Germany is the president of the foundation, and Amin Abu Rashid, nicknamed Abu Hamza, heads the foundation in Belgium. Mahmud Hijazi and Abu Tareq were also recognized as operatives of the foundation in Belgium and Germany, respectively.

Association with Al-Aqsa was not the only item included in the first count. Another was a link with the Palestinian Relief and Development Fund, known as Interpal: an institution which was founded in Britain in 1994 and among whose chief operatives was 'Issam Yussuf, nicknamed Abu Yussuf. Another was Jihad Qindil who served as the foundation's treasurer. Interpal, like al-Aqsa, was outlawed in May 1997, due to its participation in the Hamas web of front organizations, by the Israeli Minister of Defence in his capacity under the emergency regulations that are in force in the country. Several months later (January 1998), the Israeli government, acting under Article 8 of the anti-terror regulations, declared both the al-Aqsa and Interpal foundations as terrorist organizations for being part and parcel of Hamas. Another institution – the Charity Coalition (I'tilaf al-Khayr) – joined the fray in 2001, bringing under one roof dozens of Muslim organizations the world over with the declared goal of raising funds for the Palestinian territories while the intifada (not coincidentally also called al-Aqsa) was in full swing. Sheikh Yussuf al-Qaradawi, the Egyptian exile who lives in Qatar, who notoriously condones Islamikaze acts against Israelis, and socializes with London Mayor Ken Livingstone, is the titular head of that coalition, and uses his tremendous popularity among Muslim fundamentalists across the world to raise funds for Islamist causes. But the acting manager is 'Issam Yussuf, the key figure in Interpal. Al-Aqsa, the Committee of Aid and Solidarity with the Palestinians, the World Muslim Youth Conference and the Holy Land Foundation – all outlawed as terrorist organizations by the Israeli government in January 1998 for being part of Hamas – are all members of the umbrella coalition. The Israeli Minister of Defence declared the coalition and the Muslim youth organizations as illegal associations at a time when Sheikh Ra'id sat on the board of the coalition until his arrest.

Since the establishment of HRS, and particularly between July 2001 and May 2003 when the defendants were arrested, all five of them as its active members maintained contacts with Interpal, al-Aqsa, the coalition and the Muslim youth organizations and their operatives listed above, with a view to transferring funds to HRS's accounts in Israel and the Palestinian territories, thus advancing the cause of those organizations and obtaining financing for their own social welfare activities. Those contacts took place in telephone calls, exchange of faxes, regular and electronic mail, many of which were monitored by the Israeli security apparatus and seized and transcribed as documentary evidence in the process of wording the indictment sheet. It transpires from that documentation that the defendants and their associates in HRS received large sums amounting to millions of IS (IS4.5 million = c. $1 million). Not only was the money accepted from those outlawed organizations, but it was spent on joint projects designed partly by the donors and partly by the recipients. From the Israeli legal angle, those moneys were illicit inasmuch as they contravened the law on money laundering adopted in 2000, the moment they were received and deposited in the accounts opened and serviced by Mahmud Mahajneh and Nasser Agbariyyeh. The way those funds were spent by the defendants and the purposes they served is quite another issue that will be tackled below. Moreover, the received funds were mixed in the said accounts with other moneys that were legally raised or levied from Israeli Arabs and other organizations, allegedly in order to dissimulate the traces of the illicit flow of money from the outlawed Hamas-related organizations. It was the evidence that the funds were spent in Israel and the Palestinian territories in ways conducive to lending support to, and strengthening the infrastructure of, Hamas that prompted the Israeli Minister of Defence to outlaw all those front institutions which raised funds to finance Hamas and Hamas-related activities.

The defendants channelled some of the illicit income into supporting orphans of the Islamikaze *shahids* and other 'needy', as the names of HRS and HSC suggest. It is well understood from experience and research[1] that one of the main concerns of would-be martyrs, be they Hamas, Islamic Jihad or Aqsa brigade members, especially when they are the breadwinners in their families, is the fate of their loved ones whom they leave behind. Assurance that some organization was undertaking to care for the families, until they could join the martyr in the delights of Paradise, was one of the main incentives for those people to sacrifice their lives without hesitation or worry. Prima facie, nothing is wrong with this humanitarian concern for the bereaved families, but in view of the proven encouragement that this gives to recruitment of prospective Islamikaze, such seemingly charitable activity in fact has an appalling effect and serves to encourage acts of terror. (It is noteworthy that the defendants and their organizations never evince their philanthropic concerns in aiding the families of the Israeli victims of Hamas terrorism; rather, they showed sympathy for the families of the murderers, who are the avowed enemies of their country – something that should sow doubts in any fair-minded observer about the 'innocent' motives of their enthusiastic activity on behalf of their organizations.) Moreover, aid was channelled by HRS and HSC to Hamas members who were imprisoned in Israel for conspiring to act against Israeli targets or when they were caught in the act. That meant very simply supporting, both economically and morally, convicted murderers against the state security. Other funds were spent by Ra'id's organizations in a less criminal fashion on enlarging and sustaining the Islamic movement in Israel, which though legal is not exactly the best friend of the Jewish state; for dispensing social services which, in the style of Muslim Brothers elsewhere, builds up a fund of goodwill towards the movement in the long run; for refurbishing mosques and Muslim cemeteries, notably al-Aqsa in order to rally Israeli Muslims around Rai'd's leadership; to purchase food for distribution to the poor (always Muslims, never to poor Jews or Christians in Israel); to celebrate Muslim festivals (e.g., providing banquets for the end of fast in Ramadan); and for real-estate acquisitions which would strengthen the economic base of the Islamic movement.

In fact, immediately at the beginning of the proceedings, the district court was asked by the State Attorney, under the provisions of the 2000 law against money laundering, to confiscate or freeze such assets of the Islamic movement as were financed by the illicit funds in question. They included two apartments in Haifa that were registered as properties of two individuals who worked for the Islamic movement; and two bank accounts in Israeli banks: one at Mercantile Discount Bank and another at Otzar Ha-Hayal, in Ramat Gan, that belonged to HCS and encompassed deposits, savings, securities, pension funds and checking accounts in both IS and foreign currency. More ominously, Mahmud and Tawfiq Mahajneh were charged with recurring contact with Jamal Abu-al-Hija, who, until arrested by Israel in August 2003, was one of the chiefs and the spokesman of the military Hamas in Jenin, and transferring to him thousands of IS, despite being aware of his position and affiliation. This was no longer indirect support or implied sympathy for Hamas, for which there is no punishment, but an explicit and wilful act of aiding a major operator in a declared terrorist organization. Even more damning was the Mahajneh's contact with Nabil Mahzumeh (nicknamed Abu Muhammad), born in Nazareth, who had been condemned to life imprisonment for serious security violations, but had been released in 1985 in an exchange of prisoners between Israel and the Arabs. He was thereupon expelled from Israel, but he pursued his terrorist activities with Islamic groups in Syria and Lebanon, and notably with Hamas. During the years 2001–02 Mahmud Mahajneh maintained contact with Abu Muhammad by fax and telephone, at the latter's initiative, even after he became aware that his interlocutor was an enemy operative, and he transmitted to him, at his request, a list of 70 Arab security prisoners who were incarcerated in Israeli prisons, presumably for the purpose of demanding their release in any future exchange of prisoners. Mahmud Mahajneh also transmitted to Nabil Mahzumeh the email of *Sawt al-Haqq*, the mouthpiece of Ra'id's northern Islamic movement, presumably for purposes other than exchanging greetings.

What all this amounts to, from the Israeli legal point of view, is that the indicted individuals and organizations were knowingly perpetrating a series of offences punishable by law:

- They maintained contacts with foreign agents whom they knew to be hostile to their country, and received funds from them which were used to promote the agents' causes and to support a terrorist organization under whose agenda they chose to operate. That was a clear contravention of Article 29 of the Israeli criminal code of 1977.
- They violated Articles 73 and 85 of the 1945 emergency regulations which prohibited rendering services to outlawed organizations.
- They held in their possession funds originating from illegal organizations, in contravention of Article 73 of the 1945 emergency regulations, and of Article 29 of the 1977 criminal code.
- They transacted illegally owned property in violation of Article 4 of the 2000 law on laundering money.

These are all serious charges, but they constituted only the first count of the indictment. The second count which, though related to the first in substance, only concerned Suleiman Agbariyyeh (the fifth defendant on the first count) and the HCS under which he operated, which developed intricate relationships with other likeminded sister Muslim associations in Israel that were all connected to the same network, although their names and goals varied. Indeed, in 1994 (the year Interpal was established in Britain), Agbariyyeh founded in Nazareth, the largest Arab town in the country, the Islamic Relief Committee, which he headed. But in 1996 the head of the Northern Command, like the Minister of Defence in the case of the Umm al-Fahm associations, ordered that the committee be closed down due to its support of the families of Hamas members in the Palestinian territories who committed acts of Islamikaze against Israeli citizens, or were conspiring to mount terrorist attacks or were caught red-handed and incarcerated. In the justification of his order, the commanding general explained that the committee was linked financially to Hamas, therefore its activities were deemed unlawful. The committee did not give in and appealed to the Supreme Court, but its plea to reverse the military commander's order of closure was rejected in August 1996. Thus the highest instance in the Israeli legal system determined that there was enough evidence to show that the committee was bent on lending massive aid to the families of Hamas terrorists. The court also found that the committee's activities were all financed by foreign donors who belonged to the Hamas network and concluded that the commanding general's defence to the effect that the committee supported a terrorist organization was entirely credible.

However, when the activities of the committee were prohibited by court order, Agbariyyeh attempted to circumvent the prohibition by turning to HSC with a view to pursuing his activities under another guise. Being the chairman of the HSC and authorized to sign in its name, it was expedient for him to compound the activities of the two organizations and continue to act on the committee's behalf despite the court order. For precisely this reason, the head of the Northern Command acted again on the basis of his authority under emergency regulations 6 and 120, and ordered in November 1996 the closure of HSC due to the continuity it provided to the prohibited activity of the committee. The Minister of Defence, invoking the same source of legality under the emergency regulations, decreed the confiscation of HSC's assets, and his decree was periodically revalidated. But Agbariyyeh did not agree to the decree, and approached the authorities to find a *modus vivendi* which would allow him to revive the HSC. After lengthy negotiations, the commanding general repealed the decree on condition that Agbariyyeh and his employees at HSC accepted certain limitations which would neutralize the perceived security threats that had prompted its closure in the first place. The principal limitations were as follows:

- HSC would only accept donations from identifiable private donors who were also citizens of the state of Israel. This clause not only would preclude the flow of money from organizations like Hamas which were involved in an ideological struggle against Israel, but would also rule out the incoming of moneys whose source was unclear. The assumption was that such a limitation, which would have rendered every donor accountable to the authorities, would not only facilitate the monitoring of the flow of cash, but, knowing that they were accountable, prospective donors would act responsibly for fear of getting involved with the law-enforcement agencies of the country.

- HSC agreed to accept no donations from abroad, and also not to serve as a channel for foreign money. This measure was designed to prevent the money-laundering.
- HSC also committed itself to refrain from employing, either in Israel proper or in the Palestinian territories, anyone who was affiliated or identified with a terrorist organization. However, for fear that it might always claim that it 'did not know' of the affiliation of its employees who were supposedly hired for their own 'merit', this limitation stipulated that any newly recruited employee of the organization had to be cleared by the Israeli authortities.
- HSC was obligated to distribute its relief money solely on the basis of economic need, and not to the families of deceased, imprisoned or wounded terrorists who had taken part in an attack on the state of Israel or its citizens. In the early 1990s Hizbollah and Palestinian terrorist groups launched attacks against Israelis abroad, notably in Argentina and Cyprus. Hence this limitation which would not accept any defence that perpetrators did not act against the state of Israel.
- The heads of HSC and their employees undertook not to establish any other organization that would allow them to circumvent these limitations on their association, nor were they to act through other organizations in contradiction of the stipulations decreed by the authorities. Such activity would be deemed as a violation of the terms of the agreed limitations.
- HSC pledged to submit a quarterly report on its activities to the registrar of NGOs, detailing its budgets and expenditure, the sources of its income and any other pertinent financial transaction.

However, despite Agbariyyeh's signature on the agreement, in May 1997, he apparently had no intention of abiding by the limitations agreed. He signed the document personally, and also on behalf of HSC (which included the supposedly defunct committee) and his employees and any person acting in the interest of the association. This presumably included Sheikh Ra'id, who had chosen to stay out of the fray, but worked for this, as well as for all the other Islamic organizations he founded. The indictment sheet, solidly anchored in an immense investigative effort that had yielded dozens of dossiers and documents, indeed pointed to the systematic and intentional violation of all the agreed limitations. The breadth of offences meant that these were not minor breaches unwittingly made by a large-scale operation, but that HSC had consistently put its own and the Islamic interest above the law of Israel and its security concerns. The indictment sheet lists these infringements:

- Since the middle of 2001 the HRS acted to raise funds abroad to finance the activities of its sister organization, the HSC. This is indicative of the level of sophistication and of law-circumventing strategies that these Islamic organizations adopted from the start in order to conceal the traces of illegality. Had their intentions been innocent, one organization would have been sufficient to raise the funds and distribute them to the needy. The fact that several organizations operated together, some of them from the same offices or from cities other than Umm al-Fahm, but all under the aegis of Sheikh Ra'id, begs explanation. The best rationale one could come up with is that these organizations, far from being transparent and open to public scrutiny as any registered NGO ought to be, on the contrary attempted to hide their sources of income, the sums involved, and the interaction between them.

- Nor was funding innocent or straightforward. The HSR, which raised the funds, transferred payments not directly to HSC, which would have directly implicated it contrary to its commitments under the limitations, but to producers of various goods who in turn handed over their products to HSC employees in the Palestinian territories who were Agbariyyeh's subordinates. In this way, the perpetrators hoped to circumvent the ban on receiving moneys from abroad and to pursue their activities in the territories under another guise. That ploy worked even after the Islamic committee was shut down by the authorities in June 2002 and thereafter.

- Then Agbariyyeh and his assistants transferred the value of the goods they got to finance their own charitable and other projects via various local Muslim associations in the Territories. All this while, and contrary to their commitment under the limitations, the HSC failed to submit quarterly reports about their income and expenditure, obviously because they had something to hide. It is noteworthy that Arab associations in Israel in general often are inclined to break the law (tax evasion, illegal demonstrating, use of violence, ideological crime, illegal construction, etc.), knowing that for fear of being

accused of 'racism', or of raising tempers and causing unrest among them, the authorities very often look the other way. It is not improbable that Agbariyyeh and his group were capitalizing on this when they took the risk of breaking their undertakings to the general of the Northern Command.
- Agbariyyeh and HSC were also accused of violating the limitations by employing, albeit indirectly, people and bodies who identified with terrorist organizations and accepted donations from outlawed associations.

In the aggregate, the second count of indictment included charges of grave and repetitive infringements of Articles 9, 69, 73 and 85 of the emergency regulations by both Agbariyyeh and HSC, under the overlordship of Sheikh Ra'id. What made these violations particularly serious was that the defendants broke the trust that was placed in them by the military commander when he negotiated and signed the limitations that they had agreed upon. Again, the recurrence of the same violations, in the face of the lenient policy of the authorities who had consented to give them a second and third chance, only indicates the determination of the defendants to pursue their course come what may, in the hope that they would escape the scrutiny of law next time around. Small wonder, then, that even before the trial began, with the battery of lawyers on both sides struggling to prove or disprove the case, it became clear that this was going to capture the attention of the media, attract sympathy for the defendants among Israeli Arabs, and make headlines about 'framing', 'political persecution', 'discrimination against Arabs and Muslims' well beyond the merits of the case. Predictably, the defendants flatly denied all counts of the indictment, and it transpired that the prosecution would have to invest months of research and expensive resources, amass immense amounts of documentary evidence to substantiate each count, and solicit the assistance of dozens of experts in the fields of intelligence, national security, Arab and Islamic affairs and legal matters of this sort. Though the trial began in June 2003, while the defendants were under arrest by order of the court for fear that they might constitute a danger to national security during the trial, or attempt to tamper with the witnesses and the evidence if they were free, their lawyers did not seem at first in a hurry to expedite the proceedings. They prepared for a very long trial, perhaps in order to postpone the harsh verdict that was expected, even at the price of a protracted incarceration of which no one could predict the end.

For 18 months, and for the duration of the 76 full days of court deliberations which lasted from June 2003 until January 2005, when the court proceedings were interrupted by a plea bargain, the prosecution produced a long succession of witnesses who day after day detailed evidence of the breaches of national security, criminal acts regarding illicit transfers of funds and the ideological underpinnings of this whole operation. For it must be said that the violations of Israeli law perpetrated by its Muslim citizens were not geared to personal or material gain, but to enhance the ideology of the Islamic movement, which by definition was inimical to Israel, and to recruit to its ranks so as to widen its field of operation. The six young Israeli lawyers, headed by the District Attorney, Sylvia Freiman, held daily consultation meetings during the entire period of the proceedings, with each one of them specializing in one aspect or another of the defendants' activities. Data relevant to each were gathered and analysed. Arguments were prepared and presented before the court. It took so much sustained effort to present the prosecution side, not only due to the mass of documentation, but because the defence was predictably determined to shake the credibility of the witnesses, to question the methods used for the collection of evidence (e.g., phone-tapping), and to undermine the indictment in any way possible.

It would take any number of volumes to summarize the evidence produced by the prosecution witnesses, and an even more voluminous space to describe the deliberate waste of time and resources that the defence cross-examination generated. In other words, one could imagine the long procession of defence witnesses that the defendants would have had to bring forward to try to demolish the overwhelming evidence that was accumulated against them in the court, and the lengthy cross-examinations that the prosecution attorneys would have had to undertake in order to counter those witnesses. This was probably one of the reasons for the plea bargain that interrupted the proceedings, but we shall refer to that later. Here we shall focus on my evidence in court, which tackled the ideological links between the Islamic movement and Hamas: an issue that was pivotal not only to the argument of the prosecution in the trial but also to this study in general inasmuch as it concerns the role of Sheikh Ra'id as a religious actor in the political activities of the Islamic movement in Israel.

CHAPTER SIX

The Trial and its Resonance

MONTHS BEFORE I was called to the witness stand in the trial, I was approached by the Haifa District Attorney, Sylvia Freiman, and her staff in the summer of 2004, when the court proceedings were already well underway. I was asked to write an 'expert opinion' on the ideological links between Sheikh Ra'id's movement and Hamas, and also to take the stand, if necessary, in the court and prepare for cross-examination by the defendants' lawyers. I consented on both counts after undergoing a series of 'interrogations' by the prosecution to make sure that my knowledge and views on the Islamic movement were scholarly and 'objective' (if indeed anybody can be objective). Based on the books I had written until then on the Arabs in Israel and related issues, and my more recently published volume on Islamikaze (the so-called 'suicide-bombers' who embrace the Hamas ideology of violence),[1] which I made available to the State Attorney, I was given a clean sheet and we proceeded. At first, I had to get acquainted through briefings, discussions and readings of mammoth quantities of documents, with the indictment and its supporting materials, then I undertook the daunting work of putting together what I knew from previous research and the new evidence made available to me by the prosecution, to write the opinion that was to be the basis for the court deliberations and for my cross-examination by the defendants' lawyers when I was called to the stand. As it turned out, I was to be the last of the prosecution witnesses, after which the court would move on to the defence part of the trial, where the State Attorney would lead the cross-examination of the witnesses. A lengthy process loomed that would have perhaps made it the longest trial in Israel's history; however, as the prosecution made its case, it became increasingly clear that the overwhelming evidence it produced could hardly be overturned by the defendants.

Before we delve into the substance of this piece of evidence, it is essential to say something about the court proceedings, the ambience in the court-room and the unseemly fashion in which the points of contention were disputed. I was told that the appalling style of deliberations that I witnessed was no different from what had prevailed during the previous 18 months – something that hardly lessened my embarrassment. First of all, contrary to the open and friendly atmosphere that I had grown accustomed to at the District Attorney's office, where I had become a frequent and familiar visitor during the months of preparation for my part in the trial, in the adjacent district court building, a heavy and somewhat sombre mood reigned. As I entered the building, security guards were on hand to accompany me to the court-room, giving the uneasy feeling that standing as a witness on behalf of the Attorney constituted a risk in itself. By contrast, the multitudes of Muslims who had flocked to the court building to witness the proceedings where their heroes sat on the defendants' bench, were so self-confident and nonchalant, and exuding so much hatred and contempt toward anyone who was not of theirs, that one could not help but wonder about this extraordinary reversal of roles. It was as if the diffident prosecution were the culprits, so much so that their witnesses needed protection, while the sympathizers of the accused celebrated quite noisily their dominance in the court building. Even when being hustled with bodyguards to the cafeteria during the breaks, one could not escape that strange feeling of confusion as to where every one of us stood. When once, during the three days I took the stand, I ventured to the bathroom during a break and then inadvertently sat in the hallway waiting for the resumption of the proceedings, I was surrounded and stared down by the huge crowd of Muslim spectators, until the guards who were concerned for my safety came in to 'rescue' me from their apparent threat.

As I entered the court-room and made my way to the stand in the aisles between the spectators' seats (packed to capacity), a penetrating and scrutinizing stare by all those dozens of eyes, accompanied by murmurs from the crowd, did not augur well for me. I had been instructed by the State Attorney to respond briefly and to the point to the defendants' lawyers' queries, but I did not imagine to what point would the deliberations be conducted by those crowds or at least influenced by them. The five lawyers for the defendants, headed by Anis Riad and Avigdor Feldman and another three Arabs, one of them of the Mahamid clan of Umm al-Fahm, were already at their bench on the left side of the court-room, adjacent to the dock, readying their piles of books and documents. I noticed there copies of the Qur'an and the Hadith, treatises on Shari'a law, legal publications, writings by Muslim scholars, and lying modestly side by side with them some of my own books, articles and reviews of my writings. It immediately dawned on me what their two-pronged strategy would strive for: first to deflect the debate into general Islamic issues that had nothing to do with the trial, the indictments or my written opinion that they held in their hands with almost every other word underlined with markers; secondly, without any competence on their part in the subject matter other than their legal training and experience, to try to discredit me personally as a credible witness. They would take turns between the three senior lawyers among them to lead a war of attrition against me for three consecutive days, with the loud interference of both the defendants and their crowd of supporters. Never in my life have I had to face such a barrage of abuse, cursing and swearing, shouting and intimidation, as happened before my eyes in that court-room, with the judges remaining placid and oblivious at best, if not discussing among themselves at worst, as if I were the defendant and not an impartial witness who had nothing to do with the defendants or their prosecutors. More than a dozen times on every one of those three days the president of the district court would threaten to oust the defendants and the crowds of spectators from the room if they pursued their interference with the court's deliberations. But all the warnings remained unheeded as after three or four 'last warnings' no one took them seriously any longer.

The atmosphere of intimidation inside the court-room increased when one of the spectators who shouted hysterical words of personal abuse at me (I was not allowed to answer) was hustled out of the room by a security guard, but the president of the court ordered him back into his seat despite the protestations of the guard who was simply doing his duty. That was an indication to the defendants, their lawyers and the crowd of supporters that the court was theirs and that they could dictate the pace of the trial, impose their order on the proceedings and indicate in a wild and vociferous fashion their displeasure with anything said or heard. When the five defendants were led into their booth, just before the judges came in and called the court to order, the crowds who in civilized countries would sit quietly and be grateful that they were let in, burst into roars of applause, especially to the chief among them – Sheikh Ra'id – who was hailed as a hero, not as a suspected criminal. Many of them rushed to greet him and lend their support or to touch the hem of his gown, as if a messiah had landed amidst that unlikely scenery. The members of the audience, who came day in, day out, were mostly from Umm al-Fahm and the adjoining villages where Ra'id's word is law. Family and common people in all appearance, women unrecognizable under their veils and chadors, all looked up to their hero who was brimming with joviality and charisma. Young men were also there, as well as the leaders of the Muslim movement for whom this was a fateful test-case, and occasionally also Arab political figures of the past and other public personalities who followed the deliberations with curiosity and great expectation. Members of the press were also there, both Arabic and Hebrew, who were a priori sympathetic to Ra'id's cause and were to play a role in the drama by picking up on some of the themes that were tackled during the trial. After all, the fact that after 18 months of proceedings there was still an acute sense of interest in this high-profile trial, indicated that someone behind the scenes was drumming up interest in order to keep it alive and topical.

No sooner had the judges been announced and the court-room stood up, than the defendants had (in almost every instance), a 'request' to place before the panel of judges: to order the guards to let in this or that person, to take break for this or that reason, or to accede to any of their whims. The court usually approved. Whenever on the prosecution bench an objection was raised, it was usually quelled and dismissed, thus making the trial a rather one-sided affair. It may be that the panel of judges needed to show balance in the face of the incriminating evidence they had been hearing for the past year and half, and in anticipation of the harsh verdict they were about to deliver had the proceedings not been interrupted by the plea bargain. That we will never know. What is certain is that they allowed hours and hours of nonsensical interrogation in matters that they did not understand and were thus unable to settle the controversies between the defendants and the 'expert witness'. For example, long queries and citations went into the Qur'an and the Hadith, their history and interpretation, of which the judges had no knowledge. This was not relevant to the subject matter of the indictment or of the 'expert opinion'. The judges understood nothing of the exchanges that went on back and forth, nor had they ever heard names of Muslim scholars who had written this or that. It was all a test of erudition, in which the lawyers who led the interrogation were not versed. Sheikh Ra'id, who really knew his stuff, shouted his (uninvited) interpretations or rejections at will, with the judges looking on as total outsiders in this exhausting debate of one-upmanship that everyone understood could lead nowhere. There were also comic moments in those exchanges which wasted the time of the court, with the judges never attempting to interrupt the nonsense that was spouted at an incredulous and uncomprehending audience.

At first, many hours were spent by the defendants in interrogating me about articles and books that I had written in the past and had no relevance to the indictment whatsoever. Typically, since they could not or would not read English (in which most of my writings are usually published), they focused on the most esoteric interviews, press articles and a single book I had written in Hebrew on the Arabs of Israel over the years in order to demonstrate that I was biased against the Arabs, even 'racist', and therefore unfit to give evidence to the court. Had they bothered to consult the books and articles in English that were published more recently which were more directly relevant to the indictment and also presented to the court as part of the prosecution's exhibits, they might have acted differently. But the judges did not intervene. The successive lawyers who took turns interrogating me for hours could only be called to order and cease their abuse and offence for a while when they were told by the witness that they acted like ignorant thugs. But they soon reverted to their language of intimidation, encouraged by the outraged shouts of the defendants and the audience every time something was said that was not to their liking. They attempted to drag the interrogation into gutter legalism by claiming that I had imputed 'racist' attributes to the Arabs in general, something that was seized upon by the media and made headlines the next morning. The defendants needed public sympathy to escape the fate that was awaiting them, and they thought they got it by their abusive and libellous interrogation. Only one document did not come up for interrogation at that point, and that was the expert opinion that prompted my appearance in court in the first place.

Then the question of expertise came up, when the lawyers for the defence seized upon my remark to the court that in humanities and social sciences there are no 'experts' because those fields are not 'scientific' in the same way as experimental science, which can predict results every time the experiment is conducted under certain sets of conditions. Therefore I suggested that humanities are 'studies' rather than sciences, since no foolproof predictions can be made in any discipline which involves human beings, human behaviour and human societies. How then could a self-avowed non-expert, they asked, submit to the court an 'expert opinion'? Great rhetoric indeed and grand demagoguery at its worst, but that was the only device for the defendants to use against the enormity of the evidence against them.

At the height of this rather frustrating and futile deposition in court, the lawyers produced their Qur'anic books in order to try to refute my claims about the rewards of Paradise that are promised to the martyrs who sacrifice their lives for the sake of Allah (in other words the Islamikaze) whose cause Rai'd and his co-defendants and illicit institutions were defending. In one of my articles I had cited the relevant Qur'anic passages that described in vivid terms the 72 'black-eyed virgins' that every *shahid* would enjoy in heaven, where drink also was abundant. In this fashion the two taboos in traditional Muslim societies – sex and alcohol – are circumvented and the martyr will be entitled to as much as he wished of either, since the stifling rules of the Shari'a do not apply in the hereafter. The rage of the defendants and of the audience peaked and caused an explosion not previously experienced. The Sheikh stood up, again uninterrupted, to deliver a long dissertation about the ignorance of the enemies of Islam who should be discredited and dismissed by the courts. At first he claimed that such verses did not exist, but under duress he admitted that they existed but had a totally different meaning: the drinks in question were not alcoholic and the girls were earmarked for marriage to the martyr, not just for free sex. How a *shahid* could tackle 72 wives he did not explain. At the judges' request, I sent them the next morning all five relevant passages from the Qur'an in their standard English translation, so that my Hebrew rendering would not be once again refuted as 'biased'. A brief moment of relaxation, which brought smiles to the faces of all present, happened when someone quipped that since no one has returned from Paradise to report on its delights, we can never be sure of the nature of the delights that *shahids* enjoy.

It was quite pathetic to observe Sheikh Ra'id, this usually proud, self-confident and authoritative cleric and political actor, trying to escape the noose that was tightening around his neck. After days of arguments and counter-arguments, some of them silly and time-consuming, and attempts to take over the court deliberations by dominating the agenda, he stood there begging for his life and his status, incredulous at what had happened to him. From a tremendously popular leader, a world-travelled fund-raiser for Islam, the main wheeler and dealer behind the renovation and expansion of the Aqsa Mosque and the most promising leader of Muslims in Israel, he suddenly found himself incarcerated and deprived of his family and flock, with a strong possibility of being convicted and punished so as to take him away permanently from his multifarious Islamic activities which he regarded as his life's mission. That was perhaps the background for the capitulation of his defence and his consent to the plea bargain. However, his last-ditch effort before giving in was to dismiss the 'expert opinion' which was crucial in showing his association and ideological affiliation with Hamas. The evidence was overwhelming, but his lawyers tried repeatedly to divert the proceedings until they were made to revert to the main document at issue for which the witness was called. They were compelled to make references to that document when citations from it to the court cut all escapes. Even then, they first resorted to denials, but when faced with the sources that were presented in their original to the court, they offered such childish and unacceptable interpretations of the written materials that they themselves realized that they were fighting a rearguard battle that they could not win. No wonder that rumours of ongoing plea bargain negotiations were released by the defendants then, which were flatly refuted by the Attorney-General.

The main arguments that came up in the 'expert opinion' (which were only intermittently permitted to be heard) may be summarized as follows:

- The Islamic movement led by Ra'id is essentially a branch of the Muslim Brothers, as is Hamas, which had been established in Egypt in the 1920s as an instinctive reaction to Western influence and the penetration of Western ideas and mores into Islamic societies, such as democracy, a multi-party system, elections, science and technology and cultural values that Muslims considered as intrusive and undermining the traditional order. The Brothers under Hassan al-Banna called upon their co-religionists to revert to the fundaments of pristine Islam (hence fundamentalism) as in the times of the founding Prophet and his immediate successors, and restore the glory of the united Islamic Empire – the Caliphate, where Shari'a would be the code of law.

- Because the Prophet and his immediate successors were considered righteous, their deeds and pronouncements became a model for emulation by the populace. Therefore, apart from the Qur'an, the Word of Allah which obligates all Muslims, the next essential source of the Shari'a Law is the Hadith where the stories are told of the life of the Prophet and his companions. Other foundations of the Shari'a, such as analogy, consensus and local custom, which are human-made, ought to be skirted as much as possible. Thus, though the Brothers were born within the most lenient and liberal Hanafite School tradition, which prevails in Egypt, they in fact adopted the stringent puritanism and rigidity of the Hanbalite School which dominates religious life in Saudi Arabia. This item was evoked at length in court, because the defendants wished to assure the panel of judges that Ra'id and his followers were not of the same extremist brand as the Hanbalites, so as to divorce themselves from any rapprochement between themselves and Hamas. They dwelt at length upon the various kinds of Hadith, the Sira (biography of the Prophet) and the meaning of the Qur'anic commands, which were all opaque to the judges and the rest of the audience that stared into the void during those long moments of hair-splitting between the witness on the stand and the less than knowledgeable lawyers. At times they said that they wished to learn these matters from the witness, but they were invited to do so on university benches, not in the court-room.

- The lawyers questioned me at length about the positive attitudes of Muslim rulers to their Jewish minorities in history, citing the 'Golden Era' in Spain as a model of coexistence, and implying that Ra'id and his group would therefore have no reason to wish to harm Jews. But they were inclined to forget, and had to be reminded, that Jews (and Christians) had been tolerated in the Islamic Empire only due to their subordinate and humiliating status of *dhimmi*s, which obligated them to pay the special poll-tax (*jizya*) in return for the protection (*dhimma*) the state assured them, but which was not always enforced, sometimes for the better, more often for the worse. My origin in Morocco where I was born, and about which I was interrogated, was an occasion to demythologize the alleged Golden Era of the Jews there by the simple fact that when allowed to leave they all abandoned that 'land of milk and honey' and emigrated either to Israel or elsewhere. This point was essential in the trial, because the Muslim Brothers are particularly insistent on returning the Jews to their previous *dhimmi* status under Islam (the Hamas Charter explicitly declares this), especially in view of the most virulent anti-Jewish treatise written by anyone since the Nazis, at the hand of Sayyid Qutb, the great luminary of the Brothers in Egypt who is adulated by the Muslim movement in Israel too.

- Along with the revival of the traditional Islamic division of the world between *dar-al Islam* (the Abode of Islam), that is, the territory ruled by Islam regardless of the composition of its population, and *dar al-harb* (the country of war) which will eventually be subjugated by

Islam, fundamentalism has also given new impetus to the idea of *murabitun*, namely the Muslims who live in the House of War or on its borders with dar al-Islam. They are considered as the 'campers' on the boundary with the enemy and the avant-garde of Islam in hostile territory. In this regard, Muslims who live in non-Islamic lands but act on behalf of Islam, such as those in Europe, the United States and Israel, are considered pioneers of the advancing march of Islam. When Ra'id and other Muslim leaders refer in their speeches, writings and sermons to Israeli Muslims as *murabitun*, that is not exactly a statement of friendship to the country that hosts them. Moreover, as Muslim fundamentalists are committed to the revival of jihad as a violent way to retrieve lost territory, as in Israel, Andalusia and Kashmir, holders of that view of necessity encourage violence against the countries that oppose jihad.

- Short of violent jihad when it becomes necessary, propaganda (*da'wa*) is the gentle way, a sort of non-violent jihad, by which the cause of Islam is advanced. That includes the building of mosques and Islamic centres, the refurbishing of disintegrating Islamic monuments, charity, education, medical help and social welfare in general though a network of associations and fund-raising institutions. This has been the classic way that the Muslim Brothers in Egypt have built up popular support for themselves, which can be translated into political gain when that becomes possible (e.g., FIS in Algeria, Hamas in the Palestinian territories and the Islamist movement in Jordan). Built into this concept is that violent jihad is always looming on the horizon when propitious. The charitable activity that appears innocent, and which no one can oppose, is a preparatory step towards violence, as in the cases of Hamas, FIS and even some of the Islamists in Israel who were caught participating in violent operations against Israel. After all, it is all a matter of transition from economic and social jihad to political and military jihad, like two phases of the same intellectual and mental concept. Sheikh Ra'id and his associates, while playing the naïve and innocent in the court-room ('What? Is it prohibited to help the needy in this country?') knew very well the repercussions of those deeds in the long-run, both from their own experience in Israel and their knowledge of other sister movements.

- The Muslim Brothers in Egypt (like other fundamentalists elsewhere) have developed the idea that modern society, including in the countries of Islam that have been given over to Western influence, has reverted to the *Jahiliyya* (the period of ignorance that preceded Islam). Thus, the only way to struggle against it is to follow the example of the Prophet who had migrated from his native Jahili Mecca to Medina, where he built his base and then launched his jihad to conquer the Arabian Peninsula and much of the medieval world. So today many Muslim fundamentalists who are faced with strong country apparatuses which cannot be overwhelmed by violent jihad for now, counsel to 'migrate', if not physically then spiritually, from the countries of 'apostasy' where they live, pending the construction of the base from which they can launch their jihad. Through *da'wa*, they purport to ready the ground spiritually by the work they are doing via their 'charitable' institutions. In the context of Israel, Ra'id's movement which boycotts Israeli national elections so as not to send their representatives to the Knesset, retires into its villages so as to create their enclaves of Islam which as far as possible exempt themselves from national law and live locally by their own Islamic rules.[2]

- The Muslim Brothers have been hostile to the West in general and to Israel and the Jews in particular. Not only Sayyid Qutb, already mentioned for his virulent anti-Semitic writings, but also current luminaries of the Islamic movement such as Sheikh Yussuf Qaradawi who presently lives in Qatar. He gave various verdicts (*fatwas*) which encouraged Islamikaze acts of murder against Jews in general, and defined them as worthy 'jihad'. The attempts of Rai'd's lawyers in court to depict him as a 'liberal' and 'humanitarian' simply have no leg to stand on. Qaradawi, along with many other Muslim fundamentalist leaders, has learned to be duplicitous: to show a smiling face in international conferences and to Western audiences, and to incite cruelty against innocent Israeli civilians. Sheikh Yassin and Hamas acted likewise, and both of them had been the object of adulation by the Muslim movement in Israel. The best evidence can be found in the Islamists' writings, if one cares to consult some publications of the movement: *Al-Sirat* and also *Sawt al-Haqq* (see below). Niall Ferguson, commenting on Ken Livingstone's invitation to Qaradawi to visit London, had this to say:

  > Among Qaradawi's recent statements are the following: 'It has been determined by Islamic Law that the blood and property of people of dar al-Harb is not protected. Because they fight and are

hostile towards the Muslims they have forfeited the protection of their blood and property . . . Allah has also made the Prophet Muhammad into an ideal for Mujahidin since he ordered Muhammad to fight for religion. The first assignment is to prepare the hero who is willing to put his life in his own hands for Allah's sake and who does not care whether he encounters death or death encounters him. He wants to scare his enemies [in Arabic that Qur'anic scare is *irhab,* precisely the modern word for terrorism], and the religious authorities have permitted this. They have said that if he causes the enemy both sorrow and fear of Muslims, he is permitted to risk himself and even get killed . . .[3]

The main thrust of my deposition in court centred around the linkage between Hamas and its spiritual leaders, who were acknowledged as the masters of terrorism, and Ra'id's movement who tried to pose as innocent humanitarian workers who had nothing to do with those in violent Muslim radicalism. To start with, the 'expert opinion' claimed Hamas to be part and parcel of the Muslim Brotherhood by its own admission. Hamas has stated in no uncertain terms that it regards the entire land of Palestine, Israel included, as a *waqf* (holy endowment) which must revert to Islamic rule, so also did the more 'moderate' branch of the Islamic movement in Israel. This statement *eo ipso* constitutes a declaration of war against Israel and underlies the yearnings of Ra'id's Islamists to undermine their country which gives them legal protection. To achieve its goal the movement acts overtly by ways of *da'wa* which at times are legal, and at other times are not. Among other activities, they levied *zakat,* a voluntary donation which by social pressure became a tax that one could hardly escape. Those who could not donate money paid in kind, either by contributing building materials and other goods or with their skilled labour. They could thereby not only build more mosques and Islamic centres but also charitable institutions and educational and training centres for their youth.[4] The increased popularity of the religious leaders produced their involvement in local affairs, until they were elected to lead their communities and to enforce some of their Muslim policies in the 'enclaves' they established around their communities of followers, such as banning alcohol, gambling and (commendably) drugs. One of the heads of the movement expressed the attitude of his group towards Israel thus: 'The question of Palestine is not a folkloristic issue, it is a matter of faith, since it is a *waqf* land, which had been dedicated by 'Umar ibn al-Khattab [the second Caliph of Islam (634–44)] in perpetuity to all Muslims on the day he occupied Jerusalem.'[5]

This attitude of the Islamic movement towards the country in which they enjoy citizenship and from which they solicit rights has been consistent over the years since its inception. The mouthpiece of the Islamists indeed stated back in 1989 that

> We call upon all Muslims, because we aspire to see the banner of Allah fluttering over all lands that had at any time in history been Muslim, and where the voice of the mu'azzin had ever been heard ... We want our call to reach all inhabitants of the universe. We envisage certain stages that are built into our plans, with each of them encompassing its meanings and consequences, but we refrain at the moment from disclosing them ...[6]

If that were not clear enough, a more recent declaration by Kamal Khatib, the deputy head of the Islamist group under Ra'id, referred thus to the al-Aqsa intifada in which Hamas was a key player:

> The al-Aqsa eruption came to exemplify to the entire world the nature of the conflict in this area. Namely that the struggle has not been over lands or interests, but mainly between cultures and creeds, because a Holy Land has been at stake ... The expulsion of the Israeli occupier from Lebanon and the uprising [in Palestine] are merely the first signs of the wave of redemption which has been approaching us ...[7]

This deep faith in the coming redemption has been linked in the eyes of the fundamentalists with the misfortune that has been awaiting the Jews, the usurpers of the Holy Land. We have already discussed the pathological hatred of the Jews and the West in Muslim Brother doctrine, and we mentioned Sayyid Qutb, who in his anti-Semitic writings had raised the hatred of the Jews from an instinctive gut-feeling to a 'rational' and 'scientifically' based and rationalized ideology. What was 'hopeful' and 'encouraging' in his writings was that the Jews, the enemies of Allah and humanity, who constantly concocted plots and wars and were the sworn enemies of Islam, since the times of the Prophet to these days, were not as invincible as they seemed, for their power fed on the deviation of modern Islam from its sources. If only Muslims could return to their roots, and their societies were purged from the scourge of Jews and the West, and the foreign increments were rejected, then the power of the Jews would collapse and they would return to their *dhimmi* status where they would be tolerated only as long as they acknowledged the superiority and dominion of victorious Islam. These views, like others on the revival of Islam, are accepted lock, stock and barrel by Muslim Brothers anywhere, including Ra'id and his followers. The Hamas charter does not even attempt to hide its views on Jews: their evil is exposed (Article 22) and the need to rescue the world and Islam from their plots by ways of jihad to retrieve Palestine is prescribed (Articles 9, 15).[8]

Naturally, under the vigilant eyes of the authorities, Muslims in Israel could not explicitly and openly identify with the platform of such an outlawed organization as Hamas, but implicitly and covertly they do, and they leave no doubt about that. For example, they make repeated use of that infamous *hadith* from the most authoritative Bukhari and Muslim collections, that is also cited in the Hamas charter (after Article 7), to the effect that 'The time will not come until Muslims fight the Jews (and kill them); until the Jews hide behind rocks and trees which will cry: Muslims! There is a Jew hiding behind me, come on and kill him!' An article, one of many in the organ of the Islamists, reveals something of that menacing and violent sentiment:

> Satan [i.e., the Jews] has announced the superiority of his Nazi race over the rest of mankind. His successors now declare the primacy of a certain race over all the others. Satan has then found human disciples who loyally implement his doctrine. Anybody with self-respect ought to confront Satan and his military. For only the caravan of Faith, when united, can undo their schemes.[9]

The derogation of Jews and Israelis by the Islamists in Israel prompts them to compare Jews to wild dogs whose 'barking has to be shut off by swords and spears'; to snakes whose 'poisonous teeth ought to be uprooted'; or impute to them a 'cowardly, evil and lowly conduct' in their tackling of the Palestinians. The Zionist enterprise is compared to the 'Crusader invasion'; the very existence of Israel is described as founded on the 'arrogant nature of the Jews' instead of legitimate right, and therefore it is null and void. It is also claimed in those writings that the Jews are condemned to live as 'parasites among other people, but their refusal to abide by the rules of history will lead to their defeat'. 'Evidence' for all this is culled from the infamous *Protocols of the Elders of Zion*, which is liberally 'cited' and elaborated and interpreted in the Islamists' speeches, sermons, tracts, posters and video- and audio-cassettes. Thus the very fact that Jews control Palestine in effect, despite their condemnation in the Qur'anic text to live in 'eternal misery', seems to them as an aberration of the historical process, especially as they now control a Muslim minority who used to constitute the majority in Palestine, but no more.[10] Already in 1989 an editorial warned that:

> The politicians in this country have been pursuing their vain dreams of expanding their borders from the Nile to the Euphrates. We will not be surprised if they lay claim to Hijaz [in Saudi Arabia] too. The very public announcement of this idea already constitutes a Zionist expansion the like of the Crusades . . . For now, you have to be content with the fact that the world has recognized you as a nation, but you should desist from illusions lest one day you wake up into a horrifying reality . . . Your very existence that is based on arrogance and high-handedness is nothing but an empty absurdity; therefore it is by definition null and void since it is not anchored in conventional rights and truth but on fallacy, usurpation, killing, expulsion, robbery, control of others by force, and the establishment of a society of exiles from the entire world whose internal contradictions break at the seams . . . Universal laws will bring upon them a crushing defeat like the one they suffered at the hands of the Romans and others. They will always live as parasites among other nations, due to their obstinacy to confront the rules of history. Their arrogance can only push them from bad to worse . . .[11]

What is fascinating about these remarks by the Islamists in Israel towards the people with whom they live is the denial of their own existential condition when addressing their country with an external 'you'. They exclude themselves from the nation they live among as a minority yet at the same time claiming rights from it. Moreover, the call for the demise of the state they live in does not bode well for their will to integrate and become fully-fledged citizens. It is also worthwhile to dwell on some of the contradictions that make up their world view. They deny the Holocaust but at the same time lament the fact that the Nazis did not succeed in their task. They refute Israel's rights and its historic links to Palestine, defining its presence in the area as robbery and usurpation, yet at the same time acknowledge that the Romans caused ancient Israel's rout. They do not specify where the defeat happened or when, implying that while the evil Jews are ancient and belonged nowhere, they were always 'parasites' of other nations. They would rather deny modern Israel's prowess in the fields of technology, the military, development, science, etc. than acknowledge their own backwardness. Therefore, regardless of achievements that would be worthy of emulation under normal circumstances, Islamists would rather impute even those good attributes to some 'parasitic' proclivities of the Jews, while dwelling on their own ancient and departed glory, which they wish to revive by returning to the times of the Prophet when Islam was a success story. Therefore a relentless struggle will be pursued by the Islamists against their country, while at the same time charging it with discrimination against them. Kamal Khatib once again expressed the prevailing sentiment among his group; justifying the choice of Acre, a mixed Israeli–Arab town in northern Israel, and Tiberias for a rally of his supporters, he said:

> We have chosen Acre because it has been accustomed to repel waves and tyrants . . . It represents the spirit of Saladin. We have chosen Tiberias because it is sister to Haifa, Lydda, Jaffa, Ramallah and Beit She'an, all junior sisters to Jerusalem . . . Brother! Shed the cloak of desperation and don the dress of giving. I shall live to see victory, justice and repossession of my motherland, when we retrieve our usurped land, not by tears but by right, so that Jerusalem will revert to being purged from any monkey, traitor and reprehensible creature. We shall meet in the sites of yesteryear, and then the smile will regain the faces of Haifa, Acre, Jaffa and Beit She'an, and the call 'Allah Akbar!' from their mosques will resonate once again . . .[12]

The dream to cleanse Jerusalem from monkeys and traitors refers to Jews, who are dubbed by Muslim fundamentalists the 'children of monkeys and pigs'. Typical is also the invocation of Saladin, the great medieval fighter for the cause of Islam, a recurrent theme in the dreams of Muslim fundamentalists who aspire to victory, not to a settlement or a compromise. Ruminating over the great victories of such a celebrated Muslim figure not only gives hope to contemporary Muslims to see victory sweeping their camp once again, now against the 'new Crusaders', but also to signal that the rule of Israel is temporary, just as was the Crusader state (and the Holy Roman Empire). Every now and then, great leaders (in their eyes), such as Nasser in the 1950s and 1960s, and Saddam Hussein in the 1980s and 1990s, emerge to re-inject that hope until they pass away and messianic expectations of a new figure are built up. Yussuf Azzam, of Palestinian extraction, one of the most venerated Muslim radical clerics and a mentor of Osama Bin Laden, was a source of inspiration of this sort. A poem written in his honour by the Islamists in Israel goes thus:

> When will magnificence revert to our beloved East, and
> When will glory be reinstalled in our Nation?
> When the sharpened swords will return and the
> arrogant enemy will be defeated and oppressed;
> Then the bastion will collapse on the heads of its occupants, and
> Ancestors will return to rehabilitate the ruins.
> Brothers in Jordan! You are carriers of good news!
> O, Azzam! Honourable men always implement their pledges;
> Here is the Galilee and here is the Port City [Haifa or Acre]; and
> Here is Jerusalem the Pearl of the East and of the Universe,
> Where the Great Site [Temple Mount] is located
> O, Yussuf, we the prisoners [in Israel] are sending you our greetings
> And our oath for the sake of the land of the Galilee.[13]

Ra'id himself, who was customarily more cautious than some of his associates, in order to avoid dirtying his hands directly and permitting the authorities to nail him down, wrote the following poem addressing the Israelis about the Sarafand mosque:

> Just desecrate houses of prayer and murder the worshippers . . .
> Just destroy the Houses of Allah, you dwarf who pretends
> manhood . . .
> Just dig the tombs of our people and pelt the Mu'azzin with
> your rocks of hatred,
> But your fate has been sealed to fade out, you the enemy of good.
> You may manufacture weapons and position missiles on
> hill-tops, and
> Garrison your troops like locusts all over the place from north
> to south,
> Eager to sharpen the swords of treachery . . .
> But you are nothing more than a rash on my skin,
> a cough [in my throat],

> Nothing more than a new version of conqueror that will not survive for ever.
> This is your fate, O Enemy of Allah! You are doomed to fade away
> And your oppression will lead to Hell.[14]

When read in court (in Hebrew translation) as part of my deposition, as evidence of Ra'id's systematic subversion and incitement, I was at first countered by the defendants who stood up and shouted that the words were misunderstood. After a lengthy argument with the lawyers, demonstrating word by word that the discourse in the poem was full of hatred and calumny, which might incite readers to violent action, the defendants shifted to another kind of argument: they said it was allegorical and not really hostile. It was pathetic on the part of the defence to inject into a clearly and purposefully worded political poem meanings that could not be acceptable to any fair-minded person, when the words meant exactly what they said for the commited Muslim followers of Ra'id. For everyone present understood who was the 'enemy of Allah' in question, who was to vanish from the land, who was hated and despised and whose authority was challenged. The use of Islamic symbols or putting words of castigation in the mouths of children who cannot be prosecuted, has been a recurrent device in Muslim fundamentalist writings in order to escape punishment. But then the law loses its force of deterrence, and the radical Muslims are emboldened to cast scorn on the Israeli authorities. To the point that when one reads them, one is aware that they do not seek accommodation with the authorities or the society in which they live, but rather confrontation and secession. Worse, as they identify mentally, doctrinally and in terms of concrete aid with the enemies of the country, you have there all the components that lead to irredentism. Ra'id, once again, could not be more explicit:

> My Son, be the strong bastion against the enemy
> Be the justice that defies death.
> You are the carrier of hope, my son, the carrier of
> Forbearance, the *Murabit* [see above] and the hero
> Who stands up like a mountain in our Holy al-Aqsa.
> My Son, be the roots of olive trees in the Galilee . . .
> Be Jaffa's sea-side, which in spite of the passing years
> Does not rest and keeps storming . . .

He does not submit to infidels, but rushes and erupts
To uproot the treacherous enemy . . .
Be the fragrance of flowers that is carried by the breeze
Which emanates from the Valley of Flowers (*Marj al-Zuhur*).[15]
Acre, Haifa, the Triangle, the Negev, Beit She'an and Lydda
Have cried: Woe to us, we have lost our glory . . .
Therefore, Son, wake up to help and support
For proud Ramlah is exhausted by its wounds
The mosques of the Land of the Isra'[16] are waiting for Saladin
The land and the flowers are waiting for the breaking of dawn,
On which morning you shall embrace the glorious victory . . .[17]

A state for whose demise they are praying certainly does not deserve the loyalty of the radicals who are acting to implement that dream. That is precisely the reason they refuse to take part in the national elections and prefer to live their separate lives, some of which are underground to avoid friction with the law, due to their refusal to acknowledge Israeli law as superior to Shari'a law, and to submit to Israeli sovereignty on the land they consider *waqf*.[18] However, in spite of the movement's ideological identification with Hamas, and the affiliation of both with the Muslim Brothers, Ra'id and his group have prudently and consistently avoided any public show of sympathy for Hamas's platform to establish a Muslim state in the entire expanse of Palestine, Israel included. However, on all other issues of political and religious importance, Ra'id and his followers squarely aligned themselves with Hamas: something that was bound to set them on the collision course with Israel. For example, Ra'id and his colleagues decried the Oslo Accords as inadequate for the Palestinian people and usually supported Hamas in their confrontations with the Palestinian Authority. Back at the beginning of the first intifada of 1987, as Hamas came into being, the mouthpiece of the then still united Muslim movement wrote: 'we shall never forget the pioneering role of Hamas in Palestine against the occupying forces, which consists in arousing the requisite enthusiasm in the populace to remove the occupier from the Holy Land and hoist the banner of Allah over it'.[19] It was a spokesman for the Islamic movement who stated that Hamas was the 'hope of the nation', and the publications of the movement unequivocally dubbed the intifada as a jihad against Israel, geared to redeem by way of martyrdom the Holy Land that had been usurped by the enemy. Even before that, in late 1988, there were indications about the supportive position the Islamic movement was about to adopt with regard to Hamas. *Al-Sirat* (the Qur'anic Straight Path of Allah), indicated that the 'Palestinian people had hoisted the banner of Allah in order to die for Allah'.[20] Another issue of the same journal mentioned the Jews as 'successors of Satan', an editorial urged its constituency to 'raise a new strong generation, a generation of jihad and martyrs', which was an open summons to Israeli Arabs to rise against their authorities – a style that until then had been the exclusive province of Hamas, but was now becoming common currency for the Islamists in Israel as well.

Since 1989, especially after the local elections where the Islamists made an impressive showing, the calls for jihad became a matter of routine in the Islamist journals. On the cover of the November 1989 issue of *Al-Sirat* the al-Aqsa mosque photograph was published to commemorate the 20th anniversary of the mosque arson (of which Israel has been falsely accused), but this time a caption was added: 'O jihad fighter! Wake up! Acre and its shores are expecting you! Do not sleep or doze off. Come on and defend our rivers!' The delegitimation of Israel and the call for jihad to dismantle it go hand-in-hand with martyrdom (*shahada*) for the sake of Allah, as of old during the wars of conquest of Islam (*futuh*). A major debate took place before the court, as the defendants claimed that they always talk of 'liberating' territory, that is retrieving Islamic lands that had been illicitly taken away from them, not of 'conquering' new ones as they were 'falsely' accused of in my deposition. An entire dissertation had to be laid before the court as to the use of *futuh* in current Islamist writings, and citations followed from Baladhuri's *Futuh al-Buldan* (The Conquest of Countries: a classic treatise on early Islamic expansion). Finally, much to the embarrassment of the defendants, we presented to the court a clip of a recent Islamic publication that speaks about recapturing Jerusalem as a *fat'h*. All those who fall in such battles are considered martyrs and gain their special status in heaven. While originally those designated as martyrs fell accidentally in the battle, the modern concept that was developed in the context of Palestinian terrorism decreed that a Muslim jihad fighter could take the initiative and choose to become a martyr, by sacrificing himself or herself as an act of will. In other words, the mere fact that someone has decided to blow himself and others up for the sake of Islam makes him worthy of entering Paradise. Hence the Hamas sanctification of those martyrs and the care for their families after their death which has become part and parcel of recruiting volunteers for their acts of terror. The concept was approved by clerics such as Yassin and Qaradawi and also embraced by Ra'id's movement, hence the links of collaboration and fund-raising that the two sister organizations have woven together.

For the Islamists, however, these acts of wanton killing do not amount to terrorism, since the latter is reserved for states such as Israel and America who 'terrorize the Islamic world'. For them, it is totally lawful and acceptable for people under occupation to rise against their oppressors by whatever means are available to them. Unlike the West, which customarily defines terror in terms of means, not of purpose, Islamic fundamentalists believe that if a Muslim kills innocent people for the sake of Allah, then this is acceptable as long as the Muslim purpose is filled. In the West, violence against noncombatants to achieve political goals is terrorism, as in the destruction of the Twin Towers or the bombing of buses and restaurants in the streets of Jerusalem and Tel Aviv. No wonder that Muslim countries have for years blocked UN attempts to define terrorism in order to fight against it, because they wanted to exclude the United States and Israel from any definition. Ra'id's lawyers in court also reiterated that after every case of terrorism (for them jihad, or *istishhad* [self-sacrifice]), Ra'id had condemned the act. But faced with the contention that terrorism was not a *force majeure* of the elements but man-made and willed, it served no purpose to condemn the act as if it were an earthquake or a tsunami: one had to condemn the organizations who declared responsibility for it. But they were not prepared to do that and instead went over to some other banality that they wished time to be spent upon. A passage was written by Ra'id, praising a widow who was killed while trying to assault Israeli soldiers during the *Iftar* meal which ended the Ramadan fast:

> Heroism is our dress on this holiday . . .
> Allah Akbar is above the conspiracies of our enemies,
> And he is my provision in my journey of vengeance.
> The mother has left us with the pride of the fighter of Jihad
> Don't we wield anymore the sword of 'Amr [bin al-'Ass, the
>   famous conqueror of Egypt for Islam]?
> And the resilience of Qutuz [the Mamluk Chief who defeated
>   the Mongols at Ein Jalut] who routed the Tartars,
> Rise and help your people in my homeland!
> In Jerusalem, the Golan and the valleys.
> Why are you silent in the face of the dangers that envelop the
>   Path of the Prophet?

> She parted and then assaulted the soldiers with a determination
>   as sharp as a blade.
> She fought against their evil with a strong decision,
> She was like glowing embers on the heads of the wicked
> Until her soul departed upwards.
> What an honour was hers in the caravan of the martyrs and
>   the free![21]

Once again, as Rai'd regards his struggle against Israel as akin to other great Islamic battles, he also implies that the Israelis are the successors of the Tartars (and elsewhere of the Crusaders, the Mongols, etc.).[22] Other aspects of Rai'ds encouragement of martyrdom against Israel were expressed in February 2001, on the occasion of the commemoration of the thirteen Israeli Arabs who died during the violent demonstrations in support of the intifada of October 2000. He was reported to have said on that occasion:

> We have engaged in this effort to organize this event regardless of its cost, because no effort can equal the cost of one drop of blood of one *shahid*, for the *shahid* is the only person who dies in order to live, and for that reason he will always be in the minority in his society. He lives not for himself but for his God, his people, his nation and his land, thereby sacrificing the dearest thing he has – his life, because he decided to produce death and to delineate death with his blood and honour, in his fight against the evil in this world . . . *Shahadah* is a gift that is granted only to those who deserve it. This is a gift to our youth in the Triangle and the Galilee, who are eager to die and compete for dying as martyrs. This education that they have is a model for emulation.[23]

This is incitement in its most blatant form, coming from a venerated leader who commands the obedience of many Muslim young people in the country, who can then easily transit from rhetoric to acts, from acknowledging the desirability of martyrdom, to desiring it for themselves. This is terrorism at its most pernicious: when a religious leader lauds the attributes of the *shahid*, not among Palestinians in the Territories, but also among Israeli Arabs in the Triangle and Galilee. Moreover, while the clerics of Hamas have sanctioned and lent support to the young Palestinians who wish to blow up Israeli civilian targets and in the process knowingly and purposely sacrifice themselves, Ra'id extends the validity of that tenet to include young Israeli Arabs, who have no intention to kill or be killed, by inciting them to confront the Israeli authorities under the promise that if they should die, their martyr status is guaranteed. There is something contradictory in Ra'id's and other Israeli Muslims' assessment of the October 2000 clashes between them and the security forces. For on the one hand they blame the Israeli police for 'wanton murder' of the Arabs who had staged an orgy of violence – burning private property, besieging Israeli villages and hoisting the flags of Hizbollah and Hamas. But on the other hand, Ra'id praises those involuntary and incidental martyrs, as if they had initiated their death, which is so desirable in the eyes of their preacher. According to this logic the Islamic movement, if anything, should be thankful to the Israeli troops who helped those martyrs fulfil their desire to die. Sheikh Ra'id has expressed in more poems his unqualified support for, and approval of, martyrdom activity against his country. This is neither good poetry nor good moral education, but Ra'id, like other preachers and clerics of the movement, prefers to hide behind ambiguous words and allegorical allusions in order to escape the legal prosecution that might come more swiftly had his subversive doctrine been worded in plain prose that he could not deny. In an open letter to the 'mother of a *shahid*' after the Jenin clashes, which caused much death and destruction, he wrote:

> The mother of the *shahid* told us: How about drawing your swords now
> and defending the honour of the dwellers of tents [refugees],
> and of their old, children and pregnant women under the ruins?
> To defend your Jerusalem . . .
> We told her: O sister! We are peace-lovers,
> who elect friendship and love over hatred . . .
> She said: Woe to you! Has your shame completely vanished within you?
> Has the right of vengeance completely died within you?
> Wake up! For al-Aqsa has been wronged, your property turned into ruins,
> And Jenin, Tul-Karem, Nablus, Hebron and Balata have been slaughtered like sheep . . .
> O the one billion-soul Nation! Wake up and advance towards Jerusalem and al-Aqsa.[24]

It requires little guesswork or interpretation to detect the complete alignment of Ra'id and his group with the Palestinian side of the conflict. Nor is he ambiguous about the need to take arms and advance for jihad. He was so deeply affected by the events of Jenin (grossly exaggerated by the Palestinians before the record was set straight by the UN) that he allowed himself the freedom to indulge in hyperbole that is matched by other writings of this sort. 'Right of Return' speaks of the Palestinians who will flood the country, outnumber the Jews, make the Jewish state redundant and return the land to Islam once again. In 'Advance!', he wrote:

> Go forward to removing evil from Jerusalem.
> Advance Brother, do not heed the despicable [Jews]
> For you are the brave. Advance Brother
> For your path is that of sacrifice
> You are the best shield against weapons
> Very soon darkness will be removed
> And my country will rejoice at the return of the exiled refugees.
> You are the brave! Haifa is calling upon you!
> You must heed the call, for you are the remedy for injured Haifa
> Jaffa is calling upon you with tears of sadness
> With a broken heart and a miserable life.
> Acre is also calling upon you, and calling Jenin
> So, let us advance instead of putting up [with the situation].[25]

It is thus abundantly clear that Ra'id not only delegitimizes Israel and works for its demise (and condones terrorism to that end) but also incites terrorism against his own country. When explicitly interrogated about this in an interview, he responded:

> As far as martyrdom operations are concerned, our position is that of those among Muslim clerics who deliver *fatwas*. They are the source of authority in this regard. I have no right to engage in interpretations or reach conclusions . . . because clerics of the calibre of Sheikh Qaradawi and others are the authoritative source of *fatwas* for all Muslims in our contemporary world.[26]

We have already discussed Qaradawi (see pp. 78, 87) and Ra'id's citing of him in court. There is no doubt, however, that despite his protestations to the contrary, he admires and accepts Qaradawi's anti-Israeli and anti-

Jewish sentiments and his endorsement of terrorism. This attitude predominates among the rank and file of the Islamic movement and dictates its conduct regardless of the misgivings of the state of Israel *vis-à-vis* these matters. For example, the movement regards its activities as legitimate due to the divine provenance of their authority which always supersedes the law of the state, even when according to Israeli law, or the law of any civilized country for that matter, that activity can be easily branded as subversive to the security of the state or the overall interest of society. This also explains the reluctance of the northern branch of the movement to participate in Israeli national politics and its shunning of the electoral system: if one cannot abide by the rules, one cannot be part of them, they reason. Therefore, prominent in the thinking of the group is the concept that any accusation, condemnation, indictment or law-enforcement by the state apparatus, in the context of any crime it commits, including murder, are to be rejected, either by denial or counter-accusation, rationalization or total rebuttal, for no non-Muslim institutions are competent to judge Muslims. Hence whenever one of the group is arrested for violation of the law, serious as it may be, he will always be dubbed a 'political prisoner', a 'victim of oppression', a 'target of discrimination' or what have you, who should be released immediately and unconditionally, because he 'merely' opposed the conquest of Islamic *waqf* land, rebelled against the oppressors or wished to liberate the land from the rule of apostates. For all Muslims who struggle against Israeli rule in Palestine, whether in Israel proper or in the Territories, are only heeding the imperative of jihad against such rule, and if they are killed in the process, then the shield of the blissful *shahada* is there to protect them and welcome them into Allah's Paradise. The dead *shahids* become models of emulation and adulation, with a 'heritage' that others can be brought up to admire; and those who are judged and incarcerated enjoy the support of the Muslim community. Even the southern branch of the movement, which regards itself as 'moderate', participates in national elections and sports two Knesset members, charges its MPs with the responsibility of visiting 'security prisoners' in prison in order to emphasize their innocence.

Though not much ideological difference separates the two branches of the Islamic movement, Ra'id's northern branch has undeniably made al-Aqsa the focus of its activity, not only in terms of refurbishing the mosque and expanding it, but also in terms of mobilizing its powerful symbol to rally Muslims in Israel and elsewhere around them. Hence the al-Aqsa Foundation that was mentioned in the indictment as the main backbone of Ra'id's endeavour, both domestically and abroad. Under that symbol he can rally Muslims, accuse Israel of all manner of 'crimes', incite violence against his country and mobilize Muslims to confront it. In an opinion page in the organ of the movement, people were invited to express their views on the al-Aqsa intifada. One of them ominously warned:

> Al-Aqsa, for all its religious and Islamic significance, is the trigger for the Israeli Arab uprising, in order to transcend day-to-day demands and step into the existential issues [of nationhood], for the sake of disengaging from the rituals of peace and pressing for independence. The Arab minority in Israel is the spearhead of a people that was doomed to stay on its land in order to confront the secular–Western–Imperialistic enterprise that is Israel . . . Thus the Arab minority is nothing but the show-window of the struggle between the two enterprises . . .[27]

This is the essence of the evidence given to the court which reinforced the prosecution claims about the ideological affinity between the northern branch of the Islamic movement and Hamas. Other evidence on all aspects of Ra'id's activities were also presented to the court by experts who laid out the illicit economic organizations that were networking among the movement to conceal an array of projects, investments, international relations, fund-raising and incitement. Intelligence reports exposed the security hazards that such networks posed to the country and the burden of surveillance and monitoring that they had necessitated. It took months for the prosecution to go through the thousands of telephone and fax transcripts, bank receipts, records of international transactions and reports of interrogations of the arrested defendants and put together the indictment sheet. It was well-nigh impossible for the defence to refute the case, and so the plea bargain was struck.

The trial had aroused tremendous interest among not only the Arab population but also among lawyers, scholars, journalists and foreign diplomats, for it was regarded as the big bang in the showdown between the Israeli authorities and the largest and most hostile anti-Israeli group among the Arab minority in Israel. Rai'd had earned harsh words previously for his role in inciting the crowds from the Or Commission which had investigated the October 2000 events.[28] Therefore the trial was widely seen as the occasion to sort these things out, once and for all. But this was not to be, as instead, to everyone's surprise the defendants opted to sign a plea bargain.

CHAPTER SEVEN

The Plea Bargain and its Significance

NEGOTIATED PLEA BARGAINS are usually concluded between parties either when both realize that the indictment may not lead to conviction, or as the proceedings drag on, as in the Ra'id case, when the parties come to the conclusion that to cut the trial short might be more beneficial than letting it run its course. If it stems from the first reason, then it is to the advantage of the defendants, because if the prosecution is unsure of conviction, needing a 'beyond reasonable doubt' element to convince the court, then of course the defendants will jump at an opportunity to extricate themselves from the proceedings. The second argument fits the prosecution's interest, for while it can sustain the proceedings indefinitely with state resources behind it, a private individual or organization cannot do so, especially when the defendants are in gaol. The balance between the two is what produces plea bargains. Therefore, in the Ra'id case, only the first reason was relevant so far as the District Attorney was concerned, and if she was persuaded that the evidence she and her team had amassed was solid enough, she had no apparent reason to cave in and submit to the plea bargain negotiation and agreement. Unless, of course, the urge for 'efficacy of the proceedings' was so overwhelming, and the concessions of the prosecution so minor and marginal that it was worthwhile cutting the long and costly trial short and agreeing to the plea bargain. In this instance it was proved in court that the Islamic movement maintained ties with Hamas, and that it was also ideologically affiliated with it inasmuch as both negated the existence of Israel, prayed and acted for its demise, and incited their followers, as *murabitun*, to use jihadi violence against it. Hence the support that the movement lends to Hamas terrorist activities against Israel, even when it generally avoids partaking in them itself, and sometimes even 'condemns' them in a duplicitous way, for fear of indictment by the Israeli authorities. This does not prevent the movement, however, from voicing its support for jihad, for Hamas regards Israel as an enemy that has to be confronted, lauds martyrdom in Islamikaze terrorist operations and educates its followers to constant confrontation with Israel.

While these serious accusations were repeated and endorsed by witnesses and documentary evidence in the court-room, they had never been put to a legal test against the Muslim movement, if one does not take into consideration the conviction of the tiny *al-ard* group in the 1960s, which at that time was more of an ultra-nationalist than a religious factor in Arab politics. The most comprehensive legal process in which Sheikh Ra'id had to confront such accusations and respond to them was his appearance before the Or Commission which for two years investigated the October 2000 clashes between the Arab citizens of Israel and the security forces, resulting in the unfortunate death of thirteen Arabs. The head of the commission was a judge from the Supreme Court, accompanied by an experienced Arab judge at the district court level and a scholar in Arab affairs of Tel-Aviv University. Certainly, a commission of inquiry is not a court of law, for witnesses there, though questioned by the panel cannot be cross-examined. There is no indictment, just a summons by the commission to appear before it and give oral or documentary evidence. There is also no verdict and no conviction, only a report and recommendations, though some witnesses were warned that their depositions might be used to indict them. In the two-volume report that was released by the commission in September 2003, three full years after the events, a special section was devoted to leaders of the Arabs in Israel who incited and sustained unrest and violence.

THE OR COMMISSION REPORT

The Or Commission[1] reported then on the activities of Sheikh Ra'id:

Item 178
It seems that Sheikh Ra'id Salah has lent his support to the [violent] conduct that led to the unrest that preceded the October events. In the serious clashes with police at al-Roha, Salah was seen inciting the crowds with fanatic slogans. Subsequent to the events, he had words of praise for them, in a fashion that could be interpreted as a general backing of their violent style. He was cited one week after the riots

as saying that they constituted for their participants a training experience, a 'first try' which has reinforced 'our determination and strength to pursue our just and clear-cut rights'.

Item 179
Sheikh Ra'id has also urged the Arab public in Israel to confront the authorities. In an interview published in the press in 1999 [that is, prior to the October 2000 riots), he urged his fellow Arabs to transcend the local level when they raise their problems and present them on the national level, to relinquish the mood of response and reaction and to take the initiative for more confrontations. Some time later the Sheikh urged Israeli Arabs to block with their bodies the erection of Israeli military camps on the lands of al-Roha, because such a *démarche* by the Israeli government was tantamount to declaring war on the Arab public. On Land Day of March 2000 [which also preceded the October riots], Ra'id declared to a crowd in Baqa al-Gharbiyyah that 'We are not violent, but should violence be imposed on us, we would resort to even more violence.' In his deposition he explained that anyone who attempts to infringe upon the rights of Arabs is considered as a violent actor, and this in turn legitimizes the actions of the Arab public who wish to safeguard their rights. The commission interpreted this as a message of legitimation of, even a threat to resort to, violence against any attempt to confiscate lands for public or military use, as long as the Arabs considered this measure as a violent act.

Items 180–83
Sheikh Ra'id's main activity has been his political campaign under the heading 'Al-Aqsa is in Danger', meaning the entire compound of Temple Mount. His campaign consists of warnings against the menace to the Muslim domination in the mosque area and to the mosques themselves, and he summons his public to set out to defend them . . . He in fact acted upon an intention he imputed to the Israeli government to replace the mosques with a Jewish Temple, something that had no leg to stand on. Those summons urged his public to make sacrifices in the defence of al-Aqsa and to thwart any political [Arab] concession in this regard. Since Ra'id also believes that al-Aqsa includes the Western Wall, he would include in his rejection any political compromise, and calls upon Muslims to defend this Jewish holy site too. In fact Ra'id had declared to documentation

collectors for the commission that defence of the Mosques included 'resistance to their occupation by Israel', and that the threat included the presence of an Israeli police station in the compound, namely that the very presence of Israelis on Temple Mount exposed it to jeopardy. The same words were repeated in Ra'id's article in *Sawt al-Haqq*.[2]

Ra'id's campaign peaked in the annual festivals he held in Umm al-Fahm under the 'Al-Aqsa is in Danger' slogan. These festivals are attended by tens of thousands of people, among them Israeli Arab leaders, and organized by the Islamic movement of which Ra'id is the main actor and the chief engine . . . In the festival of 15 September 1999, one of Ra'id's colleagues said that 'while the oil lamp of al-Aqsa is in danger of extinction, we are ready to rekindle it with blood, for what is kindled with blood shall not be extinguished'. In the festival of 2000, merely two weeks prior to the October events, Ra'id decried any attempt to impute to Jews any rights on Temple Mount and warned that it would amount to a declaration of a war of religion on Muslims everywhere. He said among other things:

> Let us tell the Jews very frankly that you have no right on even one grain of earth of the blessed Aqsa Mosque. Therefore let us sincerely declare that the Western Wall of the blessed al-Aqsa is part and parcel of the blessed al-Aqsa. It will never be a small Western Wall or a big one . . . Let us say frankly to the political and religious leadership of Israel that the demand to leave the Aqsa under Israeli sovereignty [in any eventual settlement], is in itself a declaration of war on the Muslim world.

In the course of the festival loudspeakers clamoured, at times in the voice of Ra'id in person, 'with our soul and blood we shall redeem you, O al-Aqsa!!!' Various Muslim spokesmen, when confronted with these appeals said that they represented the deep devotion of the Faithful, not any intention of bloodshed. [But even the commission recognized the heavy element of incitement that bordered on mass hysteria during the festivals.]

Another Islamist leader in that festival addressed the crowds accusing Prime Minister Ehud Barak of planning to destroy the Aqsa Mosque, in order to rebuild the Jewish Temple on its ruins. He explicitly threatened that 'not tears but blood will flow around al-Aqsa'. He compared Barak to a Qur'anic figure who assaulted Mecca in order to destroy the Ka'ba Shrine, but Allah dispatched against him a squadron of rock-carrying birds who dropped their cargo on him and broke his neck. Barak was warned that Allah could send against him a similar squadron of birds, failing which Muslims themselves could carry out that same verdict of Allah. Those not-so-allegorical words were also given resonance in the organs of the Islamists. Ra'id Salah had himself repeated the same accusation against Barak in his interview to the Palestinian Authority daily a few days earlier, and in his own *Sawt al-Haqq*, where he urged the Palestinian people to close ranks to counter the Israeli government's threat to build a Jewish synagogue on the esplanade of Temple Mount. He emphasized the immediacy of that threat, which was likely to occur, in his words, 'within the coming few months'.

Items 184–8
Despite Ra'id's and his group's caution regarding the legitimacy of the state of Israel, they often transgress that thin and delicate border into delegitimizing their own country. In the mass rally held in Acre on 1 April 2000 [mentioned in the previous chapter], under the heading 'The Demonstration of the Thousands', with Ra'id present, one of his deputies declared that any price should be invested to retrieve the 'usurped homeland'. He enumerated the cities of Jerusalem, Haifa, Acre, Beit She'an and Jaffa in that context and depicted Israel in terms of a 'foolish and treacherous monkey' from whose grip the land had to be rescued. Those words were reproduced verbatim in *Sawt al-Haqq*, and backed by Ra'id in a speech on the same occasion. Two months later, Ra'id attended a rally of the Islamic movement in Kafr Kanna, the village of his deputy Kamal Khatib [June 2000, three months prior to the October eruption]. He projected an image of war against an illegitimate Infidel enemy that is bound to end in victory. He spoke in that rally about the ultimate victory over Infidels in general that will come after a period of forbearance. In that same rally Ra'id spoke about the Arab security prisoners in Israeli prisons as 'freedom prisoners'. Like other Arab spokesmen he put those prisoners [each of whom had been convicted for serious security infringements, including murder], as models to the Arab public. In another rally for the 'freedom prisoners' in Umm al-Fahm he said, addressing them: 'You are the light of dawn for us.

Today we all stand together: associations, frameworks, institutions and various political currents for the sake of your release.'

Treatment of Israel as an enemy also recurs in poems that Ra'id and others publish. The commission also cited the poem mentioned above about the destruction of the Sarafand Mosque, which in court he described as an 'allegory'. Though the 'enemy of Allah' that is addressed in the poem is not expressly identified as Israel, the commission found that it could not be understood otherwise, nor could its Arab readers interpret it differently. The commission found that these words, and others uttered by Ra'id and his associates, point to the delegitimation of the state of Israel as a Jewish state. For they regard Israel as Occupied Palestine of 1948, and Ra'id had confirmed this in his interviews to the press in May 2000. The commission attached great relevance to the declaration of Ra'id and his group in the months that led to the October riots. In fact, on 30 September 2000, at the outbreak of the riots, a proclamation was publicized by the Shura council of the movement which praised the Palestinian victims at the Aqsa Esplanade in their rioting against Israeli police at the opening of the intifada for their 'blood sacrifice for al-Aqsa'. Ra'id confirmed to the commission that he had himself worded the proclamation.

In another proclamation by the Islamic movement it was claimed that the clash between Israeli police and Palestinian mobs on Temple Mount on 29 September was a 'premeditated massacre', citing the fact that since the early hours the 'mosque had been surrounded by hundreds of troops equipped with weapons and clubs'. They did not explain why those who 'plan a murder' arm themselves with clubs, nor how that day was different from the many other days of tension on Temple Mount, especially when the day before serious riots had occurred there and police were routinely ready to counter them. Nor did they address the issue of the declaration of intifada by the Palestinians, not by Israelis, whatever justification they may or may not have had. The same calumny against Israeli troops was repeated by Ra'id the next day at the meeting of the Arab Monitoring Committee that is made up of all heads of Arab local councils (Ra'id was then still the elected mayor of Umm al-Fahm) and Arab Knesset members. He accused both the uniformed and covert Israeli security agents of 'conspiring to push the Arab sector to violent confrontation', as a result of which some Arab residents from all over the country had been wounded. The commission found that 'these unfounded claims only prove the lack of public responsibility on the part of Ra'id'.

Items 189–92
The commission also found that in the midst of the riots of October 2000, the Umm al-Fahm municipality headed by Mayor Ra'id published a communiqué addressed to 'all our [Arab] residents in this dear homeland', praising them for the unity they displayed 'in defence of our Holy Sites'. In the communiqués, the young who participated in the violent riots were dubbed the 'Youth of Al-Aqsa' while the Israeli troops who stood against them were called a 'gang of soldiers armed to their teeth'. It lauded the 'Youth' for 'teaching a lesson' to the gang in that this 'generation knows no fear any longer' when it comes to defending its martyrs, its lands and its honour, and in that they did not lose their cool in spite of 'the cruelty of the soldiers', but defended their rights in a civilized fashion. [If pelting security forces with rocks, burning private property (including a bank and a gas station), hoisting Hamas and Hizbollah flags and crying: 'With our blood and soul we shall rescue Galilee' are civilized ways of public protest, then what price civilization?] At any rate, the commission concluded that 'this praise for violent riots amounts to legitimizing violence'. At the same time, however, the commission mentioned that the Umm al-Fahm municipality had itself admitted that it 'negated vandalism of the sort that unfolded during the riots and included the destruction and burning of public institutions in town and on the highway in its neighbourhood'. But a similar condemnation was not voiced in the communiqué against the attacks on innocent Jewish passers-by on the highway – the implication being that only violence that hurts the town and its inhabitants was to be condemned, while hurting Jews did not matter. So much for 'civilized behaviour'.

At the peak of the riots, relentless Ra'id published an article, which was submitted to the commission as an exhibit, where he dubbed the riots in his town as 'Intifada al-Aqsa', thus joining Hamas not only in action but also on the symbolic level, and admitting that what was to be 'legitimate demonstrations' by his citizenry had grown into rebellious riots. Once again Ra'id praised the rallying of Israeli Arabs around al-Aqsa and dubbed the state of Israel, which allows peaceful and legal demonstrations and protests (and even closes its eyes to mild violence), as a 'tyrant'. Another communiqué of the Islamic movement on 6 October again praised the riots, comparing them to those of the first Land Day of 1976 and claiming that both were 'intifada' that required sacrifices: in 1976 in order to defend lands; in 2000 to defend al-Aqsa. It called the riots a 'war by the government against the Arab population of the country' in order to cause killing and thereby 'tame the Arab sector in the country'.

In sum, the commission concluded that Ra'id had contributed to the incitement that brought about the violent riots of October 2000, by his praise for violent eruptions, including specifically the October riots, his dubbing the events 'intifada' (which is by definition violent), presenting the state of Israel as an enemy while de-legitimizing it, singing the praise of the security prisoners who had committed crimes and murder against Israelis and imputing to the state of Israel dark conspiracies, including plotting a massacre on Temple Mount. The commission also said that while it had no clear-cut evidence to the effect that Ra'id intended bringing the October events to the level of violence they reached, he did not condemn them *post-factum*, nor take measures to calm them. On the contrary, he praised them and showed no sign of regretting the turn they had taken. Particularly grave in the eyes of the panel was his conduct *vis-à-vis* the mosques on Temple Mount. Thus, while there was no doubt about his sincere religious sentiment regarding Muslim control of the Religious Compound, which constitutes the third holiest place for Islam, he was at fault in playing up the alleged plot by the Israeli government to destroy the mosques and replace them by a Jewish Temple. Hence the inescapable conclusion that he used al-Aqsa to gain political influence and to mobilize more recruits to his movement by polarizing the already difficult conflict between Arabs and Jews in the land. His summons to all Muslims during the al-Aqsa festivals to liberate the mosque by blood, constituted a deliberate escalation of the tensions already prevalent among the Arabs.

Items 193–205
In a special section of its report the Commission dwelt on the legal and public significance of their findings, and those are perhaps the most relevant for us in this study. The main conclusion was that certain leaders of the Arabs in Israel, including Ra'id, whose deeds

and declarations were monitored, were found to have legitimized violence or threatened to resort to its use, especially in the months leading to the October riots. According to the commission, those statements by the leadership had a nefarious effect on the Arab populace of the country, inasmuch as they readied the mobs for confrontation against the security forces whose duty it is to protect law and order. The commission cited Supreme Court precedents where there was no need for 'expert' evaluations, since common sense sufficed for any court to reach conclusions as to the dangers of conditions of unrest, for example when declarations of communiqués of incitement are diffused in public: a thesis that was confirmed by several Arab leaders in their depositions before the panel. Kamal Khatib, Ra'id's Deputy in the Islamic movement, confirmed that he was 'proud that he could influence by his words, which the public hears and heeds'. In this light the commission found that those leaders, including Ra'id, should have known that their incitement would have serious repercussions.

[And then comes the crux of the matter: if things were so serious then why were no criminal charges brought against the instigators of violence, not even against those Arab leaders who were warned that their testimony might serve as evidence against them if they were to be prosecuted? As it turned out, none of them was ultimately brought to justice, probably to balance the fact that police chiefs and politicians, who were also pre-warned by the panel, were also not prosecuted.] The commission determined in no uncertain terms that it was not a court of law and therefore could not pronounce a verdict on the criminal responsibility of the witnesses who testified before it. It was only appointed as a commission of inquiry under the law of the country and charged with the task of identifying the events and developments that had led to the October riots. It also reassured the Arab leaders in question that though it did receive some secret material and testimonies as a background, it did not use any of them in its conclusions against them, but only material in the public domain. That made the Arab demand that such materials be put at their disposal for the most part obsolete and irrelevant. Only in the few cases where the covert materials could be used to the defendants' benefit were they handed to them.

Since Sheikh Ra'id was one of three Arab leaders warned of possible incrimination as a result of their depositions, the commission tackled his claims that his words of praise for violence that had been publicized in the years 1998–2000 in various Arab localities came only in response to police violence and were intended to strengthen the hands of Arab demonstrators against it. The commission determined in unambiguous terms that the testimonies of Arab leaders that they were innocently demonstrating until they were attacked by police were simply without foundation. On the contrary, the panel maintained, those demonstrations became serious riots in which wanton violence was used against the police. It was the police who were attacked and who responded to violence, after being prevented from fulfilling their duty to establish law and order. It was those Arab leaders in question who had described the events as 'intifada', and that meant that any word of encouragement amounted to legitimizing the use of violence against police. Sheikh Ra'id himself had declared before that the Arabs were entitled to respond when their rights were violated, and that in itself meant, according to the panel, justification of violence whenever the deeds of the authorities displeased them.

The commission also addressed the claim that to cry out 'Al-Aqsa is in danger' was part of the freedom of religion, by saying that while freedom of religion was one of the basic rights of every individual, and the state recognized also the freedom to hold rallies as part of that freedom, it was necessary to monitor the nature of the messages that were transmitted to the crowds in such rallies. When they include explicit incitement by public figures who are listened to and heeded, it becomes the duty of the commission to identify them as triggering the October riots. Another claim asserted that the very warning that the commission sent to Ra'id and two Arab MKs constituted a breach of their freedom of speech. However, while reiterating that freedom of expression was the very essence of democracy, the commission decided that since it was within its competence to investigate the circumstances that led to the October events, and since it had concluded that those words of incitement were part of the trigger to those events, the claim of breach of freedom of expression had to be rejected. The commission also explained that the right of expression, like any other right, is not absolute and it always hinges upon the equilibrium between it and other public interests, such as respect for law and order. Therefore the panel thought that since those words of incitement were found to have been connected with the violence of October, the 'indirect harm' to the freedom of expression could be said to have been part of that equilibrium.

Those Arab leaders who were warned by the panel also advanced the claim that commissions of inquiry under law were empowered to draw conclusions with regard to the behaviour or misbehaviour of government officials, not against Arab individuals who were not part of the government machinery. The commission found that it acted within the terms of competence assigned to it by the government, part of which was to ascertain the triggers which led to the eruptions of October 2000. Therefore, if the defendants found fault with those terms, they should apply to the Supreme Court and plead for their amendment. Moreover, they said that in this instance it was a matter of great public concern to investigate thoroughly those events, including the reasons that had led to the eruption of violence, that was not in the domain of the executive branch of government.[3]

In Volume 2 of the Final Report of the Commission,[4] it was explained that since Ra'id had in the meantime terminated his office as mayor, there was no longer any need to take steps against him, let alone incriminate him for his deeds. This was beyond the commission's remit. However, the gravity of his words left no doubt as to the heavy responsibility he bore for what he did and said. The commission's report, which was based principally on published materials, even though it did not encompass Ra'id's covert association with Hamas, certainly set off alarms within the legal and security apparatuses of the state, which launched a comprehensive investigation into his worldwide activities. It was this that resulted in his arrest and the trial that was cut short by the plea bargain. Though the very notion of plea bargain conflicts with the idea of absolute justice, sometimes the latter is sacrificed for the sake of expediency, or speeding up the proceedings, as outlined above. However, in view of the findings of the Or Commission, which would have in themselves sufficed to incriminate Rai'd and convict him, it remains a mystery why the prosecution did not pursue its case to the logical end, especially as his lawyers were panicking to see their defences crumbling under the barrage of testimonies by the witnesses of the District Attorney and by the copious documentation that had been assembled against Rai'd.

Against this background, rumours were rife during the proceedings to the effect that the parties were seeking a plea bargain in order to reduce the punishments and to control damage. The defendants and their lawyers knew the objective truth, which was overwhelming and clear-cut. Thus, we must try to comprehend the import of this plea bargain against the background of the Or Commission's report on the principal defendant, the massive covert investigation that followed the work of the commission which had admittedly used some of its findings, and the stunning success of the prosecution in weaving together that mass of evidence into a coherent case.

THE PLEA BARGAIN

The plea bargain, in the form of a judgment by the Haifa District Court, was the result of the negotiations that took place between the parties during those long months of psychological warfare. One may assume that the final touches to the deal were influenced by the court verdict in Cologne, that had outlawed and ordered the closure of al-Aqsa Foundation in Germany, which was a principal fund-raiser for the organization and one of the main sources of Ra'id's income. The judgment was given in the presence of the lawyers of both parties, after all details of the indictment counts and their punishments had been negotiated and agreed upon. The judges added that that they viewed the agreement as 'balanced, reflecting public interest and taking into consideration the complaints of the defendants during the negotiations to achieve it'. That meant essentially that the defendants had to save face before their constituencies after the long months of claims of innocence, pledges of victory and attempts to intimidate the Israeli legal system by trying to intimidate and humiliate the Prosecution's witnesses. Now they had to justify their 'capitulation', to explain the constraints under which they were 'compelled' to accept the deal and to be careful not to tarnish their image.

The main clauses of the bargain were:

- Mahmud Mahajneh, alias Abu-Samrah (defendant No. 1), was sentenced to seven and a half years imprisonment, four and a half actual incarceration and the rest suspended. That is a harsh judgment, and in this case the plea bargain could have been justified in view of the relatively low profile of the culprit and the subordinate role he played under Ra'id.

- Sheikh Ra'id, the main actor in this drama, and the main focus of interest for the Arab public, received a lesser sentence: six and a half years in prison – three and a half years actual incarceration and the rest suspended. This is the most problematic clause in the agreement, not only due to his leadership, his arrogance in court and disturbance of its proceedings, but mainly in view of his previous condemnation by the Or Commission, his high rank which would have made an example of him and a precedent of deterrence to others in his community, and the likelihood, not to say certainty, that he did not repent, nor is he likely to relinquish his criminal activities. In fact, his illegal record has been a source of pride and inspiration to others, so his release with a relatively low penalty is likely to guarantee recurrence, especially in view of the fact that he was released shortly after the bargain was signed, after his period in custody was deducted from the period of incarceration, as well as another third from the sentence as is customary, for 'good behaviour' (of which he showed no evidence, at least not in court). On the other hand, one has to take into account that the entire face-saving exercise of the plea bargain was done for the sake of Ra'id, who least of all others could take the humiliation of imprisonment, and be absent from his flock for any length of time, which could push him into oblivion, and was the only figure able to collect together the pieces of his movement and relaunch it to more campaigns if he were released. Why the prosecution would wish to facilitate that endeavour on behalf of the state remains a mystery. It may be that the prosecution had to pay the price of lowering the penalty that was due to Ra'id in order to obtain the admissions of all others and the punishments decreed against them. But all of the rest were small fry, while Ra'id was the main player. One could also argue that humiliating him any further might provoke a backlash precisely because he is who he is, but in view of his pledge to pursue his course, it is difficult to see how he would renounce that and slip into insignificance. These were the stakes, and no easy decision could be made either way.

- Tawfiq Mahajneh (No. 3 on the list) got five years and eight months in prison: two years and eight months actual incarceration and the rest suspended. Like the others, he was scheduled to be released shortly after the conclusion of the bargain, due to 'good behaviour'.

- Nasser Agbariyyeh and Suleiman Agbariyyeh (Nos 4 and 5) got five and a half years under the same conditions as all the others: three years short of the end of the terms and deduction of a third for good conduct. That was apparently the standard yardstick adopted by the authorities to release the culprits as soon as possible, counting from the day they were arrested in May 2003, but at the same time make them admit their guilt and serve at least part of the sentence.

- Both foundations of the Muslim movement under Ra'id's aegis (defendants 6 and 7), since they could not be incarcerated, were each fined IS 50,000. They were not ordered to be closed and their properties were not all confiscated (as both the United States and Germany had done with regard to the terrorist or terror-aiding organizations that were caught in their territory and brought to justice).
- The court also ordered that the properties and bank accounts of all the other defendants be confiscated.

All these decisions were included in the plea bargain that was signed on 12 January 2005 and received the validity of a court judgment. But one month later (February 2005) the court, with the same composition but different plaintiffs and defendants, had to deal with an appeal to revoke the verdict regarding the confiscation of property in accordance with the law against money-laundering. The plaintiffs were two Arab residents of Haifa who claimed actual possession of the two confiscated apartments who argued that those localities were intended for use as kindergartens and a sports and educational club for the benefit of all Haifa inhabitants. Even though the two assets were stripped, the plaintiffs said they would collect donations in order to refurbish them and ready them for their social purpose. However, the court was aware that the assets had been acquired thanks to a donation of the Humanitarian Relief Society (HRS), defendant No. 6 and which had been fined and its bank accounts confiscated as part of the plea bargain. Thus the court decreed that in view of the fact that those assets had been acquired with illegal funds which originated from a transgression of the law on money-laundering, and that the defendants in the trial had financed the acquisition for the plaintiffs who were now appealing, without the latter having to pay anything in return, the previous confiscation verdict which linked the assets to the convicted culprits was upheld. All the more so since the convicted defendants, by signing the plea bargain which also included the confiscation of those assets, had implicitly admitted that the apartments in question had been purchased with Hamas moneys that were illegally transferred to them. Furthermore, the panel of judges found that there was not only a criminal act of money-laundering, but an act of laundering the moneys of a terrorist organization that was bent on the destruction of Israel. The court found unacceptable the idea that people who would enjoy the hospitality of those houses should know that the assets were purchased with Hamas money, even in the unlikely event that the plaintiffs themselves, who were used by the Islamic movement to launder those funds, did not know their true origin, as they claimed, and naïvely accepted the 'donations'.

This verdict separately delivered by the court after the plea bargain had been negotiated and signed by the parties, and supposedly marginal to the main indictment-sheet and to its ultimate disposition via the plea bargain, turned out to be the most pivotal issue in the unfolding of this prolonged and intricate drama. For it not only showed the relentlessness and persistence with which the Islamic movement's cadres could pursue their goals even when their leaders were in gaol, but it also indicated the turn the trial might have taken had it been allowed to take its course. For while the judges seemed lenient towards the defendants and their lawyers during the trial and there was no way to foretell what their judgment might be after the defence arguments and testimonies were heard, their secondary verdict upon the assets of the Muslim movement and their impatience with the machinations of the Islamists who tried to 'fool' the Israeli legal system on behalf of Hamas were proof enough that the panel was made up of tough legal minds who would not let the defendants slip through loopholes. In fact, the judges, beneath their veneer of impartiality and compassion for the defendants, were not only contemptuous of their repeated attempts to manipulate the system for their benefit but were so impressed by the weight of evidence that the prosecution laid out before them, that they were shaken by the proven link between the defendants and Hamas once they became aware of it. Having recognized the terrorist nature of Hamas on the one hand and the affiliation of the defendants with it on the other, acknowledging most of the accusations made by the prosecution, and before it by the Or Commission, became inescapable. In other words, the severe way the judges treated the purchase of those houses with Hamas money, via the cover organizations of Ra'id, boded well for their eventual treatment of Ra'id and the other defendants had the trial been permitted to proceed. The judges explicitly said in their verdict that had the plaintiffs won their petition to regain control of the houses, both the defendants in the trial and Hamas would have been rewarded, and they would not let the 'sinners', in their parlance (i.e., Ra'id and his group and Hamas) gain any reward. They could not dub the defendants 'sinners' and then let them go as innocent.

This is where the plea bargain was faulty, as the prosecution who was persuaded into this deal that was neither necessary nor justified, by its own hand undermined its case which was foolproof and stood every chance of success. The fact that the judges specified in that secondary verdict that they could not accept a situation where 'the fruits of the poisonous tree [i.e., Hamas funds], which were illicitly obtained, should nurture residents of the State of Israel' meant that they established the following:

- that Hamas was a poisonous tree;
- that the Islamic movement in Israel was fed by that tree;
- that Ra'id and his co-defendants were consciously and willingly aiding that poison to seep into the country against the law of the land; and
- that the Islamists were engaged in illicit manipulation and undercover activities such as money-laundering, in collaboration with Hamas.

The judges said that the plaintiffs who pleaded for their right to regain the two houses, were only marginally damaged by the decision of the court to confiscate the houses, because they had cost them nothing. Therefore, and in view of the fact that a more substantial damage would have been caused by allowing their possession to take effect on assets that were paid for by Hamas, the confiscation verdict was inevitable. The judges also specified that the money for the houses had been handed over to the plaintiffs under suspicious circumstances: the large sum of IS 400,000 (the equivalent of $100,000 at the time) was placed in a plastic bag and brought to them by a person, presumably from the Islamic movement, whom they hardly knew. This should have raised questions in the minds of the recipients as to whether the deal was legal. This was especially true when the money was not handed from person to person, but on behalf of HRS, that is a company or an association that would customarily pay such a large sum in a straightforward fashion. So the judges conceded that though they would not necessarily accuse the recipients of having been aware of the Hamas source of the money, they should have been alerted to it by the way it was paid to them. Thus the confiscation stood, though that came too late for the prosecution to contest the thinking of the judges in the principal trial during their negotiation of the plea bargain. Had they been more confident about their overwhelming mass of evidence on the one hand, and the hysteria of the defendants on the other, perhaps they would have rethought their side of the plea bargain and opted to press for the continuation of the trial that they were certain to win. Unless, of course, someone else in the high reaches of government was interested to put an end to the trial, for political or other considerations, and ordered the proceedings to be terminated via the only means open once they had started, namely a negotiated plea bargain.

CHAPTER EIGHT

Consequences of the Trial

HAVING SERVED MOST of their sentences while under arrest, the defendants now saw the prospect of being released and going back to their families and loved ones. But the basic issues were not resolved, for not only had none of the culprits repented or pledged not to revert to illicit activity after the period of the suspended penalty had elapsed, but some of them made it clear upon their release that they would pursue it with a vengeance. Chief among them was Sheikh Ra'id, who was released in mid-July 2005, a few days short of his due date, in order not to allow his followers to turn his home-coming into a victory celebration. In fact, after Ra'id was hustled into his village unannounced, the rumour spread, and a multitude of well-wishers began to flock into Umm al-Fahm and lay siege to his house. The celebrations of victory did take place. Ra'id was the focus and the hero, but no wrongdoing was admitted either by him or any of his admirers, which meant that the legal system of Israel which had treated them more than fairly and struck the compromise with them in order to release them, was completely sidetracked. Furthermore, even though the plea bargain they signed, at their own instigation, was an admission of guilt and an acceptance of the penalties meted out to them, they and their followers remain persuaded that it is 'Islamic' to resist the authorities of the country, to subvert and undermine the country where they dwell, at the same time as they clamour for their 'rights'. This attitude again casts doubts on whether the plea bargain was a wise move on the part of the state in the first place, now that it has become clear that the release of the culprits would only mark the beginning of a new phase in their activity that they vow to pursue.

Two days after his release Sheikh Ra'id made some significant statements to his public and to the press which do not augur well for his future conduct under the restraining conditions of the plea bargain. Not only did he state boldly to the crowds of well-wishers who came to congratulate him on his 'victory' and proven 'innocence' that he would go to al-Aqsa any time he wished and would not abide by the restrictions imposed on him, but he also gave interviews to the press stating the same intentions. Wafa, the Palestinian News Agency, published an interview with him under the heading 'The Head of the Islamic Movement in the lands of 1948, declared to Wafa that the data base of Israel's dealings with the Arab citizens inside the lands of 1948 does not bode well for the future.' Thus, not only is Ra'id for the official mouthpiece of the Palestinian Authority the 'Head of the Islamic Movement' (ignoring the split in the movement and the existence of the less militant 'southern branch'), but both Wafa and Ra'id, twelve years after the Oslo Accords and two days after Ra'id's release from prison, after his lawyers signed the plea bargain, are agreed that Israeli Arabs are not 'Israeli citizens' but 'Arabs inside the lands of 1948'. This is not very encouraging in terms of recognition of Israeli jurisdiction over its territory and nationals by either of them. In response to questions by his interviewers from Wafa, Ra'id said:

> There are serious indications that the Israeli establishment is planning to brandish the whip of transferring Israeli Arabs or parts thereof, under various headings such as 'border adjustments' with a view of chastizing them, dismantling their thinking and their social projects and keeping them busy with their daily livelihood.

Challenging the Israeli authorities, he added: 'Whoever thinks that under pressure and hatred we would renounce even a portion of our convictions, is like someone who expects us to give up one of our body organs, something that is unthinkable.' He pointed, as examples, to the usurpation of Palestinian rights since 1948, the aggression against the Muslim holy places, the confiscation of the lands of Galilee and the destruction of houses in the Negev. He emphasized that 'we were born free on our land and we shall pursue our abiding by our rights, even though we were arrested for our construction of our identity and we paid the price for that. We were at peace with ourselves in prison and we left the gaol happy.' Ra'id accused Israeli political and intelligence circles of attempting to 'accumulate assets' at his movement's expense by means of lies and deception, and warned that 'they are mistaken who believe that they can get away with accusing and harassing the Arabs within the 1948 territories under the atmosphere of the post al-Aqsa uprising, as if we were on the verge of being transferred with trucks across the border'.

Ra'id claimed that he had been approached for negotiations with the Israeli authorities both before and after he was arrested, by Benjamin Ben-Eliezer who was then Minister of Defence under Prime Minister Barak (this is incorrect: in fact he held that post under Ariel Sharon, after the fall of Barak's government in 2001), but he firmly rejected the offer despite the assurances he got of Barak's intention to transfer IS 50 million to the Umm al-Fahm municipality of which he was then the head. In return he was requested to limit the movement's activities with regard to al-Aqsa. He also said that he was approached by Prime Minister Sharon via the mediation of an Israeli scholar of Arab affairs, Dr Motti Keidar of Bar Ilan University, and offered material assistance in return for his movement's participation in national elections. He also made a stunning revelation: that a representative of the Israeli Shin Bet (the security apparatus) approached his lawyer, Fahim Dawud, and offered to release Ra'id from prison if he wrote an article in the press about the Israeli elections, Arab–Israeli coexistence and the Palestinian 'resistance'. He pointed out that the Israeli government sent him several messengers shortly before he was arrested, who tried to convince him to visit the Auschwitz death camps in return for which his indictment sheet would be cancelled.

Ra'id said that the Islamic movement stood by its determination to make Palestinian rights prevail, even if that would mean him returning behind bars, and pledged to pursue the activities of his movement in the service of the Palestinian cause, because 'defending the Negev meant defending the future of the Arabs in the lands of 1948 and their geographical and cultural expansion'. He claimed that Israel had not renounced its motivation for his and his colleagues' arrest, but he added that his movement would not yield and would continue its link with the Palestinian people for the defence of the lands, holy places and the rights of the Palestinian refugees and émigrés. He also pledged to keep a watchful eye on al-Aqsa, underlining that 'we are aware of the price that the Israeli establishment will levy from us in its illusory attempt to tame us and terrorize us, but we are firm in the implementation of our convictions'.

Ra'id assured his interviewer that he would not abide by Israeli diktats, and that he would visit Jerusalem and pursue his links with al-Aqsa at any moment he so desired, even if that meant his return to gaol. He stated dramatically: 'As long as I live, I shall not ask for permission from the occupation forces to visit al-Aqsa, because this is an absolute Palestinian, Arab and Islamic right, while the occupiers do not have the right over even one grain of earth there.' He reiterated that he was holding on to his slogan that 'al-Aqsa is in danger', and that his movement would stick to it without any fear of prison or persecution, calling attention to the fact that Israel still constituted the most immediate danger to Al-Aqsa. He maintained that his movement did not plan to desist from its activity on behalf of al-Aqsa but was planning to increase it, in defiance of the threat of prison. In response to some Israeli officials who had allegedly said that the leaders of the Islamists had not learned any lesson from their incarceration, he commented that it was said in preparation of 'al-Aqsa Hostages File No. 2', which planned for the renewed arrest of the movement's leadership. Ra'id also expressed his delight about the mass participation in the rally of solidarity with him the night before, which for him amounted to a true referendum on the platform of the movement, and he predicted that the relations between Israel and its Arab population, which were on a collision course, were bound to erupt once again. On the other hand, he saw the urgent necessity to effect a sincere historical reconciliation between the various Arab and Islamic organizations and their peoples, warning that the present explosive situation would erupt in outlandish places if no change came about. He said that he would soon publish a book of reports and poetry that he had written whilst in prison.[1]

This orgy of indicting statements from someone who had just been released from prison after a plea bargain says much about the man and his ideology, about the authorities who signed the bargain with his lawyers and about the value of the plea bargain itself. Ra'id not only holds fast to his de-legitimation of the country whose rights he seeks to obtain, but also completely denies its rights in Jerusalem and Temple Mount, threatens it with more violence and vows to breach the limitations that were accepted by his lawyers in the plea bargain. Ra'id came out of prison with a victory sign, did not acknowledge any wrong on his part, and can always say that the plea bargain was signed by his lawyers, not himself, that it was signed under duress as the only way for him to be released from gaol so that he could pursue his sacred work. He was not required to repent, to express regrets for his words and deeds and for inciting jihad among his fellow Muslim citizens of Israel, for undermining the security and the very legitimacy of his country, or for his association with Hamas, the sworn politicial enemy of his country. Although a suspended sentence of three years in prison was built into his plea bargain, Ra'id promised his audience that he had no intention of heeding it. No country where the rule of law prevails would tolerate such an open and arrogant challenge to its system and destructive defiance of its instruments of law.

Thus those who concluded the plea bargain with him ought either to have refrained from it, knowing that he would not respect it, or made sure that it was enforced. Otherwise, what would stop him or others repeating their violations of the law? Perhaps he sensed the squeamishness of law-enforcement authorities in Israel when it comes to the Arab sector, for fear of being dubbed 'racists'.

A major error that recurs in Western law-enforcement systems is that the rule of law is falsely assumed to apply to all citizens. Islamic law has rules of conduct that do not recognize the concepts of Roman Law, such as *lex justicia*, law of torts, civil law of contract where mutual obligations depend on each other's fulfilment thereof, or the modern norms of international law that govern relations between countries on an egalitarian basis. Other people's lands can be invaded and occupied, but once occupation is dubbed '*fat'h*' and the land is called '*waqf*', that is *ipso facto* a licence to treat the territory as subordinated to Islamic law, classify it as *dar al-Islam*, its dwellers as *dhimmis* or *kuffars*, as might be the case, and condemned to murder, expulsion, slavery, expropriation, abuse, intimidation or forced conversion accordingly. The 'benefit/interest of Islam' is the key concept, namely that anything judged by Muslim authorities to be beneficial to the cause of Islam is to take precedence over any other considerations. When a Muslim individual signs a contract, especially under duress, then only the contractual commitments of the other party must be implemented as long as they benefit the Muslim, while the latter can always escape his obligations if they can be shown to give advantage to the non-Muslim party. So it goes for contracts between nations that we call pacts or treaties, following the precedent of the Hudaybiyya Accord signed by the Prophet with Mecca for ten years, but violated after two years because it was 'good for Islam'. Certainly, in the modern world Muslim states cannot get away with such conduct, especially if a pact obligates them *vis-à-vis* major powers, but Muslim fundamentalists who wish to turn the clock back to the times of the Prophet would certainly countenance a situation where Islamic justice reigns. With that kind of thinking, Ra'id and his cohorts will not rest until his vision of Israel as a subordinate entity within the Islamic Caliphate is realized.

In October 2003 Israel was rocked by a horrendous Islamikaze terrorist act in the Maxim Restaurant in Haifa, where a young Palestinian woman lawyer blew herself up murdering 21 diners, some of them three-generation families who were totally or nearly wiped out. Eighty-one were wounded, some of them so severely that two years later they are still in need of treatment and rehabilitation. This was one of the worst acts of terrorism against Israel, second only to the March 2002 Park Hotel Passover massacre that left 29 dead and a hundred maimed, and which prompted the Israeli government to launch the Defence Shield Operation to cleanse the West Bank from terrorist infrastructures. During the police investigation, one of Rai'd's and two of his co-defendants' Mahajneh clan was arrested for aiding the terrorist. It was found during the investigation that Mahajneh, taking advantage of his Israeli car-plate and his own Israeli identity-card and familiarity with Israeli roads and prospective targets, had driven the terrorist-murderer from the border town of Umm al-Fahm where he lives with his clan, to which his famous relative belonged, to the place of crime. He sat with her at the restaurant, ordered food, then left with the car to return home, whereupon the terrorist activated the bomb and caused that horror in which she also perished. The trial went on for over a year at the same Haifa district court where Ra'id Mahajneh was tried at about the same time, and there was reason to assume that some spiritual and ideological link existed there between the two culprits. Ra'id incited and collected funds for the Hamas, for which he was convicted as part of the plea bargain and released, for he was not accused of direct murder of Israelis, but of white-collar ideological crimes of illicit money transfers, of aiding a terrorist movement and of contact with a terrorist organization; his relative was convicted two weeks later for manslaughter by negligence and for driving into Israel an illicit passenger who had no permit to enter the country. But he was acquitted of aiding the act of murder, because the judges said that the prosecution could not prove that he knew of the intention of the Palestinian terrorist to explode and kill.

The relatives who survived the murder of their 21 loved ones and the maiming of 81 others, who followed the court proceedings, were deeply shaken once again; in the words of one of the spectators who had lost his son and parents-in-law and was still trying to rehabilitate his severely maimed wife, 'this is the second explosion for us'. They sat in court in a dignified silence, but were so stunned by the judgment that they sensed that the machinery of justice in Israel had again missed its target. The outraged relatives of the victims simply posed the questions that would have occurred to any fair-minded person:

- What did Mahajneh the culprit think, after the years of indoctrination by Rai'd, another culprit in another trial, who openly supported

Hamas, editorialized about its 'charitable deeds', raised funds for it, and acted underground to serve its purposes? That the Palestinian girl asked him for a ride in order to visit the Haifa seaside, or her Israeli friends, or to find a restaurant to her taste? Her trip, for which she paid and he knew was illegal, should have raised his suspicions that she had some disturbing goal in mind, and he should have either alerted the authorities or at the very least refused to drive her.

- Why did he sit down with her to eat and then leave just before she blew herself up, bringing down much of the Maxim sea-side restaurant and many of its diners?
- Why should Mahajneh return to his car after he left the terrorist and burn his own clothes, hers after she changed in the car and the seat-covers of the car so as to eliminate any chance for forensic experts to detect DNA or other traces of the occupants of the car? This conduct is not typical of an innocent person.
- Why, after he learned of the blast, did he not run to the police to admit his complicity, but on the contrary tried to conceal his part in that horror?

In other words, enough circumstantial evidence was there to convict the culprit also for aiding an act of terror, which is qualitatively different from just 'killing by negligence', and for which he would have been sentenced to life imprisonment instead of a few years. This is what upset the relatives, because it means that the fanatics, both those who spread the poison and those who act on it, are immune to severe prosecution and penalty. This leaves Israeli citizens exposed to more attacks. To Ra'id's followers it means that the Israeli legal system is so hopelessly squeamish and lenient towards them that they can pursue their criminal activity without fear of a high price to pay. This is precisely what Ra'id has promised after his release. The legal system has not learned to act pre-emptively to arrest terrorists and their instigators before they strike. The United States for a decade looked with indifference at Steve Emerson's reports, written and video-recorded, on the activities of jihad in America, where Sheikh Abdul Rahman, a fugitive from Egypt found asylum and began mounting his terrorist network right under the nose of the FBI, which could not act as long as there was no violence committed. Britain, during the same period of time, allowed terrorists Abu Hamza al-Masri and Umar al-Bakri to find shelter in London, feeding on the British welfare system while recruiting young Britons for training in Afghanistan. Only after the first attempt on the Twin Towers in 1993 and then 11 September in the United States, and the terrorist acts that shook Madrid and London, did large-scale arrests begin, with the FBI suddenly panicking and arresting right and left, and Jack Straw, the British Home Secretary, lecturing the world about the need to fight international (not Muslim) terrorism. This is the price that the West and Israel are paying for not daring to pre-empt Islamic terrorism and nipping it in the bud before it strikes.

After his conviction and release, Ra'id made it clear that he would not budge from the de-legitimation of his country, which lies at the root of his activities. He and his followers maintain that they are proud of their deeds, which are hailed by their constituencies as 'heroic' and that they will not be deterred by Israel and its legal system. It is thus doubtful whether, in instances of national security and corruption of officials, the plea bargain device is justified from the viewpoint of the prosecution, which is also supposed to reflect and represent public interest. For not only is there no repentance in this case on the part of the convicted culprits, and, on the contrary, an assurance of repetition, but the Israeli public has been robbed of a unique opportunity to wake up to the dangers in its midst of a rebellious Muslim minority which does not recognize the state, is devoted to its destruction and allies with its worst enemies to achieve its goal. Even the prosecution was denied the chance to cross-examine the defendants and their witnesses in court – something that would have allowed it to bring to light their staunchest supporters, to learn about their thinking and goals and hopefully uncover more about the covert activities of the defendants. One may guess that it was precisely that fear that drove the defendants to move from denial to damage limitation, rather than take the risk of exposing their deeds, their associates and their goals under oath at the court. In so doing, they avoided a full conviction which could have resulted in long-term incarceration and the dismantlement of their movement once their supporters were in gaol, their funds and assets confiscated and the leadership defeated and absent. Conversely, those are precisely the very arguments that should have reinforced the prosecution's determination to let the trial take its course and to allow a decisive verdict to cite the facts and punish the offenders.

One ought not be confused by the 'democratic', 'freedom' and 'human rights' discourse the Islamists use in order to beat democratic systems. They resort to that terminology that is so dear to the West, because Western democracies are so sensitive to it and are afflicted with a sense of unjustified 'guilt' that the Islamists are only too happy to heap on them. The soul of democracy resides in the people's sovereignty, thanks to which the people are free to elect their representatives that make their laws for them. For Muslims that sovereignty resides uniquely and exclusively in Allah, and any claim to it is considered blasphemy. Moreover, Allah having dispensed to humanity the most perfect of legal systems, namely the Shari'a law that is based on the Qur'an and the Sunnah of the Prophet, any pretension by anyone to ameliorate it by human thinking amounts to sacrilege. So, for Islamists anywhere, there is no question of accepting democratic rules or yielding to them in their countries of residence in the West. Quite the contrary, they are bent on changing their alien environment rather than yielding their identity to it. This is what they are trying to achieve in Israel and elsewhere, and Sheikh Ra'id's and his followers' conduct is no different from that of other Islamists. They do not hide their intentions and they should be taken seriously by their interlocutors. The point is that when their environment becomes irreconcilable with their ideology, violence is inescapable. This is the reason why Sheikh Ra'id who is the front-man of his various organizations has been attempting to stay out of the fray in order not to be caught, and why he delegates the practical chores of the movement to his underlings who are willing to engage in them in the service of the ideas they believe in. This 'distance' also allowed him to declare victory after the plea bargain and to remain defiant, because despite his machinations he could not be charged with the actual wrongdoing. He was, and remains, 'merely' the spiritual guide, the supreme authority and the main engine, and he uses his talents, his poetry and his writings to play with 'allegories' that his disciples understand very well and risk their lives to apply in the open. Though he perhaps never murdered anyone himself, nor engaged in illicit money transactions in person, there is no doubt about who is the boss, judging from the adulation and popularity he enjoyed both in the court-room and in the spontaneous homecoming ceremony that was staged by the crowds when they learned of his early release.

All this should suffice as evidence that there is no way to expect Ra'id or his followers to reform their ways to please the Israeli authorities. For them, the Arabs of Israel will remain 'the Arabs of 1948'. Ra'id would not vouch for any peace settlement between Israel and the Arabs, nor for coexistence between the two, because for him the entire land belongs to Islam and there is no reason for him to accept any compromise of partition, or a two-state solution on a land that was given by Allah to

Muslims for all generations to come. If he cannot accept even the fact of the Holocaust, let alone lament it, then why expect him to visit the camps in order to gain any sort of sympathy for the Jewish people? His convictions are far stronger than any historical 'fact' with which he might be confronted. In short, the northern branch of the Islamic movement has shown beyond doubt that its principles are not up for sale, and that even under duress they will not yield to pressures, penalties, trials, prison, etc. They are so convinced in their ways that they will not desist from them unless stopped by their opponents. The measures that Israel has been pressuring Western countries to adopt against Hamas, Hizbollah and other Islamist movements, such as closing them down, banning them, confiscating their properties and pursuing them in the courts, it does not apply itself, in spite of long years of relentless subversive activity. And the danger posed to Israel's existence is far greater than anything the West has been exposed to. There is a level on which one can understand the paradoxical Israeli attitude, where the more vulnerable and exposed to the mercy of the Arab population and neighbouring countries Israel is, the more it tries to show sensitivity to their grievances and demands. But on another level there is a widening gap between what Israel is allowed to do in self-defence and what other less vulnerable countries (both in the West and in the Middle East) can afford to do. This is precisely what gives the Islamists in Israel a sense of immunity to the state's counterattacks and self-assurance that if they persist they will prevail.

But there is also a level of domestic politics in Israel which Israeli politicians have to watch at all times lest the considerable Arab vote in the national elections decide who will rule the country in the future. As long as Ra'id's Islamists are boycotting national elections, one might think that scenario unlikely. But politicians from all parties who vigorously court the Arab vote every election eve would not do anything that might antagonize Arabs in general, and would pledge to respond to Arab demands after the elections should they win. The Islamists' cause, and Sheikh Ra'id in person, have become so popular among the Arabs in general that very few politicians would dare to cross him in public. In the past, parties that were negotiating with Arabs prior to elections found themselves faced with demands that suited the Islamists in the country, such as cultural autonomy, the widening of the jurisdiction of Shari'a, an Arab–Islamic university, more government support for Islamic institutions and the reversion of *waqf* properties to the control of the Islamists. These are some of the considerations that may have been behind the decision to conclude the plea bargain, and they partly explain the extraordinary leniency of the system, even when the convicted defendants stated that they would not abide by the terms of the plea bargain. Moreover, even in the unlikely event that they should abide by those terms, who guarantees what course of action they might choose to take once the three years of suspended penalty have elapsed? They have only undertaken under those terms to 'refrain from perpetrating the same violations' for the duration of three years, but they obligated themselves to nothing beyond that. One has to remember (and the Islamists certainly do) that the Or Commission had 'warned' Ra'id (and others) of the incriminating consequences of his testimony, but nothing followed in terms of indictment or penalty. The Islamists have learned to sideline those 'warnings' that they hear from various quarters now and then. Why should it be different this time?

In sum, if there is anything to be done to counter the threat the Islamists pose to Israel, it is not to be found exclusively in the domains of security and legal means. Some measures in the civic area can be adopted immediately and applied collectively to all Muslims, while others may be planned for the long-run that may at least give incentives to the Islamist population to mend its ways and gain benefits if it does. Some may and some may not, but at least we would know that they had a choice either to be rewarded or punished according to what they would have chosen to do. If they have no choice, and a uniform policy is imposed by the authorities that does not differentiate between those who reconcile themselves to their minority status and are prepared to take on their civic duties, which also entitle them to their rights, and those who decide to wage a perpetual war and would under no circumstances bend to realities, then Israel would be cultivating a rebellious population that is bound to rise against it. A young Sheikh of the Islamic movement, who gave an interview to an Israeli journalist in the mid 1980s had this to say, which should be heeded today:

> From what I know, and according to the Qur'an and Islamic religion, I believe that Palestine was Islamic under Islamic rule, until Jews came and expelled all Muslims from Jaffa, Tel Aviv and Safed. Those who came here by force can only get out by force. The Christians killed Muslims here and then came the Tartars and the Jews. But we believe that Muslims shall yet return Palestine to the Muslims. We have religious leaders [like Ra'id] and they will determine where we have to wage [jihad] war and whatever they say is binding on us.

[Whether we want] a Muslim Palestinian state to replace Israel? The truth and our real thinking on this matter we do not reveal to newspapers. We do not believe in peace, because if there is peace it would be a peace between puppet regimes in government today, not between peoples. The peoples do not want peace. The Qur'an says that Christians and Jews are on the other side of the Islamic hurdle. There will never be peace, and if there is peace there can be no just peace. Only the strongest will prevail. It is true that today I have no power and I merely sweep streets, but if I had power I cannot tell you what I would do. All our ancestors fought against Jews, now they vote for the Labour Party. The only way is to return to the faith, this way we can retrieve everything. For the time being, we live the way we live out of sheer self-interest, not ideology. After all, I am getting from you unemployment benefits. When I went to university and was an outstanding student, I got from you a grant-in-aid. One Arab saying goes like this: 'Until you get what you want, kiss the hand that feeds you.' What we want is a Muslim state, anywhere, from which we could expand in all directions. True, Israel is a fact, but I cannot give it legitimacy, for Allah enjoins us never to give up, to stand fast everywhere, to take root in the land, and not to renounce anything. I am not going anywhere from here. Even when I die I do not go from here, I am just covered with earth, but I do not budge.[2]

All this means that both in Israel and in the world context, Islamists follow a blueprint for their long-term confrontation with Israel and the West. While the plan's details are only gradually emerging, it has proven immensely popular with the masses who are in no mood for compromise, much less for beating a retreat, and who seem to go along with it as it becomes known. Their belief in Allah's blessing for their venture has become so deeply rooted in their hearts that they feel no fatigue or fear, nor do they recoil from any difficulties in implementing their scheme, even as obstacles have been blocking their road. For Allah has tested many of his followers in the past and he ultimately made them victorious, as one of his many names (al-Nasser = the Victorious) indicates. And Islamists are set to get victory, nothing less. They are equipped with the requisite faith, zeal and enthusiasm, as the acronym of Hamas (The Islamic Resistance Movement) connotes. They are boundlessly devoted to Allah as their various Hizbollah (Party of God) groups profess. They are determined to pursue their *da'wa* (mission, call, propaganda, education) the world over as many of their organizations call themselves and their organs. They are intent on waging merciless jihad if their 'peaceful' message urging surrender is not heeded, as their recurrent attacks against Israel (and the West) ought to have taught us, and as the names of many of their associations remind us. Many of them are inspired and aided by al-Qa'ida, which used to be the main base physically and spiritually, who trained the candidates for Islamikaze, financed their operations and planned the time, place and scope of the next strikes. Since the blow they incurred in Afghanistan and thereafter, their operations have been more decentralized but are carried out with the same fervour, as events in Iraq and along Israeli borders demonstrate. They have also acquired the skills of double-speech: soothing, anaesthetizing the enemy and manipulating the media, as evinced in Ra'id and his defendants' discourse during the trial. The main components of this blueprint can be summarized as follows:

1. The West and Israel must be defeated, or at least weakened, frightened and put on the defensive. For not only do they undermine the Muslim world with their debauchery, innate corruption and pragmatic alliances with corrupt Muslim regimes; but also by posing an alluring alternative to the young Muslims, with their permissive way of dress, coeducational schools, pop music, pornography, pre- and extra-marital sex, mixed dancing and frolicking, alcohol and Western movies, they threaten the future generations of Muslims. The fundamentalists, with the assent of their generally conservative public, dread the prospect of seeing their societies slip from their grip and supervision, therefore they enlist for their endeavour all Allah-fearing Muslims, even those not necessarily affiliated with them, who are concerned about the rapid drift of the young towards modernity and Western and Israeli-style living.

2. A first step towards this goal is to cultivate the rift between pro-Arab and pro-Muslim Europe on the one hand, and 'Zionist-controlled' America on the other. Thus, while both belong to the evil West, it is imperative to go easy on Eurabia at first due to its assistance, both directly to the Muslim world, and indirectly by diminishing US power, challenging it and keeping it in check. This policy has proved a success for the time being, inasmuch as the European Council has been openly favouring Palestinian terrorism over Israel's right of self-

defence, in spite of American misgivings. And the Muslims have also succeeded in drawing Europe onto their side in the Balkans (Kosovo, Bosnia, Macedonia), dragging with it US forces who have implemented European-Muslim designs in Europe. The Islamists in Israel hope to Balkanize the situation in Palestine and drag Europe into it, hence their repeated demands for the internationalization of the conflict.

3. Europe's turn will come after the United States is driven out of the game and Israel is eliminated. Those among the Islamists who are impatient, have hastened to act in London, Madrid and Amsterdam, thus indicating that those stages can be parallel and not necessarily consecutive. Islamists speak openly of reconquering Islamic territories such as the Iberian Peninsula, Palestine, Kashmir and then the rest of the world. Al-Qa'ida bases and secret lodges already exist in practically all European countries as well as on Israel's borders. The showdown with Europe and Israel has been tested by increasing the numbers of illegal Muslim immigrants into those countries, and later by internal growth (and the Right of Return of Palestinians). They would be inundated demographically to the point where they could no longer resist the Muslim onslaught.

4. The elimination of Jews is advocated by Islamists (from Qutb to Bin Laden), and by inference also Zionism and Israel, and is something that not a few Europeans also subscribe to. Only thus would the 'desecration' of Muslim holy places cease, *waqf* land of Palestine revert to its legal Muslim owners and the Jewish 'control of the media and financial centres', as well as the corridors of power in America, come to its end. Therefore, Jews are targets not only in their own state but also around the world.

5. Finally, pending the anticipated Muslim victory, much long-term groundwork is needed, which Muslim radicals, including those in Israel, wholeheartedly support and initiate and even push Muslim governments and individuals to help finance. The list is long: recruiting new converts in the West, lending financial support to families of Islamikaze martyrs, raising moneys either through 'charitable' front organizations in the West itself, to be used against it, or from donor states and individuals (e.g., Saudi Arabia, Iran, Bin Laden and

other Saudi magnates) for building mosques, Islamic centres and madrasas in unsuspecting countries, but then diverting their use to conversion programmes, indoctrination and hate propaganda, recruitment of trainees for Islamikaze operations, strengthening Islamic education in Islamic countries in the periphery, such as south, central and southeastern Asia and raising Muslim consciousness among Muslim minorities in Europe, Asia, Africa and the Americas.

6. What they cannot do today they will try tomorrow. Like a burglar in a hotel, they will try to force open any door which offers little or no resistance, but will recoil when the alarm is activated, the door is steel-reinforced and its lock armoured, or when security personnel are on the alert and ready to act, regardless of the risk of confrontation or the dangers of casualties or damage that might ensue.

CONCLUSION

The Islamic movement in Israel, which shares many of the above characteristics with similar groups in the region and worldwide, is not a passing fad, nor is it likely to subside if certain of its demands, such as 'equality' and an 'Islamic Palestinian state' are met. On the contrary, the sooner it meets its immediate goals the sooner it will press for the implementation of its ambitions in a snowball effect that will be difficult to stop. Already, judging from Ra'id's interviews to the press after his release,[3] he is losing no time in reorganizing his activities, and there are even indications that he is seeking to reunite the entire Islamic movement in Israel if he can get the heads of the southern branch, who were among his well-wishers when he returned home from prison, to toe his line and abandon their participation in national elections (an implied recognition of Israel's legitimacy, which is abhorred by Ra'id and his group). One of their heroes, the Egyptian preacher Umar Tilimsani, had urged the Muslim world to reject any acceptance of Israel, even after President Sadat signed peace with Israel in 1979 and there was talk of 'normalization' between Israel and the Islamic world. His reasons, which remain guidelines to Muslim fundamentalists everywhere, remain as valid as they ever were:

1. Normalization might erode Muslim determination to reclaim the rights usurped from them in Palestine.

2. On account of the confusion and hesitation it may create, normalization ought to be refuted because the 'very presence of Jews among us, and our dealing with them on a permanent basis, might become a habit that is liable to kill our sensitivity to their crimes'.

3. Jews are attempting to Judaize the entire region, something that is detrimental to the faith and to public welfare.

4. The Jews are known for their natural propensity to spread permissiveness among all nations in order to pave the way to their mastery of the world. Normalization would contribute to the implementation of that scheme.

5. The danger is run not only by Egypt, but due to the latter's prominent position, by the entire Islamic world.

6. Jews are likely to spread corruption which would put an end to all values and life essentials.

7. The Jews exploit freedom of speech in order to spread films to all parts of the world which are ready to succumb to Jewish money, while the Islamic *da'wa* is lagging far behind.

8. They use their expertise in order to diffuse their baseness, using the meanest and most clandestine ways.

9. They diffuse journals, newspapers, books and cassettes under Islamic names, and these media are the worst in influencing public opinion.

10. Jews have invented the treacherous ways of propaganda. They spread their so-called 'anti-reactionary' message among the youth, and in so doing they undermine Muslim traditions.

11. They use smooth and glib talk to influence the innocent and uninitiated.

12. Normalization might facilitate their financial penetration into all aspects of the Egyptian economy and cause it irreparable damage.

13. They will spread dissent among Egyptians and then between them and the rest of Muslims. Already Egyptian artists have been

welcoming and meeting some Jews, something that unless checked could bring about uprisings of Egyptians against Egyptians.

14. They find ways to spread use of illicit interest, exploiting the human weakness for money to disseminate it using methods that only seem legal.
15. Normalization might turn Israel into an accepted fact of life which might make it irreversible, while only its disappearance can prevent the rise of 'endless plights'.
16. Can anyone imagine that Jews are able to be normal with any non-Jew? They are the only ones who refuse to accept any foreigner into their faith. Therefore normalization with them is bound to fail.
17. Normalization would mean a slow but sure death to the Muslims. Therefore, Muslims ought to choose between dying today with honour or living on without honour.
18. Jews have already been competing successfully against Egyptian agriculture and industry due to their skills and know-how. They can take losses until they eliminate Egypt economically and then they will take over and recuperate their losses.
19. Normalization would facilitate Israel's penetration into Egypt's military, political, social and economic secrets. Israelis are the masters of intelligence and they are already spying on Egypt. Normalization would increase the pace and efficacy of their endeavour.
20. Jews will corrupt the relations within Egyptian families: between fathers and sons, husbands and wives.
21. And much more that cannot be discussed.[4]

Any Muslim fundamentalist who reads this message must of necessity be wary of Jews and alienate himself from them, rather than seek to 'normalize' relations with them. The Islamist movement in Israel cannot dismiss Tilimsani's teachings and at the same time, admire him, just as no one who admires Marx can denigrate Marxism. The message cannot be clearer, and the only question is one of implementation by stages in view of the widespread support for these views throughout the Muslim world. Like their kin in the West Bank and Gaza, the Islamists in Israel wish first to transform their society in Israel and then call for an open jihad against it. Like the struggle within the Palestinian people between secularists who follow Fat'h and the Islamists who support Hamas, within the Israeli Arab public there is a widening gulf between the nationalists and the Islamists headed by Ra'id. If, according to Muslim fundamentalist reckoning, the relationship between Israel and the world of Islam is beyond normalization, then what remains is confrontation. The lingering debate in Israel about whether the intifada has or has not crossed the borders into Israel proper has become largely academic. The statements of the heads of the Islamic movement in Israel before its split, to the effect that they sought a Palestinian state side-by-side with Israel, have been overtaken by the events of the intifada, which precipitated the unfolding of history and telescoped events into a brief time-span and set into motion the mechanisms of confrontation. The evidence produced during the trial as to Ra'id's Islamists' direct involvement in sustaining terrorist groups such as Hamas, together with the growing involvement of young Israeli Muslims in Hamas activities, all point in that direction.

In the long term, the Arabs of Israel, Islamists and others, must be regarded, as they regard themselves, as Palestinians, and therefore their built-in hostility to the Jewish state where they live can only be contained if they are counted as part of the solution, not only of the problem, of the Palestinian issue. When a Palestinian state is established in parts of the territories of the West Bank and Gaza, independently or in conjunction with the half of the Palestinian people that dwells in Jordan, then the Islamists in Israel will have to choose between joining their brothers and creating an Islamic order to their liking, or remaining in Israel as alien residents who owe their political loyalty to that state. In the short term, a few immediate measures seem necessary to stem the dangers:

1. The law must prohibit umbrella organizations of the Islamists on the grounds that they create an ambience of public disobedience, incitement and even rebellion, as Ra'id's affair has shown. Only local associations of Muslims, who pursue peacefully individual and community worship and charitable work ought to be allowed and subsidized.

2. There must be a network of Israeli schools in Arab-populated areas where the language of instruction would be Hebrew and where Jewish and Arab students would share the same culture, language and national values. The liberal policies of Israel, Holland and Britain, where the Muslim populations are allowed to study in schools in their own languages and to give precedence to their native culture,

has only produced alienation and bred secession and ultimately terrorism. The integration that the centralized French system forced on its Muslims did not work either, but in Israel it can be tested as the only state education system that the state finances, while all Muslims who wish to pursue their own educational programmes would do that at their expense and would thereby rob their followers of the chance to integrate. These are two powerful incentives to join the state system. In addition to the official curriculum in state schools, 'Friday Schools' would enable Muslim children to pursue their religious and cultural studies on their own on a voluntary basis.

3. When infringements of law occur, such as incitement, violence and terror, the individuals concerned should be prosecuted, like Ra'id and his colleagues, and made to pay the price. If they should become Palestinian nationals after the Palestinian state is established, then they can be repatriated to their own land. Closures of Arabic papers, or arbitrary decisions to issue or not to issue permits simply open the way to recriminations and claims of discrimination.

4. Christians and other liberal Arabs who are frightened by Muslim radicals in their mixed communities must be encouraged to distance themselves from the Islamists, to join the Israeli system and integrate with all attending rights and duties guaranteed and protected.

5. Islamists should not be permitted to maintain international links with other Muslim organizations, beyond carrying the duty of the Hajj. For the funds that they receive from abroad not only encourage them to claim the right to secede or bring down their Jewish–Zionist state, but as in Ra'id's case, enjoin them to collaborate with radical and terrorist organizations such as Hamas.

6. The Islamists in Israel should not be permitted to exclude the Jews from their holy places under threat of violence, nor should the Israeli government give way to those threats, otherwise the Islamists are not only encouraged in their confrontations with the Israeli establishment but they thereby gain prominence and popularity in the Islamic world, notably among the Muslims in Israel, which in turn strengthens their constituency and emboldens it to further confrontation. For example, the Islamic movement and Ra'id personally, have turned the Aqsa Mosque into their fief and made it the focus of their activity. They undertook to add a basement to the structure of al-Aqsa, which they call the Marwani Musallah, and in the process

dug up rare ancient Jewish archaeological vestiges, which they dumped in an attempt to efface any concrete evidence of the Jewish claim to Temple Mount and to Solomon's Stables. Israel could, as in Hebron's Tomb of Patriarchs, demand that since the place is holy to both faiths, the right of worship should be fairly divided between the two. But under threats of Muslim violence, the state of Israel which has been sovereign in Jerusalem since 1967, has yielded, with the absurd result that the Muslim exclusivists who deny others' rights and history are masters of the entire place, while the Jewish liberals who show understanding for the other claimants and are ready to share the use of those sites remain excluded.

7. Finally, the Islamists have got into the habit of believing that since they represent the final divine message it is also the only true one, while all the others are usurpers and falsifiers of Allah's message. In that light (or rather obscurity) they demand that their holidays must be respected by everyone, that their prisoners should be released, no acts of warfare should be launched against them and their sites of worship should be kept exclusively for them, since no one's sanctity can match theirs. If any place of worship of theirs is accidentally damaged or attacked on purpose (like al-Aqsa in 1969) then the entire world is alerted to the 'onslaught against Islam', to the 'conspiracies of Jews and Christians', and what have you. But they can wage war against Israel in Ramadan (the 1973 Yom Kippur War), exclude Jews from praying on Temple Mount, destroy Jewish historical evidence linking them to that place in antiquity, burn down Jewish synagogues in Jericho and the Joseph Tomb in Nablus during the intifada, and launch the intifada uprisings first in 1987 (during Chanukka Festival) and then on the eve of Jewish High Holidays in 2000. Israel should make clear that while it respects, like any civilized country, the beliefs of others, it expects the same from the Islamists, and that it will retaliate within the boundaries of the law against any encroachment on its own religious taboos.

The combination of short- and long-term measures will not calm the mood of the Islamists nor dampen their resolve to attain their goals. For they will take every liberal gesture of goodwill towards them as a vindication of their claim, and any firm stand on the part of Israel as evidence of discrimination and oppression. Therefore, only a programme of integration into Israeli society, which might attract a few among them, can serve if not as a viable alternative then at the very least as a sign that Israel has made an effort to resolve the issue. But for the majority of Islamists who are determined to follow their course, only their inclusion into the overall solution of the Palestinian problem can address their concerns. Whether they like it or not, even the most liberal and democratic state has the right to self-defence and survival in the face of imminent and concrete threats. This may not constitute an easy or acceptable solution for many, but great statesmanship does not consist of adopting the good and discarding the bad. That would be too easy. Leadership that leaves its mark on events is the one that seizes the less than ideal solution and implements it before even this becomes inapplicable. This is the last moment of decision.

Bibliography

PRIMARY SOURCES

Most of the materials for this volume were culled either from the two journals that serve as the organs of the Muslim movement in Israel, *al-Sirat* and then *Sawt al Haqq wal-Huriyya*, or the legal files compiled by the Haifa District Attorney's Office in preparation for the trial, or the minutes of the court deliberations during the year-and-a-half that the Prosecutor's part lasted.

The journals of the movement tell its detailed inside and outside story since its early days in the 1980s to the present, and they reflect in particular the views of Sheikh Ra'id, the current editor. Many of the columns, stories, reports, features, comments, editorials, critiques, book reviews, letters to the Editor, interviews and even poems are his or about him or inspired by him. Therefore, an extensive reading is bound to provide a complete coverage of Ra'id personally, the ramification of his activities worldwide, his close aides and confidants, his movement in general and the adulation he is given by the populace.

The legal documentation is of two categories:

The materials compiled by the District Attorney and her aides. This mass of materials was put at my disposal almost without limitation during the months that preceded my appearance in court; its contents are extremely diverse and include dozens of dossiers that were assembled, researched and analysed by the six attorneys employed by the Attorney's Office during the 18 months that preceded the opening of the court procedures and then accompanied the proceedings. The dossiers contained:

1. Hundreds of transcripts of faxes and telephone calls made by the defendants, who were tapped by court order, and which revealed their electronic contacts within Israel, with the Gulf countries where they raised their funds and with sister Muslim organizations across the globe.

2. Copies of the prolific correspondence which the defendants maintained with the rest of the world.
3. Bank transcripts and other financial statements which showed the scope of the fundraising, the web of 'charitable' organizations that were used as a front for the money laundering that was channelled to Hamas.
4. Reports by the Shin Bet Secret Service, which monitored some of those activities and recorded them for use by the prosecution.
5. Reports, affidavits and intelligence evaluations by the police and other investigative bodies about the Islamic Movement, Hamas, the links between them and the main actors in both.

The court records, which contain thousands of pages of statements and cross-examinations by the defendants' lawyers of the dozens of witnesses provided by the prosecution, and included:

1. Expert opinions of intelligence officers and various investigative bodies.
2. The minutes of 18 months of court sessions needed by the prosecution to build the case.
3. The interim rulings of the panel of judges during the court sessions.
4. The exhibits produced by the prosecution which were accepted by the court and introduced as part of the evidence.
5. The plea bargain which cut the court proceedings short.

As mentioned above, though the court proceedings were supposed to be open to public scrutiny, except for some intelligence materials which may have been screened and reserved by the judges as a security precaution, the President of the Court made the availability of the materials conditional on the consent of both parties. Naturally, the defendants, who could not consider the plea bargain as a victory in spite of their protestations to the contrary, were reluctant to comply when they learned that their defeat would be made public in a book. But since the bulk of the material was the result of the prosecution's preparatory work, both in the office and during the trial, most of the important and relevant material was consulted and referred to.

SECONDARY BOOKS AND ARTICLES

Arabic and Hebrew Media
al-Ahram (Cairo)
al-Da'wa (Cairo)

al-Hamishmar (Tel Aviv)
al-Hayat (London and Beirut)
al-'Ilm (Cairo)
al-Manar TV (Hizbollah, Lebanon)
al-Mustaqbal (Lebanon)
al-Riyadh (Saudi Arabia)
al-Sharq al-Awsat (London)
al-'ukadh (Saudi Arabia)
al-Usbu' (weekly, Cairo)
al-Wafd (Cairo)
Egyptian Gazette (Cairo)
Haaretz (Tel Aviv)
Iqra' TV (Saudi Arabia and Egypt)
Kul al-Arab (Nazareth)
MEMRI – Middle East Media Reports (translations of main articles in the Arab press)
WAFA News Agency

Foreign Press
Panorama, BBC (London)
Sunday Telegraph (London)

Books and Articles
Bar, Shmuel, 'The Religious Sources of Islamic Terrorism' (Hebrew), *Policy Review*, Tel Aviv (June 2004)
Bat Ye'or, *The Dhimmi* (Madison, WI and London: Fairleigh Dickinson Press, 1985)
——, *The Decline of Eastern Christianity Under Islam* (Madison, WI and London: Fairleigh Dickinson Press, 1996)
Burns, Robert, *The Crusader Kingdom of Valencia* (Cambridge, MA: Harvard University Press, 1967)
Demurger, Alain, *Chevaliers du Christ: Les Ordres Religieux Militaires au Moyen Âge* (Paris: Editions du Seuil, 2002)
——, *Jacques de Molay: le Crépuscule des Templiers* (Paris: Editions Payot, 2002)
——, *Les Templiers: Une Chevalrie Chrétienne au Moyen Âge* (Paris: Editions du Seuil, 2005)
Ghanem, A., *The Arabs in Israel on the Eve of the Elections for the 13th Knesset* (Hebrew), Survey of Arab Affairs No. 8 (Givat Haviva: Institute of Arab Affairs, 1992)

Israeli, Raphael, 'The Charter of Allah: The Platform of the Islamic Resistance Movement', *The 1988–89 Annual on Terrorism* (The Netherlands: Kluwer, 1989), pp. 99–134; reprinted in Raphael Israeli, *Fundamentalist Islam and Israel: Essays in Interpretation*, pp. 123–68

——, *Peace is in the Eye of the Beholder* (Berlin: Mouton, 1987)

——, *Muslim Fundamentalism in Israel* (London: Brassey's, 1993)

——, *Fundamentalist Islam and Israel: Essays in Interpretation* (Lanham, MD and London: University Press of America, 1993)

——, 'Muslim Fundamentalists as Social Revolutionaries', *Journal of Terrorism and Political Violence* 6/4 (1994), pp. 462–5

——, 'The Arabs in Israel: Criminality, Identity and the Peace Process', *Journal of Terrorism and Political Violence* 10 (Spring 1998), pp. 35–59

——, *Poison: Manifestations of a Blood Libel* (Lexington, NY and London: 2002)

——, *Green Crescent over Nazareth: The Displacement of Christians by Muslims in the Holy Land* (London: Frank Cass, 2002)

——, *Arabs in Israel: Friend or Foe?* (Hebrew), Ariel Centre for Policy Research, 2002

——, *Islamikaze: Manifestations of Islamic Martyrology* (London: Frank Cass, 2003)

Khadduri, Majid, *War and Peace in Islam* (Baltimore, MD: Johns Hopkins University Press, 1969)

Layish, Aharon (ed.), *The New East* (Hebrew), special issue on the 'Arabs of Israel between Religious Revival and National Awakening', 32, (Jerusalem: 1989)

Lewis, Bernard, 'How Did the Infidels Win?' *National Post*, 1 June 2002

Mawdoodi, Abu-al-'Ala, *Nationalism in India* (Malihabad, 1948)

Mayer, Thomas, *The Muslim Awakening in Israel* (Arabic) (Nazareth: 1986)

Or Commission Report, 2 vols. (Jerusalem: Israel Government Printing, 2003)

Osecki-Lazar, Sarah, *The Elections to the 13th Knesset among the Arabs in Israel*, Survey of Arab Affairs, No. 9, Tel Aviv University, 1992

Qut'b, Sayyid, *Our War against the Jews* (Arabic) (Beirut)

Tal, Nahman, 'The Islamic Movement in Israel' (Hebrew), *Strategic Update* (February 2000), pp. 8–12

Theis, Laurent, 'Les Templiers', *Le Point* (Paris) (August 2005), pp. 53–66

Tsimhoni, Daphna, 'Christians in Israel: Between Religion and Politics', in E. Rekhess (ed.), *The Arabs in Israeli Politics: Dilemmas of Identity* (Tel Aviv: Tel Aviv University, 1998)

Yaniv, Ya'kov, 'The Islamic Movement in Israel Between Integration and Secession (Hebrew), *Vision and Praxis* 4 (1995)

Endnotes

PREFACE

1 This preface is based on Alain Demurger, *Chevaliers du Christ: les Ordres religieux militaires au moyen âge* (Paris: Editions du Seuil, 2002); *Jacques de Molay: le crépuscule des Templiers* (Paris: Editions Payot, 2002); and *Les Templiers: une chevalrie chrétienne au moyen âge* (Paris: Editions du Seuil, 2005). A write-up by Laurent Theis in *Le Point 1717* (Paris), 11 August 2005, pp. 53–66, summarizes the topic.
2 This term has been coined by this author as the combination between Islam and the Japanese Kamikaze of the Second World War, to designate the so-called 'suicide-bombers' in the path of Allah. See Raphael Israeli, *Islamikaze: Manifestations of Islamic Martyrology* (London: Frank Cass, 2003).
3 See Theis, in *Le Point*, p. 54.
4 Translated and annotated by this author as 'The Charter of Allah: The Platform of the Islamic Resistance Movement', in Y. Alexander and H. Foxman (eds), *The 1988–89 Annual on Terrorism* (The Netherlands: Kluwer Academic Publishers), pp. 99–134; reprinted in Raphael Israeli, *Fundamentalist Islam and Israel: Essays in Interpretations* (New York and London: University Press of America, 1984), pp. 123–68.

CHAPTER ONE

1 Abu al-'Ala' al-Mawdoodi, *Nationalism in India* (Malihabad, 1948), pp. 5–11.
2 Robert Burns, *The Crusader Kingdom of Valencia* (Cambridge, MA: Harvard University Press, 1967), p. 303.
3 See R. Israeli, *Islamikaze: Manifestations of Islamic Martyrology* (London: Frank Cass, 2003).
4 For a most comprehensive and authoritative study, see Majid Khadduri, *War and Peace in Islam* (Baltimore, MD: Johns Hopkins University Press, 1969). See also Bat Ye'or, *The Dhimmi* and *The Decline of Eastern Christianity Under Islam* (Madison, WI, and London: Fairleigh Dickinson University Press, 1985, 1996).
5 Bernard Lewis, 'How Did the Infidels Win?', *National Post*, 1 June 2002.

6 *Al-Ahram*, 25 April 2002.
7 Al-Manar Television (Lebanon, Hizbollah), 24 April 2002.
8 Iqra' Television (Saudi Arabia and Egypt) 24 April 2002. See *Memri* 373, 30 April 2002.
9 Ibid.
10 In fact the number of Israeli casualties has long surpassed the 20,000 mark, that is four times the author's estimate.
11 *Al-Usbu'* (Egypt), 28 May 2001; *Memri* 224, 4 June 2001.
12 *Al-Sharq al-Awsat* (London), 8 June 2002.
13 Al-Manar Television (Hizbollah, Lebanon), 2 June 2002.
14 *Al-Mustaqbal* (Lebanon), 19 March 2002; *Al-'Ukadh* (Saudi Arabia), 22 November 2001; *Al-Riyadh* (Saudi Arabia), 22 November 2001.
15 *Al-Wafd* ((Egypt), 13 February 2000; *Al-Ahram*, 19 April 2000; *Egyptian Gazette*, 20 April 2000.
16 *Al-Ahram*, 30 December 1999.
17 *Al-Hayat*, 31 January 2000; *Al-Akhbar*, 26 January 2000; *Ak-Ahram*, 18 April and 17 May 2000; *Egyptian Gazette*, 17 April 2000, and more.
18 *The Secret Ties between the Nazis and the Zionist Movement Leadership* (Arabic) (Amman: Dar Ibn Rushd,1984).
19 See R. Israeli, *Peace is in the Eye of the Beholder* (Berlin: Mouton, 1987), especially pp. 33–4, 231, 326 and passim.
20 *Al-Akhbar*, 27 May 2001. See *Memri* 231, 20 June 2001.
21 See R. Israeli, *Poison: Manifestations of a Blood Libel*, (New York and Oxford: Lexington, 2002).
22 *Al-'Ilm* (Egypt), November 2001; *Memri* 322, 28 December 2001.

CHAPTER THREE

1 R. Israeli, 'Muslim Fundamentalists as Social Revolutionaries', *Journal of Terrorism and Political Violence*, 6/4 (1994), pp. 462–5.
2 See Sayyid Qutb's *Our War Against the Jews*, often quoted by Muslim fundamentalists everywhere. See also A. Layish (ed.), *The New East* (Hebrew), a special issue on 'the Arabs of Israel between Religious Revival and National Awakening', 32 (1989).
3 For the entire story, see Thomas Mayer, *The Muslim Awakening in Israel* (in Arabic), (Nazareth, 1986).
4 For details on the rise of the Islamic movement and its history in the 1980s, see R. Israeli, *Muslim Fundamentalism in Israel* (London: Brassey's, 1993).
5 For the miracle of turning water into wine, see John 2.1–11; for the miracle of the cure of a child, see John 4.44–54.
6 For the entire story of Sheikh Khatib and Kafr Kanna, see Israeli, *Muslim Fundamentalism*, pp. 66–76.
7 Ibid, especially Chs 2, 5, 6.
8 *Al-Sirat*, 7 November 1987, pp. 10–13.
9 Ibid., pp. 20–23.

10 See A. Ghanem, *The Arabs in Israel on the Eve of the Elections for the 13th Knesset* (Hebrew), Survey of Arab Affairs No. 8 (Givat Haviva: Institute of Arab Affairs, 1992),
11 Sarah Osecki-Lazar, *The Elections to the 13th Knesset among the Arabs in Israel*, June 1999, Survey of Arab Affairs, No. 9 (Tel Aviv: Tel Aviv University, 1992).
12 Ibid., table, p. 21.
13 Ghanem and Osecki-Lazar, Survey of Arab Affairs, No. 13 (Tel Aviv: Tel Aviv University, 1994).
14 See D. Tsimhoni, 'Christians in Israel: Between Religion and Politics' (Hebrew), in E. Rekhess (ed.), *The Arabs in Israeli Politics: Dilemmas of Identity* (Tel Aviv: Tel Aviv University, 1998), pp. 66–7.
15 Ibid., p. 67.
16 Ibid., p. 68.
17 Ibid.
18 *Sawt al-Haqq wal-huriyya*, 29 December 1989.
19 R. Israeli, 'The Arabs in Israel: Criminality, Identity and the Peace Process', *Journal of Terrorism and Political Violence*, 10 (Spring 1998), pp. 39–59.

CHAPTER FOUR

1 Israeli law requires two concurrent but separate votes in local elections: one for the mayor personally, where the candidates are to present their tickets with their full personal details for the voters to choose from; the second for the municipal council. It happens at times that the elected mayor is opposed by a council made of other parties than his, in which case municipal work may be handicapped, but usually popular mayors bring with them a majority council too.
2 *Al-Sirat*, December 1988.
3 See for example *Al-Sirat*, July and November 1989.
4 *Al-Sirat*, 21 July 1989.
5 Ibid., 18 August 1989.
6 For years Israeli authorities have been excavating around Temple Mount, the location of the two ancient Jewish temples (which are denied by Muslims), for archaeological purposes, and digging a long tunnel along the western wall in order to uncover the long-buried strata of the original wall surrounding the ancient temples. This work was largely completed by the early 1990s and the premises were opened to tourists. To secure an emergency exit for visitors, Israel opened the tunnel at its other end near the Via Dolorosa in October 1996, which occasioned severe armed revolts by Muslims who believed, or at least claimed, like Ra'id, that the tunnels and the new openings were calculated to destroy the mosque. There was no substance to these claims, because the tunnels were dug along the wall and not underneath the mosque, and no damage was caused to the mosque compound.
7 In August 1949 an Australian Christian tourist, Michael Rohan, attempted to burn down the mosque in a bout of messianic lunacy. Israeli authorities put

out the fire, arrested the culprit and indicted him, but most Muslims across the world have been accusing Israel ever since of arson. Umm al-Fahm's locally published journals, leaflets and posters have been repeating that accusation on the anniversary of the arson.

8 *Sawt al-Haqq*, 27 October 1989.
9 Ibid., 24 November 1989.
10 R. Israeli, *Muslim Fundamentalism in Israel* (London: Brassey's, 1993), pp. 134–5.
11 Atallah Mansur, *Haaretz*, 10 and 15 October 1989.
12 Ibid., 20 October 1989.
13 See R. Israeli, *Islamikaze: Manifestations of Islamic Martyrology* (London: Frank Cass, 2003).
14 Undated announcements by the organizing committee of the camp (headed at the time by Sheikh Ra'id of the opposition), circulated in Umm al-Fahm in the summer of 1986.
15 Qassem Zayd, *Al-Hamishmar*, 12 May 1986.
16 Ibid.
17 *Al-Sirat*, November 1987, pp. 23–5; *Al-Ittihad*, 26 April, 15 May 1988.

CHAPTER FIVE

1 See R. Israeli, *Islamikaze: Manifestations of Islamic Martyrology* (London: Frank Cass, 2003).

CHAPTER SIX

1 *Muslim Fundamentalism in Israel* (London: Brassey's, 1993); *Fundamentalist Islam and Israel* (Jerusalem Centre for Public Affairs), (Lanham, MD: University Press of America, 1993); *Green Crescent Over Nazareth: The Displacement of Christians by Muslims in the Holy Land* (London: Frank Cass, 2002); *Arabs in Israel: Friend or Foe?* (Hebrew) (Tel Aviv: the Ariel Center for Policy Research, 2002); *Islamikaze: Manifestations of Islamic Martyrology* (London: Frank Cass, 2003).
2 For an elaboration of these themes, see Israeli, *Islamikaze*, pp. 38–45, 95–6, 103 and 184–7; Shmuel Bar, 'The Religious Sources of Islamic Terrorism', *Policy Review*, June 2004; Israeli, *Fundamentalist Islam and Israel*, p. 35.
3 *Sunday Telegraph*, London: 24 July 2005.
4 See Ya'kov Yaniv, 'The Islamic Movement in Israel between Integration and Secession' (Hebrew), in *Maof u-ma'aseh* (Vision and Praxis), 4 (1995): pp. 162–5.
5 Sheikh Kamal Khatib, Ra'id's deputy at the head of the northern branch of the Islamic Movement, in an interview to *Sawt al-Haqq wal-Huriyya*, May 1998.
6 *Sawt al-Haqq*, 29 December 1989.
7 Ibid., 1 June 2001, p. 4.
8 See 'The Charter of Allah: The Platform of the Islamic Resistance Movement–Hamas', in Y. Alexander and H. Foxman (eds), *The 1988–89 Annual of Terrorism*

(The Netherlands: Kluwer, 1988–89), pp. 99–134, rep. in Israeli, *Fundamentalist Islam and Israel*, pp. 123–70.
9 *Sawt al-Haqq*, December 1988.
10 See more on this in Israeli, *Green Crescent over Nazareth*, pp. 55–63.
11 *Al-Sirat*, 18 August 1989.
12 *Sawt al-Haqq*, 7 April 2000.
13 Ibid., 1 December 1989.
14 Ibid., 18 August 2000, p. 11.
15 The place in southern Lebanon where the leaders of Hamas were expelled in 1992. Ra'id attempted at that time to rush aid of food and medicine to them, but was thwarted by Israeli police.
16 Isra' is the mystical night journey by the Prophet on winged horseback, from his native Mecca to al-Aqsa (the furthest place), which after the construction of a mosque bearing that name in the seventh century, has become identified with Jerusalem.
17 *Sawt al-Haqq*, 19 April 2002.
18 See Nahman Tal, 'The Islamic Movement in Israel' (Hebrew), *Adkan Istrategi* (strategic update), February 2000, pp. 8–12.
19 *Al-Sirat*, 29 April 1989.
20 Israeli, *Muslim Fundamentalism in Israel*, p. 40.
21 *Sawt al-Haqq*, 20 December 2002, p. 8.
22 See Tal, 'The Islamic Movement in Israel', p. 11.
23 *Sawt al-Haqq*, 9 February 2001.
24 Ibid., 12 April 2002.
25 Ibid., 26 April 2002.
26 'Panorama', BBC TV, 27 April 2001.
27 *Sawt al-Haqq*, 1 December 2000.
28 See the report of the 'State Commission to Investigate the Clashes between the Security Forces and Israeli Citizens in October 2000' (Hebrew), 2 vols (Jerusalem, 2003), Vol. 2, pp. 542–52.

CHAPTER SEVEN

1 I have paraphrased the relevant material, offering my own comments and observations. See the Or Commission report (Jerusalem: Israeli government printing, 2003).
2 Also cited in *Ayyam al-'Arab*, 15 September 2000.
3 The relevant material for Sheikh Ra'id is Vol. 2 of the Or Commission's report, pp. 542–59.
4 Ibid., Vol. 2, pp. 643–4.

CHAPTER EIGHT

1 Wafa News Agency, 20 July 2005.
2 Cited by R. Israeli, *Muslim Fundamentalism in Israel* (London: Brassey's, 1993), p. 173.

3 See the above Wafa report, *Haaretz*, 1 August 2005 and *Kul al-Arab*, Nazareth, 29 July 2005, where they all predicted the growth and strengthening of the Islamist movement as a result of Ra'id's incarceration and release.
4 *Al-Da'wa* (Cairo, April 1981), pp. 4–5. See also the issues of January 1977 pp. 58–9; September 1978, p. 10; March 1977, pp. 54–5; October 1977, pp. 50–1; October 1979, pp. 5–6; September 1979, pp. 14–15 and September 1980, pp. 7–9. A true calendar of 'Israeli corruption' during all the months of negotiations between Egypt and Israel that ultimately led to the peace treaty between the two countries. But the Islamists would not relent and their impact on the negative images of the Jews and of Israel in Egypt would be strong and lasting.

Index

11 September 9, 16, 18, 22–4, 32, 145

Abdul Rahman, Sheikh 144
Abraham (Patriarch) 27
Abu Ahmed, Salman 58
Abu Hija, Jamal 89
Abu Mazen 31
Abu Rashid, Amin (Abu Hamza) 86
Abu Sayyaf 4
Abu Samrah 132
Abu Shaqrah (clan) 67
Abu Tareq 86
Abu 'Ubaydah 52
Acre x, xiii, 58, 68, 110–11, 113–14, 118, 125
Afghanistan 3, 5, 8–9, 18–19, 24, 47, 78, 82, 145, 150
Africa xv, 33, 40, 152; North Africa 7, 18
Agbariyyeh (clan) 85ff
al-Akhbar 31
al-Ahram 26
Algeria 4, 15, 47, 104
Allah Akbar 5, 110, 115; *see also* God/Allah
Allies (Second World War) 12, 28
Al-Roha 122–3
Amir al-Mu'minin 35
Amr, Mahmud 86
Amsterdam 151
Andalusia 19, 60, 81, 104; *see also* Spain
Antioch x
anti-Semitism 25ff, 45, 48, 71, 105, 107–8, 118–19, 152–4
Apache (helicopter) 28
al-Aqsa ix, x, xi, 4, 26, 68, 70, 75, 80, 87ff, 101, 112, 114, 117, 119, 123ff, 126, 128, 130, 139ff, 156–7; Brigades 14, 88; Festival 80, 84, 124, 128, 140ff; Foundation ix, xiii, 4, 70, 77, 80, 86ff, 119, 132; Intifada *see* Intifada; Youth 127
Arab/Arabs 27; countries 2, 38, 47, 49, 57, 59; Arab–Israeli dispute 3, 9, 23, 38, 43–4, 47, 118, 128; League 53; Nation 30; of Israel 10, 36ff, 116, 120, 122ff, 126, 155ff; world xi, 2, 32–3, 43–4, 59
Arabia 61, 105
Arafat, Yasser 31, 34
al-ard 122
Argentina 92
Ashura 16
Asia xv, 14, 33, 47, 152
Assyrians 27
Auschwitz 140
Australia 8, 76, 80
Autonomy 10
Ayatullah 2
Al-Azhar 31, 34; Sheikh 34
Azzam, Abdallah-Yussuf 34, 111

Babawi, Dr 26
Bakri, Sheikh Umar 17, 144
Baladhuri, Ahmed 114; *Futuh al Buldan* 114
Balata 117
Baldwin, King x
Balfour Declaration 69
Balkans 151
Banna, Hassan al- xii, 9, 59, 102
Baqa al-Gharbiya 72, 123
Bar Ilan University 140
Barak, Ehud 124–5, 140
Basilica of Annunciation 20
Bedouin 36, 58, 65
Beit She'an 110, 113, 125
Belgium 86
Ben-Eliezer, Benjamin 140

Blood Libel 26, 31; *see also* anti-Semitism
Bosnia 3 151
Boubaker, Dean 9 34
Brazil 10
Britain/British 10, 17, 45, 74, 87, 90, 144–5, 155
Bush, President George 23, 27, 82
Bukhari and Muslim 108

Cairo 26
caliph 35, 107; caliphate 17, 57, 59, 102–3, 142; Rashidun caliph xiv
Canaanites 23
Canada 8
Capucci, Archbishop 52
Chanukka 157
Charity Coalition 87
Chechnya xii, 19, 81–2
China 8, 33, 47
Christ, Jesus ix, x, 27, 51–2
Christians/Christianity ix, xii, 11, 14, 16, 20, 23, 26–7, 36, 38, 51–2, 55, 57, 62–3, 66, 75–7, 82, 89, 103, 148–9, 156; Catholics 7; Christian Church xv, 7, 16, 19–20, 51–2, 56, 71; Pilgrims x, 77; versus Muslims 3, 27, 38, 48, 52–3, 55ff, 148
CIA 22
Clairvaux, Bernard de x
Cologne 132
colonialism 8, 21, 59, 81
communism 11, 28, 43, 51, 54, 63, 67, 71, 73–4; anti-communism 52; *Communist Manifesto* 28; *see also* Rakach; Hadash
Committee for Aid and Solidarity with Palestinians 87
conspiracy 28–9, 62, 70, 80, 159; theories 16ff; world Jewish conspiracy 26, 31ff, 107–8
Copts 26–7, 52–3
Crusaders x, xi, xiii, xiv, xv, 3, 5, 14, 17, 68–9, 82, 108–10, 116; New Crusaders 52, 61, 82, 110
Cyprus xiii, 1, 10, 92

Damascus xiv
Dar, Justice Y. 85
dar al-harb 60, 103–5
dar al-Islam 8, 11, 18–19, 59–60, 103–4, 142
Darwish, Sheikh Abdallah 34, 49–50, 53, 56, 58, 63–4, 68, 74–5
David, King xiv

da'wa 17; *see also* propaganda
Defensive Shield Operation 143
democracy 1, 10–11, 16, 36, 38, 57, 59, 61, 63, 66, 102, 130, 145–6, 158; democratization 2, 37, 62
demography 9–10, 36–8, 43, 60, 151
dhimmi 26, 48, 55, 57, 103, 108, 142
Dome of the Rock 20; *see also* Temple Mount
Druze 36, 38, 66

Eastern Bloc 71
Edessa x
Egypt x, 2, 4–6, 8, 15, 19, 23–4, 27, 29, 31–3, 45–9, 53, 57–9, 61, 76, 78, 87, 102–4, 115, 144, 152–4
Ein Jalut 115
Emerson, Steven 144
Erbakan, Prime Minister Necmettin 76
Europe xii, xiv, xv, 7–8, 10, 14, 16, 20, 26, 28, 31, 36, 60–1, 82, 104, 150–2; European Council 150; Eurabia 150; Jews of xiv; Muslims of 47, 104

Fadl'allah, Sheikh 3
Fahim, Dawud 140
Fascism 11
Fat'h 114, 142, 158
fatwa 4, 78, 105, 118
FBI 144–5
Feldman, Attorney Avigdor 85, 97
Ferguson, Prof. Niall 105
fidayun 14, 29, 73; *see also* Islamikaze
FIS 104
France xv, 9–10, 18–19, 156
Frank x
Freiman, Attorney Sylvia 95–6

Galilee 36, 42, 50–2, 65–6, 111–12, 116, 127, 139
Gama'at 2, 8, 34, 59
Gaza xiv, 72, 78, 83
Geneva 32
Gentile 31
Germany xiii, 10, 28, 31, 45, 86, 132, 134
Ghali, Boutros 52–3
God/Allah x, 1, 16, 18, 24, 29–30, 56, 59, 62, 71–2, 83, 101, 106–7, 113, 119, 125, 146, 149–50, 157; Enemies of God xi, 14, 27, 107, 112, 126; Path of God xi, 17, 22–3, 81, 106, 114–16

Golan 115
Greece 18
Guantanamo 25
Gulf; States 8, 34; War 5, 46, 53

Habash, George 52
Hadash Party 51, 54; *see also* communists; Rakah
hadith 67, 97, 99, 102ff, 108
Haifa 74, 89, 110–11, 113, 118, 125, 134, 142, 144; District Attorney vii, viii, 84–5, 89, 96–7, 121, 131; District Court viii, 85, 89, 97ff, 132, 143; President of District Court 98
hajj 66, 156
Hamas vii, xff, 2–4, 6, 14, 16, 18, 30, 34, 52, 61, 63, 65, 68, 72, 74, 76–7, 79, 81, 86ff, 127, 131, 134, 136, 141, 143–4, 147, 149, 155; Platform/Charter of x, xi, 103, 108, 113; political leadership of 77
Hanafi 47, 59, 102
Hanbali 59, 60, 103
Hebrew 155
Hebron 72, 79, 80, 117, 157; Islamic College in 50, 66; Tomb of Patriachs in 80; 157
hijra 61
Hijaz 69, 109
Hijazi, Mahmud 86
Hinduism 10–11
Hitler 28, 31
HIV Positive/AIDS 23, 32–3, 82
Hizbullah 2–4, 6, 14, 27, 30, 34, 44, 84, 92, 117, 127, 147, 149
Hobsbawm, Eric 6
Holocaust 147; Denial of 23, 26, 30ff, 53, 109
Holy Land x, xiii, xiv, xv, 48, 52, 107, 113; Foundation 87
Holy Law/*shari'a* xii, 2, 4, 11, 54–5, 57, 59, 97, 101–2, 113, 146–7
Holy Places ix, xi, 20, 48, 73–5, 80, 123, 127, 139–40, 151, 156–7; for Christians x, xiv, 20, 52; for Jews ix, xiv, 123, 156; for Muslims ix, xi, 20, 48, 73–5, 80, 123, 127, 139–40, 151, 156–7
Holy Sepulchre x
Hospitallers xv
Hudaybiyya 142
Humanitarian Relief Society (HRS) 85ff, 134, 136

Humanitarian Salvation Committee for Orphans and the Needy 85ff
Hungary 10
Hussein, Imam 16
Hussein, Saddam 5, 46, 53, 111
Hussein, Haj Amin 70

Iberia xii, xv, 11, 151; *see also* Spain
al-'Ilm 32
imperialism 21, 81, 120
Imam; Association of 10; Hidden Imam (Shi'a) 6
India 3, 10–11, 22, 47
Indonesia 2, 4, 7, 19
Innovation/*Bid'a* 7
Interpal (Palestinian Relief and Development Fund) 87ff
intifada 23, 32, 68, 84, 128, 130, 157; first 12, 52, 113, 155; second (al-Aqsa) 12, 29–30, 36, 42, 79–81, 87, 107, 116, 120, 126–7, 139
Iran xv, 2, 4–5, 8, 10, 14, 30, 35, 47, 72, 151; Iranian Revolution 9, 49, 78; *see also* Persia
Iraq 5, 8, 10, 46, 82, 150
Islam; Islamic conferences 11; Islamic countries xv, 7, 11, 27, 29–30, 49, 115; Islamic festivals 55, 89; Islamic fundamentalism 2–3, 7, 9–10, 15, 18, 35–6, 37, 47ff, 73; Islamic minorities xii, 7–10, 34, 60, 152; Islamic world/Islamdom xi, xiii, xiv, 2, 4, 7, 12, 14, 18–19, 22, 24, 30, 35, 62, 72, 77, 124, 150, 152ff
Islamic Jihad 14, 18, 30, 88
Islamic Liberation Party 49
Islamic Movement x, xi, 89; in Israel vii, ix, x, xiii, xvi, 47ff, 72ff; Shura of 126; Trial of 85ff
Islamic Relief Committee 90–1
Islamikaze ix, x, xiv, 3, 14, 19, 22–3, 28–30, 73, 83, 87–8, 90, 96, 101, 105, 122, 142, 150–2; *see also* terrorism; martyr
Israel 3, 5, 7–8, 10, 12, 15, 18ff, 61, 103–4, 115, 120, 145; anti- 52, 68, 84, 120; see also anti-Semitism; Attorney General 102; Minister of Defence 87, 90–1; Northern Command 90–3; Supreme Court 91, 122, 129, 131
Istiqlal Cemetery 74

Jaffa x, 58, 110, 112, 118, 125, 148
jahiliyya 61, 105
Jaljulya 58
Japan 15, 31, 45
Jenin 23, 32, 82, 89, 117–18
Jericho 79, 157
Jerusalem ix, x, xiii, 20, 34, 52, 72, 75–6, 107, 110–11, 114–15, 117–18, 125, 140–1, 157; Arab and Muslim 76; Festival 76
Jews xiv, 7, 12, 19–20, 23–5, 76, 80, 103, 107–8, 147–9, 152–4, 156–7; anti- 52–3, 61, 79, 81, 84, 118; Jewish festivals 80; Jewish nationalism 40; Jewish state 12, 28, 37-8, 54, 57, 63, 69, 89, 118, 126; Jewish synagogue 19–20, 79–80, 125; of Europe xiv; *see also* anti-Semitism
jihad (Holy War) xi, xv, 3, 14, 19, 53, 60, 68, 73, 81, 83–4, 104ff, 108, 113–14, 118–19, 121–2, 141, 144, 148, 150, 154; fighters xii, 106; *see also* mujahidin; groups 2, 30, 59, 61; Laskar 2
jizya 103
Jordan 5–8, 31, 33, 44–5, 47–8, 57, 111, 155; River Jordan 42
Joseph's Tomb 79, 157
Judea xiv; *see also* Palestine
Judeo-Christian 22, 62

Ka'ba 125
Kabul 3
kafir/infidel 3, 142
Kafr Bara 50, 58
Kafr Kanna 51–2, 56, 58, 125
Kafr Qara 58
Kafr Qassem 34, 49, 58
Kamikaze 15; *see also* Islamikaze
Karbalah 16
Karine A 23–4
Kashmir xii, 3, 22, 60, 81, 104, 151
Kedar, Dr Motti 140
Khadr, Mahmud 31
Khaled, Ibn al-Walid 52, 68
Khatib, Sheikh Kamal 51–2, 56, 58, 107, 110, 125, 129
Khomeini, Ayatollah 2, 30, 35–6, 78
Knesset 42–4 54 56 58 64 66 105 119 126; Arab members of 130
Knights ix, x, xv
Korea; North 33
Kosovo 3, 19, 82, 151

Kul al-Arab 55
Kurds 9
Kuwait 34

Labour Party (Israel) 149
Land Day 42, 44, 123, 128
Laskar Jihad 2, 3, 7
Lebanon 2, 4, 6–7, 14, 27, 47, 73, 84, 89, 107; Southern 76
Levant xv; *see also* Middle East
Lewis, Bernard 20
Lindenstrauss, Judge Micha 85
Livingstone, Mayor Ken 87, 105
Lod/Lydda 58, 110, 113
London 10, 28, 87, 105, 144–5, 151
Lusitania 28

Macedonia 151
madrasa 152
Madrid 145, 151
Mafia 74
Mahajneh (clan) 66–7 143; defendants 85ff; Mahmud 132
Mahamid (clan) 67, 97
Mahdi 6
Mahzumeh, Nabil (Abu Muhammed) 89–90
Makarios, Archbishop 1
Mamluks xv 115; *see also* Qutuz
Mansur, Atallah 55
Maqsud, Clovis 53
Marj al-Zuhur (Valley of Flowers) 113
Marseillaise 18
martyr/*shahid* 3, 14–15, 22–3, 29–30, 81, 83, 101, 113–14, 116–19, 122, 127, 151
Marwani Musallah 76, 156
Marx and Engels 28, 71, 154; Marxism 154
Mash'al, Khaled xiv, 3
Masri, Sheikh Abu Hamza 17, 144
Mawdoodi, Mawlana 11
Maxim Restaurant 142, 144
Mecca 11, 61, 66, 105, 125, 142
media 3, 13, 15, 30, 32–3, 71–2, 78, 83, 94, 99–100, 126, 139, 148–53; Arab 27, 31–2, 53, 55, 69–70, 156; European 32; Muslim 4, 26–7, 30–1, 53, 82; Palestinian 139
Medina/Yathrib 61, 105
Mercantile Discount Bank 89
Middle Ages ix, xi, xii, 17, 20, 46, 82, 105, 110

Middle East/Orient x, xii, xiii, 26, 28, 43–4, 46, 147; Conflict 43; *see also* Arab-Israeli dispute
mi'raj and isra' xiv; Land of 113
al-Mithaq 58
Molay, Jacques de xv
Moluccas 3
Mongols/Tartars xv, 115–16, 148
Morocco 103
mosque 3, 9–10, 18–20, 30, 33, 48–9, 55–6, 60, 66, 73–5, 80, 83, 89, 104, 106, 110–11, 113, 123–4, 152
Mossad 22
m'uazzin 62, 107, 111
Mufti 80; of Jerusalem xiii, 34, 70, 72
murabit/ribat 60, 104, 112, 121
musallah 76, 156
Muslim Brothers x, 6, 8, 34, 48–9, 58–61, 74, 89, 102ff
Muslim Youth Movement 49

Nabi Sa'in 56
Nablus 72, 79, 117, 157
Nahdat al-'ulama' 7
Nakbah 40, 74
Nasrallah, Sheikh 3, 5, 13, 30, 34
Nasser, President Gamal Abdul 46, 59, 61, 111
National Democratic List 45
nationalism 4, 27, 36–7, 40, 42–3, 44, 50, 57, 72, 122, 155; Arab 52, 57; bi-nationalism 40; religious 47
Nativity Church 26
Nazareth 20, 51–2, 54–6, 58, 75, 77, 89–90
Nazism 28, 31, 45, 82, 103, 108–9
Negev 58, 65, 113, 139–40
Netherlands/Holland 86, 155
Nigeria 8, 19
Nile; Delta Valley 32; Nile to Euphrates 69, 109

October Riots 122ff
Omar, Mulla 35
Or Commission 120, 12ff, 133, 135, 148
Orontes (River) x
Orthodox (Jews) 41
Oslo; Accords 57, 63, 113, 139; Peace Process 12
Ottomans 28
Otzar Ha-Hayal Bank 89

Pakistan 2, 5, 8, 11, 24, 47, 78
Palazzi, Sheikh 34
Palestine/Palestinians xi, xiii, xiv, 2–4, 12, 19, 21, 23, 26–30, 32–3, 36–7, 42ff, 52–7, 60–1, 81, 84, 106, 108–9, 116, 140, 142, 148, 151, 155–6; collaborators 15, 41, 44; organizations 14; Palestinian Authority 4, 6–7, 63, 79, 113, 125, 139
Paradise x, xii, 22, 83, 88, 101, 114, 119
Park Hotel 143
Paris 9 34
Passover Massacre 143
Patriarch of Jerusalem x
Payns, Hugues de xi
Peace xi, xv, 27, 31, 120, 146; anti- 28, 120, 149; negotiations xi, 41, 53; treaty 30, 33, 45, 63, 152; *see also* Oslo
Persia xv; *see also* Iran
Philippines 4, 10
PLO, Charter of 63; *see also* Palestine
Pope xii, 77
propaganda/*da'wa* xii, xiv, 3, 8, 17, 28–9, 52, 60, 66, 71, 104–5, 106, 149, 152–3
Prophet xiv; of Islam xiv, 7, 14, 20, 35, 59, 79, 102–3, 105–6, 107, 110, 115, 142
Protocols of the Elders of Zion 26, 31, 70, 109

al-Qa'ida 2–3, 14, 18, 24, 61, 81, 84, 150–1
Qaradawi, Sheikh Yussuf xii, 3, 15, 61, 78, 87, 105, 114, 118
Qassam, Izz al-Din 74; Brigades x, 74–5
Qatar 61, 78, 87, 105
Qindil, Jihad 87
Qom 78
Qur'an 20, 24, 59, 67, 97, 99, 101–3, 106, 109, 114, 125, 146, 148–9
Qut'b, Sayyid xii, 60, 62, 103, 105, 107, 151
Qutuz 115

racism 45, 55–6, 73, 94, 100, 142
Rakah Party 43, 67; *see also* Hadash; Communism
Ramadan 31, 76, 89, 115, 157
Ramadan, Tariq 9, 80
Ramallah 79, 110
Ramat Gan 89
Ramla 58, 113
Ramlawi, Abdallah 32
Rantisi, Sheikh xiv
Red Cross 32

Riad, Attorney Anis 97
Right of Return 43–4, 118, 151
Roger of Antioch x
Rome 34; Holy Roman Empire 110
Romans 69, 109–10; Roman Law 142
Russia 47

Sadat, President Anwar 59, 152
Sadeq, Dr Adel 27
Safed 148
Saladin 46, 52, 68, 82, 110, 113
Samaria 74; see also West Bank
Sarafand Mosque 111, 126
Sartre, Jean-Paul 71
Satan 27, 108, 114
Saudi Arabia xv, 2, 4–5, 9, 12, 22, 30, 34–5, 60, 72, 77, 103, 109, 151–2
Sawt al-Haqq wal-huriyya 52, 55–6, 58, 68–9, 75, 90, 105, 124, 125
Scandinavia 18
Schieff, Judge A. 85
Schindler's List 30
Seniora, Hanna 52
Serbs 3, 82
Shah 78
Shararah, Umar 51
Sharon, Prime Minister Ariel 26, 81, 140
Shi'a 14, 16; Twelver 6
Shin Bet 140
al-Sinara 55
Sira (biography) 103
al-Sirat 53, 68–9, 105, 114
Solomon, King xiv; Stables 76, 157; see also Musalla Marwani
South Africa 10
Soviets 3, 8
Spain 61, 103; Golden Era in 1–3; see also Andalusia
St Bernard ix
Straw, Foreign Secretary Jack 145
Sudan 2, 8–9, 35, 47
Sudeten 10
Suez Canal 33
Sunna 6, 47, 59
Swiss 9, 72
Syria 8, 44, 49, 66, 89

Takfir wal-Hijra 59
Taleb, Ja'far 'Amr 4
Taliban 25 35

Tanzim 14
Taybeh 72
Ta'ziah 16; see also Shi'a
Tehran 30, 78
Tel Aviv 50, 115, 148
Temple (of Jerusalem) xiii, xiv, 76; Solomonic/First ix, x, xiv; Second xiv; Third (projected) 70, 123, 128; Mount x, 20, 70, 80–1, 111, 123–6, 128, 141, 156; see also al-Aqsa
Terrorism/*irhab* xii, xiii, xv, 2–3, 7, 14–15, 18–19, 22ff, 45, 60, 73, 76–7, 81–2, 84–6, 89ff, 106, 114–16, 118–19, 121, 135, 140, 142–3, 145, 150, 155–6
Third World 13, 33
Tiberias 110
Tilimsani, Umar 152, 154
Transylvania 10
Triangle 65–6, 72, 113, 116
Tripoli x
Troyes Council xi
Truman Institute vii–viii
Tul Karem 117
Tunisia 15
Turabi, Hassan 2
Turkey 10, 76
Twin Towers 23–5, 115, 145; see also 11 September

'Ulama 6 11
Umar, Caliph 52, 68, 106
Umar, Ibn al-As 115
Umayyad 11, 76
Umm al-Fahm vii, ix, 50, 55, 58, 65ff, 85, 90, 93, 97–8, 124–5, 126ff, 138, 140, 143; Islamic College in 76
umma 4, 12, 47
United Nations 21, 32–3, 115, 118; Human Rights Commission 32; Secretary General 53
United Arab List 64
United States 5, 7–8, 16, 18–19, 21–5, 28, 32–3, 45, 47, 53, 79, 81, 104, 115, 134, 144–5, 150–2; United States Congress 26
Usrat al-Jihad 49 53

Valencia 11
Vatican viii, 7
Versailles 28

Vietnam 32
Voivodina 10

Wafa (Palestinian News Agency) 49
Wafd Party 59
Wahhabi 9, 59
waqf (Holy Endowment) 20, 48, 54, 56–7, 74–5, 106, 113, 119, 142, 147, 151
Wars 29, 48, 68, 107; First World War 28; Gulf 53; see also Gulf War; Second World War 28, 31, 45; 1948 26 38 74 126; 1967 38, 42, 48; 1973 33, 44, 157
West xi, xii, xiii, 3, 8, 10, 15, 18, 19ff, 36, 62, 78, 81–2, 105, 107, 115, 142, 145, 147, 149; versus Muslims 9–10, 61; Western invasion 17, 19, 62; Western values 10, 13, 14, 17ff, 59–61, 79, 102, 105, 107–8, 120, 150
West Bank and Gaza xi, 5, 18–19, 42–4, 48–9, 52, 66, 72, 80, 84, 87, 90, 92–3, 116, 119, 143, 154–5; *see also* Palestine
Western/Wailing Wall 80, 123–4; *see also* Temple Mount
World Muslim Youth Conference 87
Wye Agreement 63

Yassin, Sheikh Ahmed xii, xiv, 3, 5, 13, 77-8, 105, 114
Yussuf, Issam 87

Zahar, Dr al- 77
zakat 73–4, 106; Board 58
Zarqawi, Sheikh 13, 34
Zawahiri, Sheikh Ayman 3, 5, 34, 61
Zimbabwe 10
Zionism xi, 27, 29, 38, 40, 44, 54, 69, 79, 82, 108–9, 150–1, 156; anti- 26, 52
Zyad, Tufiq 51, 54, 56

Recently Published by Vallentine Mitchell

Palestinians between Nationalism and Islam
Collected Essays
Raphael Israeli

This book is a thematic collection of mostly already published articles by this author, a recognized authority on contemporary Israeli–Palestinian relations, providing a retrospective on the development of the tension between nascent Palestinian nationalism as articulated by the PLO and Islam as incorporated by Hamas. It illuminates the dynamics of a rapidly changing situation, plotting the development of this volatile region.

The death of Arafat and the rise of the comparatively moderate Abu Mazen provided the final impetus for the dramatic rise of Hamas in Palestinian politics. Hamas strengthened permanently in the grassroots by dispensing welfare to the poor, criticizing the corrupt Palestinian Authority, and providing religious solace for the misery of life. Its stunning victory over the veteran PLO in the 2006 elections has made the matter all the more pertinent. Difficult days lie ahead for those behind international attempts to bring peace to Palestine.

November 2007, 304 pages
978 0 85303 731 6 cloth £49.50 / $85.00
978 0 85303 732 3 paper £20.00 / $35.00

Recently Published by Vallentine Mitchell

The Palestinian Press as a Shaper of Public Opinion
Writing Up A Storm
Mustafa Kabha
Open University of Israel

This book deals with the development of the Palestinian Arabic press during the years 1929–1939, years in which the national identity of the Palestinian Arab public was formalized and shaped by the development of the Palestinian National Movement. During this period the Palestinian National Movement, in addition to its struggle with the Zionist Movement, was also involved in a struggle with the British Mandatory government. The primary professed goal of this struggle was to prevent realization of the programme for a Jewish National Home, and to lead Britain to a situation in which it would be compelled to grant independence or a certain degree of autonomy to the Palestinian Arabs, as had been granted to other Arab countries such as Iraq and Egypt.

The press became integrated as a central factor in shaping the development of the Palestinian National Movement. It began to emerge in the mid-1920s, its weight increased significantly during the events of 1929, and it peaked in the Great Strike of April–October 1936. The few studies conducted to date on the functioning of the Palestinian press during the Mandatory period dealt with the political aspects of the newspapers and with their articulation of the various political groups and powers in the Palestinian National Movement. In this book the author emphasizes social, cultural and institutional aspects, in addition to the national-political aspect.

March 2007, 320 pages
978 0 85303 671 5 cloth £49.50 / $85.00
978 0 85303 672 2 paper £18.50 / $27.50

Recently Published by Vallentine Mitchell

Shia Power
Next Target Iran?
Michel Korinman and John Laughland (eds.)

This book, the first in a new series from the Daedalos Institute of Geopolitics in Cyprus, asks whether Iran has pretensions to become the leader of the Muslim world. Does the Islamic Republic intend to acquire a nuclear bomb? What is its energy policy and how does the world's need for hydrocarbons bolster the country's geopolitical position? What does the election of Mahmoud Ahmadinejad mean for the factionalism and power struggles of Iranian politics? What is the relationship between the clergy and the 'neo-conservatives' who now control the presidency? What are Iran's relations with the other great powers, especially Russia and India? *Shia Power* contains incisive comment from the world's leading experts on this, one of the planet's most intriguing and mysterious states. It is a first-class source of reference material for a country which is seldom far from the centre of world affairs.

March 2007, 374 pages
978 0 85303 750 7 cloth £55.00 / $95.00
978 0 85303 751 4 paper £20.00 / $35.00

Recently Published by Vallentine Mitchell

Israel on Israel
Michel Korinman and John Laughland (eds.)

Nowhere is the debate about Israel and its future stronger than in Israel itself. Politicians, academics and journalists from Israel and the wider world join forces in this volume to discuss the various existential questions which face their state. What, if anything, has changed in Palestinian politics since the death of Yasser Arafat? What are the differences between European and American approaches to the Israeli question? Why does the Palestinian cause continue to excite so much support in the West? Is the idea of a two-state solution still viable? What is the reality of Zionism and why is it so often demonised? What is the role of historians in understanding the history of the state of Israel and influencing the policies of today? What is the role of Arab citizens in Israel? How was the construction of the security barrier decided, and how was the precise route traced? What has been the effect has the immigration of Russian and Ethiopian Jews to Israel? What is the role of religion in Israeli politics?

October 2007, 332 pages
978 0 85303 757 9 cloth £49.50 / $85.00
978 0 85303 758 6 paper £18.50 / $27.50

Recently Published by Vallentine Mitchell

Israel and the Jews in Arab and Western Cartoons
Joel Kotek

The outrage sparked by the Danish cartoon affair of August 2005 – the publication of images of the Prophet Muhammad in the European press – was a sharp reminder of the potency of the cartoon in the modern media. It is one of the most popular and effective means of communication.

By exaggerating and exasperating, cartoons by their very nature lack neutrality, and the cartoon is an important weapon in the contemporary crisis in the Middle East. In response to the Danish cartoon affair, in February 2006 an Iranian newspaper announced a competition for cartoons about the Holocaust, even though the events of the previous summer had had nothing to do with Israel or the Jewish people.

Antisemitic cartoons have long been rife in the Arab-Muslim media. The September 2001 Durban Conference against Racism, intended to denounce and combat racism in all its forms, also featured the distribution of antisemitic cartoons by an Arab organisation, yet this elicited no reaction from the delegates representing Western NGOs at the conference. This event set the author on a trail that revealed thousands of such drawings. In the name of anti-Zionism, Jews are daily depicted as sadistic and bloodthirsty monsters, solely interested in money and power. This return to anti-Jewish hatred is of a new order, in line with current trends – an Arab-Muslim form of antisemitism unexpectedly metamorphosed from the type of antisemitism traditionally linked with the Christian West.

By reproducing more than 400 of these cartoons (two-thirds in colour), taken from both the Arab and Western media and on occasion plagiarising Nazi propaganda, this book denounces the use of hatred in the media and hopes to raise the alarm.

February 2008, 224 pages
978 0 85303 752 1 paper £15.50 / $29.50

Recently Published by Vallentine Mitchell

Jacques Faitlovitch and the Jews of Ethiopia
Emanuela Trevisan Semi

The architect of the ingathering of the most problematic group of the Jewish diaspora was Jacques Faitlovitch. He was an adventurer, scholar and Zionist, a Polish-born Jew who lived in Paris and Palestine. His life was marked by his devotion to the cause of the Beta Israel, the black Jews of Ethiopia. Faitlovitch was an Ashkenazi Jew of the neo-Orthodox school and took up the task, already initiated by Joseph Halévi, of assisting the Beta Israel, particularly in their struggle against the Protestant missionaries. He had close links with the chief Jewish institutions and with leading scholars and Ethiopian leaders, notably Emperor Haile Selassie.

May 2007, 224 pages
978 0 85303 654 8 cloth £49.50 / $75.00
978 0 85303 655 5 paper £19.95 / $29.95

Recently Published by Vallentine Mitchell

Contemporary Israeli Women's Writing
Risa Domb (ed.)

During the nineteenth and early twentieth century, women could not participate in the development of Modern Hebrew literature. As pointed out in 1996's New Women's Writing from Israel, to which this is a successor volume, they could give vent to their poetic talents either in Yiddish, their spoken language, or in Russian, but not in Hebrew. Whilst Yiddish writing did not insist on the national element as a required poetic norm, Hebrew literature did. The ideological dictum insisted on the symbiosis of the collective experience with the private, of the myth of the nation with the myth of the individual. Since women did not take part in public life or in the initial stages of the Hebrew revival which took place in Eastern Europe, they could not respond to these poetic demands.

In the 1920s Hebrew prose was more open to autobiographical and confessional writing, and women were able to contribute to this genre, as they could incorporate the full range of their experience. In addition, their horizons and experiences were further extended as they began to assume a full part of the national revival in Palestine and because they were as ideologically committed as their male counterparts. On the whole they were not provocative in their writing and cannot be defined as 'feminist' writers. They did not strive to differentiate themselves from male writing, but rather to complement it.

It was only with the next generation of writers, the 'New Wave' writers of the 1960s and 1970s, that women's prose writing found its niche. The shift of marginal characters to the central stage in Israeli fiction, as well as the departure from the male-orientated national concerns, opened the doors to an influx of women writers. The change in the mainstream Israeli experience meant greater openness in literature, and a pluralism of voices emerged, incorporating those of women writers. As a result, they could, at last, as abandon their traditional place in Hebrew literature and assume their rightful role in its development. This poetic stance changed in the 1980s. Although women writers did not overtly call for sexual equality, they exposed erotic feelings and emotions which are exclusively feminine, and which their predecessors were too inhibited to express.

Since the 1980s a great deal has changed. Israeli women's writing has become more consciously feminist, asserting feminist ideology. Furthermore, we hear for the first time the voices of women who express their experience of religious life. Either from within Jewish orthodoxy, or more often having left that world, they offer us a glimpse into this hitherto unknown literary terrain. Interestingly, many still use the marvellous genre of the short story. Contemporary Israeli Women's Writing reflects these dramatic changes.

October 2007, 320 pages
978 0 85303 758 3 cloth £15.50 / $29.50
978 0 85303 759 0 paper £15.50 / $29.50

Recently Published by Vallentine Mitchell

Israeli Society, the Holocaust and its Survivors
Dina Porat
Tel Aviv University

This collection of twenty essays analyses the encounters of the Yishuv (the Hebrew community in pre-state Israel) and Israeli society with the Holocaust while it occurred, and with its survivors. Sixty years after the end of the Second World War this is still a painful topic, very much at the centre of the agendas of both Israel and the Jewish communities worldwide, focusing on a soul-searching issue: was the tragedy unfolding in Europe part and parcel of public life in the Yishuv, its priorities and anxieties, and did Israeli society embrace the survivors as they deserved? Based on a wide scope of primary sources and on many years of research, the essays deal with a variety of poignant sub-issues, such as the attitudes of David Ben-Gurion, Martin Buber and other leaders, the understanding of the information about the 'Final Solution', relations and tensions between the Yishuv and the Jewish communities and youth movements in Nazi-occupied Europe, rescue plans and their failure, decisions regarding rescue made during a global war, and parallel changes in the attitude to the survivors and in Israeli and Jewish identity. The balanced answers provided in this collection take into consideration the limited resources of a small community under a mandate and of a young, post-war country flooded by immigration, and the many dominant factors present during a world war and in its aftermath on which the Yishuv and Israel could have no impact, yet could not avoid criticism and pin-pointing of failures and deficiencies.

October 2007, 460 pages
978 0 85303 741 5 cloth £49.50 / $75.00
978 0 85303 742 2 paper £20.00 / $35.00